D0803512

THE LEGENDARY DETECTIVE

# THE LEGENDARY DETECTIVE

## THE PRIVATE EYE IN FACT AND FICTION

## JOHN WALTON

The University of Chicago Press    *Chicago and London*

JOHN WALTON is distinguished research professor of sociology at the
University of California, Davis, and the author of many books.

The University of Chicago Press, Chicago 60637
The University of Chicago Press, Ltd., London
© 2015 by The University of Chicago
All rights reserved. Published 2015.
Printed in the United States of America

24 23 22 21 20 19 18 17 16 15     1 2 3 4 5
ISBN-13: 978-0-226-30826-5 (cloth)
ISBN-13: 978-0-226-30843-2 (e-book)
DOI: 10.7208/chicago/9780226308432.001.0001

Library of Congress Cataloging-in-Publication Data

Walton, John, 1937– author.
The legendary detective : the private eye in fact and fiction /
John Walton.
pages cm
Includes bibliographical references and index.
ISBN 978-0-226-30826-5 (cloth : alkaline paper) —
ISBN 978-0-226-30843-2 (ebook)
1. Private investigators—United States—History. I. Title.
HV8088.W35 2015
363.28'9097309041—dc23
2015015806

⊗ This paper meets the requirements of ANSI/NISO Z39.48–1992
(Permanence of Paper).

FOR MIA AND AIDAN,
BOOK LOVERS

# CONTENTS

# ACKNOWLEDGMENTS

The material for this book was assembled over a long period from a wide variety of sources. I am grateful to countless librarians—those still-vital professionals who stand behind the writer's efforts to assemble the evidence that is out there, somewhere, if someone will help us find it. My thanks to archivists and staffs at Bancroft Library, University of California, Berkeley; UCLA Library Special Collections, University of California, Los Angeles; Peter J. Shields Library, University of California, Davis; Harry Ransom Center, University of Texas at Austin; Harvard Law School Library Historical and Special Collections; Labor Archives and Research Center, J. Paul Leonard Library, San Francisco State University; Special Collections and University Archives, Stanford University Libraries; Newberry Library, Chicago; National Archives, Washington, DC; California State Archives, Sacramento; California State Library, Sacramento; and San Francisco Public Library.

Frank and Joe Hardy got me started on this project. More recently, I have benefited from the published work and editorial comments of Robert Weiss and Erin Smith. Doug Mitchell, executive editor at University of Chicago Press, has provided hearty support and good humor. Tim McGovern and Kyle Adam Wagner relieved me of worry over permissions and illustrations. Levi T. Stahl, Jenni Fry, and University of Chicago Press staff have contributed greatly to editing and promoting the work. I am impressed anew by the observation that books are a collective endeavor. Friend and colleague for fifty years and fellow detective story fan Howard S. Becker encouraged me to write this book when I had my doubts and then reviewed an early draft with a sharp critical eye. Howie has earned many accolades, the most apt being teacher. My wife, Priscilla, has given much more than I can return.

# INTRODUCTION: THE STORY

Under the laws I'm labeled on the books and licensed as a private detective. . . . My position is not exactly a healthy one. The police don't
like me. The crooks don't like me. I'm just a halfway house between
the law and crime; sort of working both ends against the middle. . . .
My ethics are my own.

CARROLL JOHN DALY, *The Snarl of the Beast* (1927)

## The Case of the Detective

At age twenty-one, Samuel Dashiell Hammett went to work for the
Pinkerton National Detective Agency, continuing his private eye career from 1915 to 1922 with interruptions for service in World War I
and subsequent hospitalizations. He learned the trade in Baltimore,
one of the firm's twenty-two regional offices at the time. Although
the term *private eye* derived from the Pinkerton logo, the agency preferred to call its field agents *operatives*, a position Hammett held in
Spokane and San Francisco. Known to his colleagues as Sam Hammett, he achieved an enviable reputation for his prowess at surveillance, strike breaking, and investigation. He participated in Pinkerton
actions at the Butte–Anaconda miners' strike of 1920 in Montana and
for the defense during film star Fatty Arbuckle's 1921 manslaughter
trial in San Francisco.

The Pinkerton National Detective Agency, a name evolved from
the firm's modest origins in Chicago during the 1850s, was the first and
for a time the largest detective agency in the United States. It was the
leader and trendsetter of a new business enterprise that burgeoned

from the 1870s on with the national expansion of commerce and industry. By the mid-1930s, Pinkerton maintained offices in twenty-seven
cities throughout the country, employed at least twelve hundred operatives engaged in industrial espionage alone (the most profitable of
several departments), and reported earnings of $2.3 million. Among
its three hundred clients were General Electric, Inland Steel, RCA, BF
Goodrich, American Cyanamid, Continental Can, Campbell Soup,
Warner Brothers Studio, Kroger Grocery, Shell Oil, Montgomery
Ward, and General Motors (which employed seven other agencies in
addition to Pinkerton at a total cost of $994,855 in services rendered
over a two-year period). The top seven national agencies alone num-
bered 1,475 clients in every branch of industry and commerce.[1]

Another seven to eight hundred agencies spread out across fifty US
cities; 187 were concentrated in New York City alone. By 1935, Pinkerton's great rival, the William J. Burns International Detective Agency
with forty-three branch offices, had taken over the lead of an industry
that employed tens of thousands of people and earned an estimated
$80 million that year. In addition to the great agencies, many of the
major US companies employed in-house detectives in one guise or another for the general purpose of employee surveillance. Strikebreaking was a lucrative service provided by the large firms, until it earned
them a bad reputation, and by firms specializing in labor conflicts that
embraced the reputation. Hotel detectives kept order among guests
and expelled or managed prostitutes, while department store detectives watched for shoplifters among customers and employees. Street
railways, pervasive in American cities at the time, used detectives as
"train spotters" in search of grifting conductors.

The great agencies like Pinkerton and Burns served mainly corporate clients, but hundreds of independent firms catered to troubled
individuals and local business. These small agencies typically were
run by an owner-manager with the help of two or three field operatives employed case by case. Additional operatives would be added as
needed, which required a large floating reserve of agents available on
demand. Some independent agencies specialized in matrimonial cases
(including infidelity, divorce, breach of promise, and fortune hunt-
ing), which the large corporate agencies regarded as beneath their
professionalism. Independents were versatile, sometimes assisting
police in criminal matters but mainly dealing in complaints of fraud,

extortion, blackmail, and missing persons. Commercial enterprises sometimes hired independent agencies in preference to maintaining in-house detectives. Seldom if ever did private detectives investigate major crimes such as murder, the province of municipal police.

Sam Hammett retired from detective work in 1922 and began a career writing fiction as Dashiell Hammett while supporting himself, his new wife, and their infant child by turning out advertising copy for a San Francisco jewelry store. Drawing on his own experience, Hammett began with short stories, many featuring the otherwise nameless "Continental Op," a field operative for the fictional Continental Detective Agency. The Continental Op was unglamorous, stout, sardonic, gruff—a working man. He took orders from the "Old Man" who managed the national agency's San Francisco office, "a gentle, polite, elderly person with no more warmth in him than a hangman's rope."[2] Although Hammett was not the only exponent of the hard-boiled detective story, he was the best and rapidly gained a national reputation for his prolific contributions to the flourishing "pulp" magazines (known as such for being printed on cheap paper with a high wood pulp content).

Hammett's Continental Op stories first appeared in the pulp classic *Black Mask* magazine in 1923. His sensational first novel, *Red Harvest* (1929), is a story of labor conflict and local corruption in "Poisonville" based on events occurring in Butte and Anaconda, Montana, from 1917–1920. The story's realism derives from the violent world of the miners' struggle and the Op's employment by an agency that engaged in industrial disputes. There is good evidence that Hammett was in Butte in 1920 while working for Pinkerton's Spokane office.[3] While there he would have witnessed the conflict between miners and the Anaconda Copper Company and absorbed the region's long history of violence, including the torture and lynching of Industrial Workers of the World (IWW) union organizer Frank Little in 1917, allegedly with the assistance of Pinkerton agents. The mayhem described in *Red Harvest*, some of it the work of the Continental Op, was real.

As a private investigator, Sam Hammett assisted police in solving a robbery of $125,000 in gold coins from the passenger ship *S.S. Sonoma* when it docked in San Francisco in 1921.[4] In *The Maltese Falcon* (1930), Hammett's best-known novel, private eye Sam Spade solves the case of a jeweled figurine stolen on board the passenger ship *La Paloma* carrying a trio of conspirators to San Francisco. The novel's commercial success and three subsequent film adaptations have overshadowed the real events from which the story derived.

Hammett also derived realism from the book *Celebrated Criminal Cases of America* by San Francisco Police Chief Thomas Duke and drew on its authority in his own stories. The book even makes an appearance in *The Maltese Falcon*; Spade keeps a copy on his nightstand. Hammett's 1933 novel, *The Thin Man*, quotes extensively from Duke's book as evidence that cannibalism was known to occur in the United States and was not a mere fabrication of the story.

In the 1924 short story "Who Killed Bob Teal?," Hammett wrote, "Those who remember this affair will know that the city, the detective agency, and the people involved all had names different from the ones I have given them. But they will know also that I have kept the facts true."[5] Is this a literary device, a truthful aside, or a bit of both? In any case, Hammett knew what he was talking about. Like the Continental Op, he was a working man who knew his job. His contemporary and friend Raymond Chandler said that, far from any artistic aims, Hammett "was trying to make a living by writing something he [had] firsthand information about. He made some of it up; all writers do; but it had a basis in fact; it was made up of real things."[6] Sam Spade, hardboiled antihero, embodies the cultural ambivalence that attaches to the private eye — part law enforcer and part underworld figure — an ambivalence that reflects the historical figure of the private detective.

Dashiell Hammett's work illustrates the relationship between the business and popular culture industries — how cultural representations derive from the service economy and in turn become commodities in the marketplace. This study focuses on the interdependence of two commercial enterprises, detective agencies and popular culture production. The chapters that follow show how the business of private investigation has developed in tandem with the business of storytelling. Hammett provides a bridge between these two worlds. The facts of the detective industry and the fictions of the culture industry continue to grow from a common root and intermingle as they grow. Anthony Lukas describes this situation as "the cult of the American detective," in which one of the country's major, and often controversial, industries is cast in collective memory as the story of romanticized loners in pursuit of devious criminals.[7] The Continental Op grounded in the occupational world of the private detective contrasts sharply with the mythical Sherlock Holmes of Victorian invention. Yet the private detective of legend embraces figures drawn from a rich provenance. Eccentric genius or working-class knight errant, the private detective infused pulp fiction, radio, film, adolescent literature, comic strips, product promotions, literary clubs, and the lecture circuit—all cohering in a universally recognized figure of popular culture. Although I introduce the investigation by speaking of two enterprises, the private detective business and the popular culture industry, these interdependent phenomena contribute to a single product, the legendary detective.

## The Investigation

Curiously, given the historical salience of the detective industry and of the fictional private eye, their historical connection is something of a mystery. A great many works have been written on the detective of crime fiction and, far fewer but still numerous, on Pinkertons, labor spies, and strike breakers. Seldom, however, has the relationship between these worlds been examined despite their demonstrable interdependence. I argue that these two institutions arose under common historical conditions and pursue parallel objectives as they seek, respectively, to control and to represent the world around them. My objective is not simply to analyze the business history of detective agencies and operatives nor to describe the popular culture of the detective story alone. Rather it is to show how these two enterprises arose in tandem, intermingle, affect one another, produce their respective stories, and confound distinctions of fact and fiction, while simultaneously inventing a convenient collective memory. The private detective is immediately known, readily envisioned, yet seldom explained.

Intrigue surrounding the image of the private detective is based on its inherent ambiguity, its duality deriving from both the criminal and disreputable underworld and the realm of public agents of protection and order. The detective's skills come from intimate association with miscreants, although they purport to serve the righteous. Detectives do society's dirty work. The sociologist Everett Hughes writes about "good people and dirty work," how society responds to the dilemma of bad things done in its name. Although Hughes developed the idea in the context of Nazi Germany, he argues that a general problem arises from work done with society's forbearance by people known to employ odious means: "the whole problem [is] the extent to which those pariahs who do the dirty work of society are really acting as agents for the rest of us." The societal reaction includes an "unwillingness to think about the dirty work done [and] this common silence allows group fictions to grow up."[8] Here lies an important clue to the legend of the private detective. The occupation is plagued with a problem of legitimacy—whether, when, how its recognized dirty work can be justified. From the beginning this problem preoccupied those who practiced as, employed, or wrote about detectives. Famous detectives acknowledged the unseemly activities and unscrupulous agents of their trade but argued that they were different, a new breed of professionals. Their self-aggrandizing memoirs inspired story writers and novelists. The whole dilemma encouraged fictions to grow up, as Hughes observed. The legendary detective is a product of this special set of social conditions.

The private detective, one of our most familiar cultural figures, provides a case study of how legends are socially constructed. The term *legend* captures more effectively the explanatory forces at work than does *myth*, although the terms are sometimes used interchangeably. But *myth* connotes error, delusion, or skepticism, something people have been fooled into believing. "Legend" is more substantial and more nuanced, referring to a collective understanding that melds fact and fiction in robust narratives. Myths invite refutation while legends prompt inquiry, appreciation of their contents and origins. Neither of these is captured in the provocative if slippery notion of "invented traditions," which refers to specific practices, rituals and performances.[9] I use *legend* and serviceable synonyms like *figure* and *image* to identify and discuss cultural understandings that people share and act upon collectively.

The first detective agency was established in Paris in the 1830s when former criminal and police informant Eugène Vidocq joined the police force and later set up his own private bureau, which spawned a new kind of business enterprise.[10] England followed a somewhat different path as mercenary "thief-takers" were superseded by the metropolitan police force, with private detectives following in relatively smaller numbers. Allan Pinkerton founded the first US detective agency in 1850, specializing in protecting railroad and express companies from robbers within and outside their employ. The number of detective agencies and operatives expanded dramatically in late nineteenth-century America as the growing labor movement, peopled mainly by immigrant workers, began to unionize. As noted, the major detective agencies worked for corporations generally in surveillance of workers. Some companies maintained an internal staff of operatives or contracted with employer associations, which acted essentially as detective agencies. The big agencies themselves became imposing corporations in a prospering service industry. The services they provided included information gathering (labor espionage), protection of property, and enforcement of client company policies such as strikebreaking. Smaller, independent agencies did some of these things but concentrated on matrimonial, personal, and financial services. Because their product was a service, detective agencies were directly affected by economic conditions and changing corporate and government policies. In concert industrial development, labor markets, collective action by employers and unions, state regulation of industry, and labor, as well as regulation and licensing of the agencies themselves, all shaped the operation of detective agencies.

The culture industry in these years was a different kind of business, equally subject to the market and its changing demands, but devoted to a product, both material and imaginative, rather than a service. The detective story was just one genre purveyed by the business of publishing, broadcasting, and film-making, but it was the most popular and profitable genre of the era. The introduction and development of the detective story began in the print medium, which shaped adaptations to radio and film. The term "culture industry" comes to us from social theory and was fashioned in a critique of cultural forces that engendered domination, capitalist hegemony, and individual alienation.[11] Insightful as that analysis may be, the culture industry merits a broader analysis. It is, as Terry Eagleton says, "a vital project . . . which must not be surrendered to a melancholic Left or Right mythology of the media as impregnably monolithic."[12] The culture industry here refers to the producers and products of popular culture and specifically to the various business enterprises and actors who fashioned the detective in story papers, middlebrow magazines, dime novels, pulps, radio, film, and an array of consumer products. In this study, the culture industry is analyzed for the ways in which developments in print technology, growing literacy, mass distribution, publishing firms, "fiction factories," writers, and editors, as well as radio broadcasters and filmmakers, all shaped the figure of the private eye.

The key point is the convergence of these enterprises. They developed under coeval historical conditions of urbanization and commercialization. From its beginning with Vidocq, the detective business fostered a legend in literary memoirs that double as agency publicity. Edgar Allan Poe wrote the first detective story drawing on Vidocq and a contemporary literary genre known as urban mysteries. Detective agencies imitated the new literary form with embellished chronicles of their exploits, designed to sell and to advertise. Pinkerton and his ghost writers produced a score of loosely factual book-length tales. Arthur Conan Doyle took his lead from Poe, sometimes using real events as in "The Valley of Fear," a Sherlock Holmes novel featuring a brutish Pinkerton operative in the Pennsylvania coal fields, much to the displeasure of the agency. The agencies present themselves to clients and, later, to investigative commissions in reports and testimony that fictionalize their methods and promote a preferred image of professionalism. Reality and representation shaped one another in moving interplay.

This convergence is revealed in a natural history of the business enterprises. The detective agency is created in a new historical situation in which the growth of cities and commerce engender conflicts that are beyond the policing capacity of the state to manage. Entrepreneurs possessing some familiarity with the worlds of crime and disorder come forward with a new service: detection. The new service is suspect, owing to its shady origins and invasive methods. The agencies are perceived as necessary evils and so are faced with a perennial struggle for legitimacy—itself a stimulus to image making. These forces play out in contrasting and contingent ways across nations. A unique set of conditions in the United States of the late nineteenth and early twentieth centuries fosters the largest detective industry and its most celebrated figure, the private eye.

Together these enterprises, their clients, customers, and critics produce a legend. The legendary detective is an international figure owing much to its development in the United States but with distinct pedigrees in France and England and cultural amalgams of surprising geographical portability. The salience of the detective legend varies internationally from pervasive in the United States to marginal in societies where policing is exclusively a state function. Intranationally, the legendary detective exists alongside other cultural icons like cowboys, outlaws and Okies. Legends and the process of legend creation may be compared fruitfully. How was the formidable figure of the cowboy constructed from a narrow empirical foundation in contrast to the historically pervasive detective? Is it true, as Eric Hobsbawm claims, that "the private eye has killed the Virginian"?[13] Do some legends, like the detective and the Okie, arise in similar ways? Such comparative questions reveal culture-producing practices not previously deemed problematic and so not properly investigated or understood.

The history of the private detective is all the more compelling because it is a history intended not to be told—a history, in important part, that has been silenced, suppressed, and substituted with fiction. Many of the activities of the great agencies were duplicitous, ranging from offensive and marginally legal to criminal and destructive. Business records were seldom preserved and certainly not made available for inspection. Case reports sent to clients and to agency files were destroyed as a matter of policy when business was concluded. Although federal investigations successfully subpoenaed some records, agencies hastily trashed case files and financial data as investigators closed in. This suppression stemmed from agency promises of confidentiality as much as from concealment of shady methods. Secrecy hung over the industry. Operatives went by code numbers rather that names and often were not known to one another. Code language and circuitous communication channels were employed to preserve anonymity. Yet evidence survives, buried in archives, leaked by insiders, or forcibly extracted and reassembled by resourceful investigators. To a large extent, the story of a once-grand industrial operation requires reconstruction from fortuitous outcroppings.

Historians are adept at researching secret organizations from discovered transcripts and ancient societies from archaeological fragments. The paradox in this case is that the ubiquitous detective was effectively suppressed and re-presented in a heavily retouched image by the historical actors themselves, yet in ways that produced an even more revealing story. In what follows I endeavor to recover that story and explain its cultural transformation. Legend reveals what the detective became in collective memory and how that happened. Fact and fiction merge. Agents, operatives, and writers are restored to their times, given voice.

# I

# ENTER THE DETECTIVE

## The First Detectives

François-Eugène Vidocq (1775–1857) was the first detective and founder of the first private detective agency. He was also a notorious criminal, a thief and jailbird from adolescence until he joined the Paris police force in 1811 as an informer with invaluable knowledge of the underworld. Indeed, his criminal activity persisted and facilitated his fifteen-year career as a sûreté bureau chief. Police work at the time consisted largely of apprehending thieves and recovering stolen property. Purloined goods conveniently reappeared after the detective-negotiator brokered an exchange for a customary fee. The prudent thief could also purchase police protection. Vidocq was at the center of this world, retiring a wealthy man to found his own detective agency, the Bureau des Renseignements, in 1827. The agency prospered, with offices in one of Paris's exclusive glass-covered arcades, a staff of forty agents, and a business model that spawned a number of rival agencies.[1] Vidocq and his imitators had discovered a lucrative niche in the growing urban economy, notably in the areas of theft recovery and debt collection.

Vidocq personified the forces shaping Paris in the early nineteenth century. He was an urban immigrant who joined a legion of petty criminals. The city's population increased fourfold in the period, reaching two million by 1860. The French historian Louis Chevalier describes a condition of "social deterioration" as new "ethnic" (i.e., regional) minorities overtaxed the city's infrastructure, creating slums, congestion, and disease such as the cholera epidemic of 1832. Poverty was pervasive, reflected in an underclass of prostitutes, peddlers, beggars, and street urchins, the *gamin*. The old craft guilds suffered the challenge of new working classes.[2] In the midst of this perceived disorder, police relied on informers: "In any urban community there would always be a certain degree of complicity between the police and those the police considered potentially dangerous."[3] Vidocq was a natural for the role that combined criminal knowledge and associations with insouciance and entrepreneurial skill. Yet the detective's niche derived from a peculiar conjunction of the state and economy—compromised police and explosive growth.

An important part of Vidocq's success was the publication of his ghostwritten *Mémoires de Vidocq* in 1828.[4] Already a Parisian celebrity, Vidocq now was becoming legend as the sensational memoir was translated into English as *Vidocq! The French Police Spy* and inspired a London play of the same name. The picaresque detective was a friend of Honoré de Balzac and Victor Hugo and informed their portrayals of the Parisian underclass. Reflecting this social world, Eugène Sue's *Les mystères de Paris* created a new literary genre soon imitated in other cities. Vidocq's place in history was forever assured in 1841 when Edgar Allan Poe published the first detective story, "The Murders in the Rue Morgue," featuring the shrewd patrician C. Auguste Dupin, who was modeled after Vidocq. Chevalier observes, "The legend of Vidocq, combining in one person as he did order and disorder, police and crime, dirty work and high politics, was an important element in popular thinking. The massive silhouette, now reassuring and now terrifying, not only loomed in the background of the major contemporary works, but also dominated the people's fears and beliefs."[5]

Private policing in Britain followed a different path, partly in reaction to contemporary France. From the late eighteenth century onward, the movement for parliamentary reform and the right of workers to form associations was harried and repressed by the state. Government spies infiltrated the network of nascent corresponding societies and worker groups suspected of violating the Combination Acts that outlawed unions. National scandal was provoked by Oliver the Spy when he publicly promoted militancy as a friend of reform while secretly naming rebels to the authorities, who arrested, tried, and, in a few instances, executed the leaders. E. P. Thompson claims, "The employment of informers had become virtually a routine practice on the part of magistrates in the larger industrial centers. . . . But the practice was regarded by a very wide section of public opinion as being wholly alien to English law [and] the clamor grew throughout to country against the 'continental spy system.'"[6]

In preference to the continental pattern, policing of British cities was delegated to the magistrate's courts, which received criminal complaints and apprehended accused persons for trial. London's Magistrate's Court employed six agents called "thief takers" or "Bow Street Runners," owing to the court's location in Bow Street near Covent Garden. At the beginning of the nineteenth century, London had become the largest city in the world, doubling its population in seventy years (1750–1820), with all the potential for disorder deriving from immigration, burgeoning slums, working class agitation, and crime—or at least the fear of crime. Dickensian London required a metropolitan police force, one that could claim respectability by clearly refusing the services of spies and criminal informers. In 1829, Parliament passed the Metropolitan Police Act, which provided full-time day and night patrol of city streets. Preventative policing emphasized the presence of authority, identified by military style uniforms, height-enhancing helmets, and a professional demeanor that spoke order. Often called "bobbies" or "peelers," after parliamentary exponent Robert Peel, these officers did not come by respectability immediately. Half the original recruits were dismissed for drunkenness and police spies plagued the labor movement. Yet the metropolitan force worked deliberately to eliminate such unprofessional behavior and establish a reputation for providing public order.[7]

The English language word "detective" derives from the Latin verb *detegere*, meaning to expose or reveal, a practice with odious connotations in Britain. It would be 1842 before a separate investigative branch was added to the prevention-oriented force and the first detectives began working to gain acceptance. Private detectives were still barely known in England. Charles Frederick Field retired from the Metropolitan Police in the mid-1850s to establish himself in private practice, although he got into trouble for continuing to represent himself as a public official. Ignatius Paul Pollaky founded Pollaky's Private Inquiry Office in 1862, certainly among the first of its kind, advertising discreet inquiries in election, divorce, and libel cases. Better known as "inquiry agents," these investigators dealt mainly with matrimonial matters. One student of the period writes, "But for the Matrimonial Causes Act of 1857, which was responsible for the divorce court as we know it, we would never have had the many hundreds of private detectives and agencies that now make a profession out of matrimonial investigation. . . . The very terms, 'private detective' and 'private investigator' would never have come into use."[8]

## American Exceptionalism

The detective agency achieved its greatest success in the United States beginning in the mid-nineteenth century when Allan Pinkerton established the North-Western Police Agency in Chicago. Early detectives were creatures of the railroads, which dated from the 1830s in southern and midwestern regional lines. The midwestern railroads expanded in the 1850s, and after the Civil War, massive federally subsidized construction extending from the Missouri River to Sacramento, California, resulted in the first "transcontinental" connection of the Central Pacific and Union Pacific Railroads in 1869.[9] These early railroads created new opportunities for business and crime. Brazen train robberies multiplied, as did pilfered freight shipments and passenger thieves. Railroad employees and express agents sometimes succumbed to temptation. Security posed special problems. Trains that crossed political jurisdictions had no consistent police protection. Special railroad police were created, but they could not match the geographic mobility and guile of the outlaws.

Pinkerton devised a new business service for the local railways, a private police force that would employ investigative methods not only to apprehend thieves and recover their booty but also to prevent theft. Pinkerton hired former police and experienced investigators who surveilled trains and railroad stations alert to the commission of crimes and observed the haunts of railroad predators—saloons or boarding houses where the thieves would gather information about potential targets. Pinkerton adapted the method of the spy to undercover police work then marketed the new service. Initially, Pinkerton contracted protective services to a consortium of six railway companies headed by the Illinois Central Rail Road. The contract dated February 1, 1855, called for agents in three different salary (and presumably skill) categories who would protect against any threat to the tracks, to the mail, or from the "depredations of any gang" which affected two or more of the companies. Although Pinkerton agents famously pursued train robbers like Butch Cassidy and the Sundance Kid, their principal task was surveillance, particularly of railroad employees. In contract

Figure 1.1. The Pinkerton logo incorporates the ancient and frequently appropriated symbol of the all-seeing eye. Founded in 1850, the agency had several names before adopting the Pinkerton name, the logo, and a claim to national coverage after the Civil War. (Library of Congress)

language, Pinkerton operatives would "at all times communicate any information they may have concerning the habits or associations of the employees of said [railroad] companies."[10]

In 1858, the young agency was renamed Pinkerton's Protective Police Patrol, first in a field of similar enterprises growing in tandem with commerce and industry. The business model spread. Train robbers were gradually arrested or killed off, along with a few detectives, thanks to the agencies. The Pinkertons, or simply "Pinks," became a familiar American institution owing to successful marketing and public relations symbolized by the trademark "private eye." Pinkerton appropriated the classical "eye of Providence" or "all-seeing eye of God," an ancient symbol found in Hebrew and Egyptian religions, which had been adopted for a variety of purposes before the Pinkerton use, including as a symbol of Freemasonry and as part of the designs of the Great Seal of the United States and the one-dollar bill. Below the eye on the original Pinkerton logo, the agency motto promised "We Never Sleep."

Equally important, Allan Pinkerton initiated a series of popular books celebrating his adventures and his agency, including *The Ex-*

*pressman and the Detective*; *Strikers, Communists, Tramps and Detec-tives*; and *The Model Town and the Detectives*. Ghostwriters produced most of the sixteen volumes, published in the 1870s and 1880s, which cast detective work in melodrama. Playwright and novelist Cleveland Moffett continued the tradition with a series of "True Stories from the Pinkerton Archives" that appeared in *McClure's Magazine* and were subsequently collected in a book. Moffett and the Pinkerton ghost-writers invented dialogue among train robbers and attributed intrepid action to detectives in stories that spawned the true crime genre.

Allan Pinkerton's business flourished, moving beyond the railroad contracts. He joined the Civil War effort, protecting trains, investi-gating war profiteers, spying on Confederate plans, and directing the Secret Service. He admitted making a good deal of money working for the government. But public attention was a mixed blessing. In 1861, the *Chicago Tribune* gave Pinkerton credit for foiling an assassination plot allegedly planned for Lincoln's inauguration, although it is unclear how the newspaper got the story of a secret operation or whether it was planted by agency publicists. The existence of a plot was denied by southern newspapers and the *Chicago Democrat* denounced the story: "How much longer will the people of this country be the dupe of these private detectives.... How are they to have cases unless they get them up? There was no conspiracy at all, save in the brain of the Chicago Detective."[11] Public suspicions about the practices of private detectives that originated in Europe reappeared in the United States, an intrinsic feature of the business.

After the war, detective agencies adjusted to a growing national economy, especially the rise of heavy industry. Chicago steel mills made rails and Pullman cars that ran on them. Detectives extended their services. Agency experience in undercover work and surveil-lance, aimed originally at employee theft, transferred well to investi-gations of worker efforts to organize unions. Industrial espionage and the labor spy emerged and grew to a principal income source. Protec-tive services developed for trains and tracks were easily adapted to industrial plants.

America's Gilded Age (1878–99) derives its name from a set of social and economic changes, including economic growth; industrial concentration; and wealth creation, excess, and inequality, which re-sulted in a pervasive rearrangement of social classes and geography. Urbanization took charge. From 1870 to 1920 the number of people

Figure 1.2. Allan Pinkerton (seated, right) during his Civil War service. Also shown is Kate Warne (standing, center), who became the first female private detective when Pinkerton hired her in 1856. (Library of Congress)

living in cities doubled from 25 to 50 percent of the population. The urban population of the Northeast reached 75 percent in 1920. Remarkably, in 1900, 60 percent of city dwellers nationwide were immigrants or the children of immigrants. Coast to coast, the great US cities were predominantly first- or second-generation immigrants as early as 1880, with Chicago at 87 percent, New York at 80 percent, and San Francisco at 78 percent.[12] The nation's cities and rural hinterlands were connected in a transcontinental railway network: from 1860–1880 the miles of railroad track tripled, and tripled again by 1920. Apropos of the age, the transcontinental railways were ill-advised schemes financed by government in a maze of corruption and destined for bankruptcy.[13] This was the age of monopoly, of the great trusts like John D. Rockefeller's Standard Oil, J. P. Morgan's U.S. Steel, and many more, from farm machine manufacturing to sugar refining to meat packing. The expanding infrastructure and the plentiful labor force supported unprecedented economic growth that favored all sectors, albeit in unequal measure.

Economic boom and bust punctuated the Gilded Age. Major depressions visited the 1870s and 1890s, which brought dislocations in the form of unemployment and wage reductions. Labor's plight motivated the early unionization movement. A series of protests over wage and job cuts by the railroads occurred in scattered locations and culminated in the General Strike of 1873–74. Although the strike failed, it signaled a new reality in American society. "The significance of the strikes lay not in their success or failure but rather in the readiness of the strikers to express their grievances in a dramatic, direct, and frequently telling manner."[14] Precipitated by depression, the railroad strikes of 1877 pitted a better organized labor movement against the National Guard in violent conflicts. Social unrest increasingly occupied public attention.

Railroad strikes provided the backdrop for the sensational struggle of the Irish immigrant "Molly Maguire" miners in Pennsylvania's anthracite coal fields. The conflict cast the miners against the Philadelphia and Reading Railroad, which had come to dominate the operation of the mines. The miners' battle for fair wages and unionization in the face of aggressive management ended in violence and the hanging of ten alleged conspirators from the Irish communities. In fact, the original Molly Maguires, a secret society of peasants in Ireland who fought against oppressive landlords, was not coincident with the fraternal and union organizations that waged the miners' fight in Pennsylvania. The erroneous connection stemmed from mine owners' antipathy for unions and sensational popular literature that portrayed the movement simplistically as a product of alien terrorism. In the second of the series of books devoted to his agency's exploits, Pinkerton published *The Molly Maguires and the Detectives*, a biased intrigue that lionized Pinkerton operative James McParland, demonized the Irish, and served mainly as "a sales pitch for his detective agency." Marked improvement in the prose over that of the first book in the series, *The Expressman and the Detectives*, suggests that the boss had already turned to ghostwriters.[15]

Urban disorder attained its most dramatic expression in Chicago's Haymarket Square in May 1886. In the wake of a general strike for the eight-hour day, labor organizers called for a rally in the city center to protest a bloody clash on the previous day at the McCormick farm equipment factory. As speakers warmed the crowd of three thousand mainly ethnic (especially German) working people and Chicago police moved precipitously to disperse the crowd, a bomb of unknown origin exploded, killing seven police and three civilians and injuring scores.[16] Once again, the press blamed "foreign savages" and a show trial led to the hanging of four accused anarchists. Judicious critics were unconvinced of their guilt or of the innocence of possible agents provocateurs. Charles Siringo, the fabled Pinkerton "cowboy detective," claimed to have been working for the agency during the Chicago rallies along with other operatives who, he said, engaged anarchists in conversation, unsuccessfully attempting to evoke threats of violence and subsequently writing "flashy reports [that] suited the agency" and giving "perjured testimony" alleging planned violence.[17]

The historian Paul Boyer observes, "Urban disorder was familiar enough from the antebellum period, but in the Gilded Age it took on a more menacing aura as a direct expression of labor unrest."[18] Following the European experience, it was fear of moral breakdown, the rabble, lawlessness, labor demands for a share of the largesse, and erosion of normative authority that generated new mechanisms of social control. Moral reform societies and coercive police power grew in tandem. The expansion of police power, however, raised deep-seated fears of another evil, the tyrannical state. The private detective agency answered this dilemma.

> Only in the mid-nineteenth century, with the growth of industrial cities—and the specters of proletarian mob, vicious hooligan, and degenerate wastrel—did fears of social order overwhelm distrust of the omnipotent state. . . . But scandals revealed that many of America's public detectives, like Britain's thief-takers before them, were little more than 'bagmen,' collecting payoffs from amiable felons and arresting those who failed to pay tribute. . . . Thus it was scarcely surprising when 'municipal' crime detection was largely returned to overtly private hands. The first American private detectives were former municipal constables. . . . By the 1850s six private agencies had sprung up across the country; by 1884 fourteen flourished in Chicago alone.[19]

Rapid urbanization, powerful corporate trusts, and sprawling commerce facilitated by the eastern and midwestern railway network provided the material foundation for increasingly essential detective agencies. A New York journalist observed in 1871, "All the large commercial cities are now liberally provided with 'Detective Agencies' as they are called."[20] Pinkerton continued to dominate the industry but rivals moved in. Thomas Furlong operated out of St. Louis as special agent for the Missouri Pacific Railroad and employing regional representatives, including the young William J. Burns. Furlong took a lesson from Pinkerton, publishing his own self-congratulatory memoir *Fifty Years a Detective*, furthering both his agency's reputation and the growing true crime genre.

Gus Thiel, a former Pinkerton operative, established his own agency in 1873 in St. Louis, specializing in railway "spotting" (employee surveillance) and, moving west, in mining disputes. By 1909 the Thiel Detective Agency maintained offices in fifteen cities. James Wood left the Boston Police Department in 1879 to create the "pioneer detective agency in New England." William Baldwin founded the Baldwin Detective Agency (partnering later with Thomas Felts), working for Virginia's railroad and coal mining operations. James Farley established the first agency devoted entirely to strike breaking in 1902, operating nationwide from New York City. In 1909 the industry was rocked by the opening in New York of the William J. Burns National (later International) Detective Agency, which spread to thirty cities by 1920, sparking an intense rivalry with Pinkerton. The Pinkerton–Burns competition centered on claims as to who was the more efficient and, especially, the more "professional" (meaning less given to unseemly practices like intimidation, strikebreaking, and matrimonial work). The pursuit of respectability (with mixed results) shaped the character of these two great firms and, indeed, in different ways, the character of the industry as a whole.

### Homestead

Forty years after its debut in the United States, the detective agency had achieved a familiar, if ambivalent, place in the nation's way of doing business. Then, in 1892, events surrounding a strike in Homestead, Pennsylvania, changed everything. A calamity that would challenge the national conscience began inauspiciously with a labor dispute at the Carnegie Steel Company's Homestead factory, six miles upriver from Pittsburg. The conflict centered on technological innovations in the labor process that portended wage reductions for many of the 3,800 workers represented by the country's largest trade union, the

Amalgamated Association of Iron and Steel Workers. With Andrew Carnegie away in his native Scotland, Homestead's hard-driving chief of operations, Henry Clay Frick, refused a wage compromise offered in negotiations by the union and imposed a lockout. Union and towns-people mobilized in an effort to block any influx of replacement work-ers while continuing to press for negotiations. US census records for 1890 no longer exist, but the 1880 census describes a representative, if smaller, population of six hundred, including a majority of immigrant and native-born first generation German, English, Irish residents. Among those engaged as factory hands and domestic workers, first-generation persons were more numerous than recent immigrants. Steel workers were mostly native-born first generation and over half the men were in skilled occupations.

Frick was uncompromising. Claiming threats of property damage, which workers had pledged to prevent at this stage, the chief raised a fence around the plant and, in a fateful step, called for reinforcements. Pinkerton offices in Chicago, Philadelphia, and New York quickly mustered a force of three hundred guards, forty of whom were regular agency employees, the rest recruited from the streets as was standard in strikebreaking situations. With a wink at federal law prohibiting the transport of private armed forces across state lines, the Pinkerton men came on one train, their guns and ammunition on another. The plan was to transport the guards up the Monongahela River on two barges, land within the fenced perimeter on the plant's riverside, and secure the facility—perhaps for replacement workers had things gone that far. Expecting trouble, workers maintained a vigil outside the factory and along the river approach. As the barges prepared to dock, an an-gry crowd broke through the fence, confronted the Pinkerton force, and warned that harm awaited any who set foot on land. Threats were exchanged; each side dug in. Then shots were fired, although it is im-possible to know who fired first. In the ensuing melee, four workers and two guards were killed and more were wounded.

The standoff lasted through the night and into the next morning when the Pinkertons, still trapped on the barges and facing an immov-able crowd, agreed to a surrender in exchange for a peaceful landing and safe passage out of town. The crowd was pacified momentarily by assurances that the Pinkertons would face murder charges in the shooting deaths of the four workers. The situation appeared in hand until the lines that had formed on each side of the departing guards

Figure 1.3. The violent Homestead Strike of 1892 sent shock waves through the country, generating congressional investigations and censure that damaged the Pinkertons, the steel workers union, and Carnegie's corporation alike. (*Frank Leslie's Illustrated Weekly*, July 14, 1892).

became an angry gauntlet of curses and then of remorseless physical abuse. Despite all the circumstances contributing to the violence at Homestead, this final act of humiliation wreaked on a retreating foe by the frenzied mob became the centerpiece of subsequent public perception—much of that facilitated by sensational press accounts.[21]

Homestead diminished everyone. The very name of Carnegie's mill became synonymous with a shameful history of labor relations. The steelworker's union was destroyed, organizing efforts were arrested for the next forty years. Congress weighed in with lengthy investigations in both the House and Senate that laid blame all around. Their reports recognized a potential threat to national sovereignty from private armies and passed the symbolically important "anti-Pinkerton law" forbidding government employment of the agency. The firm suffered a severe blow to its reputation and business interests. Twenty-six states passed laws against the private employment of armed guards.[22] A posthumous introduction to Allan Pinkerton's memoir acknowledged, "There is little doubt the events [of Homestead] shattered the reputation of the Agency"[23] The "Pinks" were reviled in labor circles. Songs and doggerel portrayed them as oppressors. Under the direction of Robert Pinkerton, Allan's businesslike son and successor, the agency responded with policy changes that shifted their focus from "industrial" work to "security" services. Employee training was introduced, commercial clients pursued, and professionalism advertised. They quit strike work—or at least said they would. Not satisfied with burnishing their own image, the agency disparaged their rivals, notably the flamboyant Burns and his methods. In the late 1940s, as James Horan and Howard Swiggert were preparing their authorized book *The Pinkerton Story*, agency watchdogs kept a close eye on manuscript drafts, ensuring that the firm would bear no responsibility for the violence at Homestead in this version of the agency's history.[24]

If Homestead shook the agency, the general reaction was mixed. A study of public opinion in the aftermath of Homestead revealed that violence was denounced whether employed by labor, detectives, or police. But owners were conceded a right to defend their property with force if necessary. Workers had a right to give or withhold their own "property," their labor, but no right to coerce others. They always had the freedom to select another employer if grievances were irresolvable but not to force concessions on ownership.[25] The rights of

labor at this time were largely negative; they could meet and talk but
they could not constrain their employers. Collective bargaining was
far down the road. Indeed, during the Red Scare of the 1920s, criminal
syndicalism laws in many states threatened rights of speech and assembly of radical labor advocates.[26] In the end, Homestead and the
national dialogue it informed were contested matters.

### Legitimacy

From Vidocq to Pinkerton, the private detective was always a figure
of dubious legitimacy. The very act of "detecting" was easily conflated
with illicit spying, and the original agents of the trade came from the
criminal underworld. As early as 1871, a New York City journalist had
uncovered evidence of "flagrant operations which have made the term
of private detective a synonym for rogue. . . . The interests of society
plainly demand the suppression of this peculiar institution."[27] One
Thomas Beet wrote the widely circulated article "Methods of American Private Detective Agencies" for *Appleton's Magazine* in 1906.[28]
Beet's name appeared over the byline "American Representative of
John Conquest, ex-Chief Inspector, Scotland Yard." Some may have
questioned whether Scotland Yard actually had an American Representative, but the aura of authority seemed to work, judging from the
frequency with which Beet's views were cited. Critics claimed that
agencies pretended to fight crime but were really "a vital menace to
American society . . . hotbeds of corruption, trafficking upon the honor
and sacred confidences of their patrons and the credulity of the public,
and leaving in their wake an aftermath of disgrace, disaster, and even
death. . . . Fully ninety per cent of the private detective establishments,
masquerading in whatever form, are rotten to the core."[29] Beet came
to be regarded as a reliable source by some journalists and historians.
Arthur Train, a bone fide ex-assistant district attorney of New York,
later revealed that Thomas Beet was actually a divorce detective from
New York City but nevertheless cautioned that there were few "real
detectives" in a field where the temptation to dishonesty was great.[30]

    The shady detective might have been a less convincing portrait
had it not been for ambivalence expressed by the industry's greatest
advocates. Reflecting at the beginning of his book *Thirty Years a Detective*, Allan Pinkerton conceded, "The time was when a halo of romance was thrown around the disreputable *mouchard* of the Parisian

Corps—when the Bow street runner of London and the 'shadow' of the American police were the ideal . . . [but now] the detective himself has undergone a complete metamorphosis." [31] Pinkerton's contemporary, Thomas Furlong, lamented that the "general public is not so charitable to detectives. The pettifogging lawyers and irresponsible penny liners of the press have educated it up to believing that all detectives are thieves, thugs and black guards, just because there are some men in the business who make the peddling of family secrets and the working up of evidence in divorce cases a speciality." [32]

With typical bombast, Furlong's protégée William J. Burns noted,

> I have openly stated, in many of my public utterances from the platform, that private detectives, as a class, are the greatest lot of crooks that ever went unpunished . . . [but, fortunately,] since organizing the William J. Burns National Detective Agency, I have been cognizant of the outrageous blackmailing methods pursued by private detectives, and I made up my mind that I would do everything possible to expose this class of lawbreakers and parasites on society. . . . The honest private detectives applaud this statement, and are with me in my effort to give to the business an air of respectability, if that is possible.[33]

While distinguishing themselves from the unscrupulous "gumshoe" (a term derived from the cheap, thick-soled shoes worn by lower-class men), these leaders of the industry also reinforced the stereotype. Critics and reformers doubted the distinction, pointing to Homestead or Burns and the methods of his agency as prima facie evidence supporting their criticism. The business may well have become increasingly professional but not necessarily more reputable. The problem, in this view, lay in the nature of the business itself—an enterprise in a capitalist economy that derived its profit from, among other things, selling the products of spying and controlling the cost of labor.

In 1872, George McWatters wrote one of the earliest and best memoirs of an American detective. McWatters was an immigrant Scot, like Pinkerton, who also shared a sense of social justice. Pinkerton was a member of the Chartist movement in Britain and an abolitionist in the United States, while McWatters embraced socialist principles in both places. His *Knots Untied: Ways and By-Ways the Hidden Life of*

*American Detectives* concludes (at the request of the publishers, he says) with an assessment of "the detective system in general." McWatters notes that society at large demands the detective system for its protection and support:

> The wonder to me is that the intelligent classes do not look things squarely in the face, and see for themselves how utterly hopeless it is to ever do without the detective in society, so long as our legislators make ten laws for the protection of property to one for man. . . . [The detective] is the outgrowth of a diseased and corrupted state of things, and is, consequently, morally diseased himself. His very existence is a satire upon society. He is a miserable snake, not in a paradise, but in the social hell. He is a thief, and steals into men's confidences to ruin them.

The irony in all this is that "detectives are, for the most part, excellent citizens [and] the detective system is one of the very best institutions or features of our corrupt civilization . . . a necessary part of an unnecessary system of wrong." [34]

The problem of legitimacy underpinned the conduct of and writing about the detective business, the practice and the prose. Agencies struggled to claim legitimacy while critics and reformers sought to deny it. Their respective stories grew from one root, the intrinsically ambivalent character of the enterprise, its duality as a supposed requirement of order and threat to civility—the problem of dirty work. Charles Siringo captured it bluntly: "Detectives are a necessary evil." [35]

The legend that grew up around the private detective drew as much on nonfiction writing (pro and con), public controversy, and industry promotion as it did on the popular fiction that arose coincident with the occupation's birth and development. From Poe's foundational stories in the 1840s and a collection of detective novels appearing in the 1860s and 1870s, the publishing industry and the detective industry developed in tandem, shaping and infusing one another. Real detectives like Burns, and Allan Pinkerton's son Robert, were at pains to distinguish themselves from the stereotypical "gumshoe" or fantastical sleuth yet happy to share in the limelight of the romanticized crime fighter. Much of what society came to understand of private detectives derived from this dialogue.

## Detectives in Theory

Why did the private detective industry achieve its most fully developed form in the United States? Why did this unique phenomenon occur in the late nineteenth and early twentieth centuries, and what inspired its contested legitimacy? Despite a vast literature on detective fiction, there are surprisingly few attempts to explain the detective system in its time, place, and social condition. "The social role of detectives has been misunderstood by succeeding generations, and ignored by historians." [36]

In Europe and America, detectives arose with modernity in the presence of rapid and disruptive changes: expanding commerce and industry, dramatic increases in population (especially urban population), new immigrants to crowded cities, slums, and disease alongside growing wealth and ostentation, opportunities in the fields of crime and punishment. Urban disorder was the diagnosis of the time, pronounced by public commissions investigating health and safety and by literary observers from Victor Hugo to Charles Dickens. France, Britain, and the United States traveled different revolutionary paths to bourgeois democracy. Authority now resided in the state, although states varied widely in the power and timely development of public institutions. Metropolitan police forces indexed state strength. And so, inversely, did private detectives. The relatively strong French state instituted metropolitan police who used detectives as informers and intermediaries, not as quasi-official authorities. The police force created a detective division early on, which graduated the first private detectives. In Britain, a metropolitan police force developed later and slowly, owing to public distrust created by government repression of political reform and the labor movement. The "continental spy system" was anathema to the parliamentarians struggling to create a state that compromised monarchial strength with representative institutions. As reform progressed, police took over from private thief takers, although the pace was halting. A detective branch eventually was added to the metropolitan force and private detectives reappeared in limited numbers.

Conditions were different in the United States, different in ways that fostered the uniquely extensive American private detective enterprise. In the latter half of the nineteenth century, a national system of law enforcement had yet to develop, and municipal policing was barely off to a controversial start. The United States also lacked a vigorous labor movement on a scale anything like the British tradition. Conversely, as Gilded Age economic expansion reached across the country, large corporate trusts dominated growing portions of the economy. The federal government was relatively weak, especially in the era of Gilded Age corruption exemplified by the railroad monopolies. States offered a patchwork of regulation, and interstate commerce was unregulated territory. Neither the national state nor the nascent labor movement restrained private policing. Corporations exercised the power to defend their property against threats whether they came from real criminals or, more often, from labor. Corporate economic expansion and a dearth of law enforcement combined to open an entrepreneurial space for the likes of Pinkerton, Thiel, Furlong, and Baldwin, who fashioned a new business model well in advance of calling themselves detective agencies.

Among the very few historians or social scientists who have attempted to explain the advent of the detective agency, two general accounts prevail. In the first and obviously compelling interpretation, Robert Weiss understands the detective system as part of the apparatus for controlling labor: "The early development of the private detective agency was largely concerned with helping provide a disciplined supply of labor to power capitalist industrialization." Weiss goes on to identify three phases in the historical career of the agencies stemming from "changes in the nature of the political economy as these affected the 'labor question.'" [37] The first begins with the pioneering agencies of the nineteenth century through World War I, a period in which policing labor was exclusively the responsibility of private detectives. For the next twenty years private firms cooperated with the Federal Bureau of Investigation in attempts to contain labor organizing and strikes. Third, from the time of the La Follette Senate investigation of the late 1930s, labor discipline shifted away from the private agencies to developing business unionism in league with the FBI.

Weiss's theory of labor discipline captures an important yet limited part of the detective agency's origin. The early agencies, particularly the independents, were directed at various forms of disorder and chaos. Although the large American agencies dealt disproportionately with labor issues, part of their business and much of the work of the independents concerned protection of property, insurance fraud, matrimonial affairs, and the like. Labor control, with its repressive implications, was only one among several services the agencies provided. Detectives sometimes pursued criminals or, by their presence, discouraged crime. They even did some good, defending innocents or speaking truth to the employers. Exclusive emphasis on labor control obscures other social forces that affected the development of the detective enterprise, such as state strength, social movements including labor and reform, and a cultural aversion to spying. Nevertheless, Weiss's much-cited 1986 article remains one of the few analytic efforts to explain private detectives.

A second explanation, from Rhodri Jeffreys-Jones, observes that private detectives were business opportunists, not enemies of labor or capitalist lackeys:

> The history of private detective agencies suggests that the reason for their special dynamism in America prior to the 1920s was the scarcity of well-organized police forces. Private detectives came into being, therefore, to meet a real need. . . . Private detectives were not, in fact, agents of an American ruling class. They neither opposed trade unionism as a principle, nor working men as a class. They simply saw an opportunity to make money out of conflict. . . . The industrial sleuth was out for himself.[38]

The observation dissolves any apparent contradiction in Pinkerton's Chartist and abolitionist beliefs or Burns's magnanimous announcement, "I believe in organized labor, and believe that it has helped the workingman" (although he went on to denounce labor leaders given to graft and murder).[39] In contrast to Weiss, Jeffreys-Jones attributes the timing and "special dynamism" of the American industry to a dearth of policing, the resulting opportunity for serving unmet needs, and a spirit of entrepreneurship. The sleuth out for himself resonates with the biographies of all the original PIs.

The theories are more complementary than opposed. Weiss's structural explanation does not attribute motives to detectives but emphasizes, rather singularly, industry's determined pursuit of a disciplined and docile labor force. Incentives and opportunities presented to would-be agency founders are not part of this social control account. Similarly, Jeffreys-Jones focuses on an entrepreneurial account of detectives themselves, neglecting the state, economy, and corporate employers who created them. Although the theories complement one another by highlighting different features of the industry, neither goes deeper into the struggle over the very legitimacy of private detectives, an issue that shapes their organization and their reputation. In the following account, I argue that the historical practices of the detective industry as well as the problem of the detectives' legitimacy—that is, both material conditions and cultural understandings—must be evaluated jointly to arrive at a full understanding of this uniquely American story.

Any effort to theorize the significance of the private detective business will suffer from a dearth of empirical evidence. Who can say, for example, that recruits to the business came largely from the criminal world when, to date, we have little or no evidence on their social backgrounds? What evidence supports the claim that detectives were mainly about controlling labor, or just "out for themselves," when we don't know what their day-to-day work involved? Given that much of the evidence relevant to these questions has been lost or destroyed, where will we find answers? In the chapters that follow, I reconstruct this story by culling a wide range of sources, including those carelessly dismissed as fiction, and reassembling them in continuous narrative.

Chapter 2 asks Who was the detective? and produces some long-buried data about the occupation and its practitioners. Next, looking into the agencies, great and small, chapter 3 reveals how the private detective business was structured and how firms competed with one another. Chapter 4 examines the actual work detectives performed, drawing on their own reports from the field. The evidence shows that their principal task was surveillance, watching other people over long and tedious hours. As critics have argued, detective work then and now derives from conflicts of one sort or another and involves invasion of someone's privacy by covert, often unscrupulous means. The evidence presented in chapter 5 reveals that some of the early detectives' actions were marginally ethical and many were outright criminal; private detectives committed crimes at least as often as they solved them. As a result, the detective business has been controversial, a matter of public concern manifest in investigations of the investigators themselves, as detailed in chapter 6. From Homestead onward, commissions launched by reform societies and, more formidably, by the government have probed the industry's activities. In addition to exposing a need for regulation of abusive practices common to the industry, the commission documents provide a rich source of empirical evidence about the private detective business, its operatives, and their times. In chapter 7, the analysis turns to how the legendary detective is socially constructed, how the business of storytelling interacts with the business of detecting. Finally, I argue that these worlds dovetail, that a full understanding of the detective business requires a cultural understanding of legend, and vice versa. On the surface, the argument seems straightforward, yet working through its implications is full of surprises.

# 2

# WORKING MEN AND WOMEN

### Two Pinkertons, Two Paths

In the early years, detective agencies attracted a variety of recruits who, as a group, shared a common status—they were outsiders. The shady occupation was hardly attractive to the better classes of people possessing education, valued skills, and legitimate opportunities. The new detectives came from the margins of polite society, immigrant and working-class stock looking for a way up, for adventure or the promise of a career. Charlie Siringo and James McParland were two such men, contemporaries in the young Pinkerton service, friends and resourceful operatives whose exploits made each of them famous. Yet they were very different people who ended their careers and their friendship on opposing sides of the Pinkerton controversy.

Charles Angelo Siringo was born in 1855 into an immigrant family, with an Italian father and an Irish mother. He spent his childhood on the family ranch in New Mexico, mostly on horseback he claimed. Throughout life he called himself a cowboy, an identity superseding all others. In his autobiography (he was a writer, too), he styles him-self a "cowboy detective."[1] He became a working cowboy at age eleven and joined cattle drives north to Kansas City and Chicago. For a short time he ran a store in Caldwell, Kansas. By the age of twenty-two he was married and living in Chicago when the Haymarket riot and bombing took place on May 4, 1886. After consulting a phrenologist, he says, "I concluded to try my hand as a detective . . . my main object being to see the world and learn human nature." Siringo knew of the Pinkerton Agency, the "greatest detective school on earth," conveniently headquartered in Chicago. With a letter of recommendation from his banker, he approached the office manager and eventually was summoned by William Pinkerton, who, with his brother Robert, now headed the agency. Pinkerton hired him, explaining they were soon to open a Denver office where a cowboy detective would be useful for "cattle work," tracking down rustlers. Siringo marked "the great anarchist Haymarket riot" as his first case, despite dating his hire to late June, almost two months after the event.[2]

After several years of pursuing "city crooks," including Chicago street car conductors, he was assigned to the Denver branch, where he discovered that crooks were actually running the office. Local operatives were profitably overcharging clients while running their own protection racket. Chicago headquarters became suspicious and sent their most experienced agent, James McParland, to Denver as assistant superintendent. McParland uncovered the scheme and fired everyone except Siringo, who was not part of the ring. So began a long association of the two detectives. McParland managed the office, which covered the entire western United States, picking high-profile cases for himself, while Siringo worked in the field in his métier, pursuing cattle thieves and train robbers. By train and horseback, Siringo crisscrossed the western states following the trail of infamous gangs, traveling under assumed names and in various guises intended to allay suspicion. The colorful and effective Siringo earned a reputation in the agency that lead to offers of promotion. McParland tried to interest him in the assistant superintendent job at a new branch in San Francisco, but Siringo refused. "The truth is, I didn't want to be tied down to an office, even with an advance in salary and a chance to swell up with self importance."[3] Later he added, "My conscience would not allow me to act as a superintendent of the Agency in a big city where so much dirty work would be expected of me. I had decided I would rather remain a sleuth."[4] Siringo's final assignment with the Pinkerton Agency was during the controversial Idaho trial of officials of the Western Federation of Miners (WFM) in the assassination of former governor Frank Steunenberg in 1905. Siringo acted as bodyguard for McParland, who headed the investigation under the auspices of the state, and for the accused assassin whose confession McParland had obtained. The sensational trial featuring Pinkertons and the State of Idaho against WFM President Bill Haywood and Clarence Darrow for the defense exposed the kind of dirty work Siringo despised, including allegations on both sides of jury tampering and perjury.

In 1907, Siringo retired to his Santa Fe ranch to write his memoirs.

The business had changed, lost its attraction for a cowboy detective. Western outlaws were disappearing along with cattle drives and cowboys. The agencies were now primarily engaged in industrial work, and operatives were mainly acting as labor spies—dirty work in Siringo's estimation. As Frank Morn has observed, "He was an adventurer, and as the demand for his kind of operations declined, so did his commitment to the agency. . . . Siringo was a late-nineteenth- century and early-twentieth-century marginal man. He was in a business he disliked to do work he loved."[5]

Before joining Pinkertons, Siringo was already the recognized author of *A Texas Cowboy: Or, Fifteen Years on the Hurricane Deck of a Spanish Pony*, published in 1885, one of the early realistic accounts cowboy life. S. S. McClure, founder and editor of *McClure's Magazine*, who got to know Siringo in Idaho while covering the Steunenberg murder trial, praised his work and suggested adding him to the magazine's staff.[6]

When Siringo finished the manuscript of *Pinkerton Cowboy Detective* and submitted it for approval, the agency sued to block publication of what it considered libelous and proprietary material. The agency was under fire as a result of the publication in 1905 of another insider exposé, Morris Friedman's *The Pinkerton Labor Spy*. Siringo's account, though generally favorable, was nevertheless held up in court with demands for extensive editorial changes. The book was finally published in 1912 with names changed and details altered or eliminated. The revised title, *A Cowboy Detective*, obscured the Pinkerton name, the text referring to the pseudonymous "Dickenson National Detective Agency" (except on one overlooked page).

Embittered by the censorship, Siringo began a far more critical reassessment of the agency's conduct. His 1914 book, *Two Evil Isms: Pinkertonism and Anarchism*, alleged numerous ethical and criminal abuses, renewing Pinkerton's attempts to block publication. When Siringo had the book printed privately, Pinkertons rushed to gather up all the copies and the printing plates, but enough survived to make news and, later, photo reproductions. Charlie Siringo left the detective business as he had entered it, a man of the people. He despised equally bosses and radicals. His study of human nature led him to conclude, "Most of the viciousness in man could be smothered by doing away with liquor and greed for the almighty dollar . . . [by creating] a large flow of the milk of human kindness. For then we would have

Figure 2.1. Charles Siringo (left) and James McParland (right), two famous Pinkerton operatives and colleagues who followed different career paths, ending up on opposing sides of the controversy over the agency's methods. (Library of Congress)

something to feed greedy capitalists and blood-thirsty union agitators."[7]

James McParland was born in 1843 near the town of Armagh in what is now Northern Ireland. His family was Catholic, rural, and poor. Under British rule, County Armagh in the province of Ulster was heavily Protestant. Catholic farm tenants and smallholders suffered acute political and economic disadvantages. Social mobility was practically impossible, leaving emigration as the main avenue to a better material life. Lacking education or skill, McParland left the family farm at age nineteen for labor in the Newcastle coal and Belfast linen industries. Three years later, he took passage on a Liverpool–New York ship, soon finding jobs on Great Lakes steamers that landed him in Chicago. A fateful opportunity arose "with the Merchants' Police Agency, the 'watch' division of W. S. Beaubien and Co., one of the city's first detective bureaus [although] he was little more than a night watchman."[8] Looking for better money, he tried the liquor business until the Great Chicago Fire destroyed his store and saloon in 1871. Familiarity with detective work then led him to the Chicago offices of fellow immigrant Allan Pinkerton and an entry-level job as a train spotter, watching for dishonest street car conductors.

Two years later, McParland's career and the agency's fortunes received a big break. Pinkerton's firm was facing serious financial difficulties owing to business stagnation and stock market losses in the great depression of 1873. Desperate for clients, Pinkerton instructed the Philadelphia branch superintendent to solicit the president of the Philadelphia and Reading Railroad, a company that had employed them previously, suggesting they might need help with their labor problems. The railroad dominated mining and shipping of coal from vast anthracite fields in Pennsylvania. The agency proposed an investigation of agitators with rumored links to a dangerous Irish secret society called the Molly Maguires. When the railroad agreed, Allan Pinkerton decided he had best learn something about the obscure fraternity and turned to the young Irishman on his staff who should know about such things. In fact, McParland was unfamiliar with the subject (Armagh is a long way from County Donegal, where most of the Mollies originated), but he embraced the assignment ambitiously and produced a laboriously written background paper for the boss within a few days. Pinkerton was impressed by the document, which described an ominously threatening gang consistent with the agency's successful sales pitch. McParland was on his way to an undercover job among the miners that lasted two and one-half years with sensational results.[9]

In a violent struggle, the Philadelphia and Reading Railroad eventually destroyed the Miners Benevolent Association, the actual organizing pivot of the insurgents, convicting and hanging for murder twenty of their leaders, based largely on McParland's testimony. He was a clever investigator and an adroit undercover agent. The popular press seized on the story, embellishing the myth of the Mollies and the detective's derring-do. Yet his trial testimony led to suspicion that he had participated in killings by the miners, or that he had prior knowledge of the miners' plans that he failed to report to avoid sacrificing his cover or his knowledge of deeds he could later testify about. All that was submerged in sensational accounts of the conflict.[10] McParland enjoyed the organizational rewards of his success, and the agency profited from the Molly Macguire job and the publicity, which helped right the agency's financial ship. Published in 1877, *The Mollie Maguires and the Detectives* provides a breathless and richly illustrated fable of enlightened industrialists beleaguered by primitive Irish slugs, whose treachery is singularly undone by the canny detective. McParland was promoted to superintendent of the Denver office and eventually to divisional director of branches throughout the entire western United States.

McParland's last celebrated case concerned the 1905 assassination of Idaho's ex-governor Frank Steunenberg, leading to the murder trial of Big Bill Haywood and two Western Federation of Miners (WFM) associates. The detective extracted a confession from the alleged assassin and then set about building a case that would prove the killer had been hired by Haywood. The investigation and trial and their repercussions throughout the country are the subject of Anthony Lukas's magnificent book *Big Trouble*. McParland went to great lengths to convict Haywood and his colleagues, including falsification of evidence, perjured testimony, and jury tampering. In the end, a Boise jury was unconvinced and the defendants went free. The assassin was convicted and spent the rest of his life in prison without recanting his story. If there was a murder conspiracy, the mystery was never solved. The failure of McParland's theory did not seem to tarnish his reputation. He had no regrets about his methods, which he deemed justified in the war against radicalism—methods that Allan Pinkerton would have repudiated had he lived long enough to see the changes taking place in his business.

In *Big Trouble*, Lukas paints the following portrait of McParland: "A picture emerges of a brash, self-confident thirty-six-year-old dressed in the latest fashions, a bit of a dandy who enjoyed his nights in the city's cafés and saloons, a little boastful in the Detective Room about his achievements, impatient with Pinkerton bureaucracy, not eager to spend much time studying the agency's mug books and other records, a loner inclined to forge ahead on a case a bit more quickly than his deliberate superiors preferred, but a dogged, determined, relentless operative if allowed to call the shots. Once in response to a reporter's question, he said, 'There's no romance in the life of a detective. It's just work; hard, hard work. That's all.'"[11]

In Denver for the rest of his life, McParland became a successful executive, a pillar of the community, a devoted supporter of the Catholic Church, and a well-dressed representative of the upper middle class, too fond of food and drink but something of a celebrity—all to his considerable satisfaction. The Denver Irish were less approving, believing he had betrayed his countrymen in the Pennsylvania labor conflict. Members of the local Knights of Columbus blackballed his coveted membership, although the San Francisco chapter of the lodge later granted him the honor. An internal evaluation of his performance with the agency judged him genteel in appearance, adaptable to the laboring class, good at investigations, determined and self-reliant, but inclined to extravagance, talkative, impulsive, and prone to operating too fast.[12]

Private detectives of the first generation were a motley lot. Personally, they were as different as the intrepid Siringo and the ambitious McParland; different, too, in their pursuit of adventure or social mobility. As agents their career paths diverged, yet they had much in common. They came from humble origins with little education and few marketable skills—outsiders and immigrants. They pursued opportunity through petty employments until good fortune brought them to an emerging business that would carry them to success. Their employer enjoyed equally good fortune despite near failure. Contingencies worked in everyone's favor. It was the American success story, at least for some. But this first generation was steadily being eclipsed by the professional corporate agency.

### American Sherlock

William J. Burns relished the title "America's Greatest Detective." Although the encomium was probably self-awarded, it was not altogether undeserved. During the first two decades of the twentieth century, Burns was certainly the best publicized American detective, thanks to his prodigious efforts at self-promotion coupled with a decided talent for investigation and some fortunate career moves. Although in age he was close to the first generation of private detectives, he represents best a second, twentieth-century generation in the development of the industry. Burns's begins his agency with a national orientation and a corporate organization. Its clients and investigative subjects are mainly institutional actors, business enterprises and labor unions rather than outlaws and assassins. As the industry changes, so too do the men and women who serve the agencies. Adventurers and upstarts yield to managers and working people.

Born in 1861 to Irish immigrant parents, Burns grew up as an apprentice in his father's tailoring shop and a devotee of his mother's Irish folk tales. From the beginning, he was clever, gregarious, and mischievous. He developed a penchant for acting in amateur productions and thought about a career in the theater, despite his father's plan to bring him into the family business. But events altered the courses of father and son. The senior, Michael Burns, by now a successful businessman in Columbus, Ohio, joined the municipal reform movement and was elected police commissioner. William was exposed to police work and began hanging out at the station, where he learned the practice and the lore of the city's police detectives. The work combined a sense of excitement, intellectual challenge, social engagement, and a touch of the actor's talent for guile. Burns was hooked.[13]

Fraud was suspected in the 1884 election for county prosecutor in Columbus. The incumbent prosecutor wanted to investigate but did not trust the police, who might have been involved with the officials attempting to alter ballots in their favor. At the time, cities sometimes found it cost-effective to employ private detectives to assist investigations on a short-term basis. William, strictly an amateur, was asked to look into the problem. His first step was to formulate a theory of the crime: how could a set of fraudulent ballots be produced and placed in a safe for honest election workers later to count? The deed would require someone to forge the original tally sheets, someone to crack the safe, and someone to conceive the scheme, roles that might be shared but likely involved two or more persons, one with criminal skills and another who would benefit from the fraud. Moving to the operational stage, the beneficiary candidate was obvious, but Burns wondered where a forger and safecracker might be found. The answer he came to was the nearby state prison, and through a series of intermediaries Burns learned how the perpetrators had been recruited from prison inmates and provided access to the ballot boxes. His theory was valid in general, although its proof involved several complications, including his successful effort to elicit a confession from one of the accessories. In the end, the scheme turned out to be a clever instance of ballot-box stuffing and his successful first case.[14]

Resolving to pursue a career as a private detective, Burns answered an advertisement placed by the Thomas Furlong Detective Agency of St. Louis. Furlong was well known as a railroad detective. Like many of the newer "national" agencies, Furlong employed agents in various cities on a case-by-case basis. Burns was hired and given his first assignment, a wave of suspected arson fires in St. Louis. First he checked the obvious possibility of building owners attempting to defraud insurance companies but found no evidence supporting that hypothesis. Thinking through the case once more, Burns hit on a novel theory: maybe building occupants rather than owners were responsible. Some clever sleuthing revealed that crooks were renting space for storage of expensive, insured furniture, which was then switched for cheap furniture before the buildings were torched and heavy losses claimed. The culprits were apprehended. Burns had a decided talent for his chosen occupation.

By 1889 Burns was a family man seeking the kind of job security offered by the fledging US Secret Service. For the next twenty years, he served in various capacities with the Secret Service, initially investigating counterfeiting, their specialty, and later, land fraud. Created in 1865, the Secret Service was the only federal police force until the Bureau of Investigation was established in 1908. By all accounts, Burns became a star in the Secret Service. He traveled the country solving well-publicized cases and ingratiating himself with important people in government and the press. His biggest break came in 1903 when Secretary of the Interior Ethan Hitchcock, alarmed by flagrant land fraud in western states, asked the Secret Service to lend him their "best man." Beginning in California, Burns unraveled the complex scheme by which colluding Forest Service agents, General Land Office agents, and speculators were able to trade worthless land for valuable tracts by manipulating a series of public land laws.

As Burns was exposing the California scheme, prominent San Francisco attorney Francis Heney was recruited to investigate and prosecute a sensational case of land fraud in Oregon. Burns was assigned to Heney's team. The marriage was happy, productive, and enduring. In the Oregon case, the network of official and private corruption was so wide that investigators, including Burns, armed with revealing evidence from public records, were able to extract confessions that netted a number of conspirators ranging from members of the US Congress and agents of the General Land Office to men and women of the business world. Heney and Burns emerged as heroes in the national movement for civic reform. Yet a shadow of impropriety fell on Burns when later it was revealed that he had tampered with jury selection in the Oregon prosecutions. In 1912, Attorney General George Wickersham reviewed the case and the prosecution's methods, publicly citing Burns for malpractice. Tactics that strained the bounds of legality would recur throughout Burns's career.

The Oregon land fraud led directly to Burns's last and most cele-

brated case as a Secret Service agent. The twentieth century opened
with Teddy Roosevelt's administration pledged to implement the
Progressive movement agenda. Municipal reform suited Roosevelt's
philosophical beliefs and embodied strategic political benefits for the
Republican president because urban political machines that relied
on corrupt patronage were associated with the Democratic Party.
San Francisco was a special case in which the Union Labor Party had
come to power in 1905 with the support of workers, a heavily ethnic
and immigrant population (Irish, Italian, German, and Chinese) and
a thriving vice industry. San Francisco was also home to some of the
great reformers, including the sugar magnate Rudolf Spreckels and
the newspaper editor Fremont Older, righteous opponents of boss
Abe Ruef's machine, which ran Union Labor. Older petitioned Roosevelt to assign Francis Heney (San Francisco native and friend of local
progressives) to the investigation and expected prosecution of official graft. A deal was struck: Spreckels would finance the operation;
Heney would prosecute, continuing his ascent among progressives
(later he ran for district attorney); Older would write the story; and
Roosevelt would reinforce California Republicans. Heney recruited
a team of investigators headed by Burns, his new partner in fighting
corruption.[15]

Contemporary San Francisco journalist Franklin Hichborn described "The System." Abe Ruef was the undisputed boss whose
debonair style and University of California education defied the machine politician stereotype. The front line consisted of Union Labor
Party Mayor Eugene Schmitz (head of the musicians union and an
accomplished violinist) and a majority of the eighteen-member Board
of Supervisors of the City and County of San Francisco. As a private
attorney, Ruef was able to receive as fees the stream of graft payments
flowing in from businesses enjoying favored protection. These included the vice industry epitomized by the "French Restaurant" devoted to dining and prostitution and by Chinatown gambling parlors.
But favors were also purchased by powerful companies, notably the
street railway franchise United Railroads (URR), which paid Ruef
$200,000 for permits to build overhead power lines—the cheaper if
unsightly alternative to underground lines.[16]

Calling himself a "special agent of the district attorney," Burns set
up headquarters in three rooms of the Claus Speckels Building, where
he supervised a well-financed team of twenty operatives. Here Burns

Figure 2.2. Burns (right) cultivated an association with Arthur Conan Doyle (left), who was supposed to have bestowed the title America's Sherlock Holmes.

fashioned the methods that would later govern his own agency. Surveillance was key. Operatives were deployed to follow and report not only about Ruef, the supervisors, United Railroad officials, and their associates but also about people on the jury lists who might be selected to judge the grafters. Prolific, mostly handwritten reports were delivered to Burns describing the tailed subjects and offering conclusions like, "By no means allow the following to qualify" (for the jury) and "should any of these 3 show any desire to qualify go after them with hammer and tong." Italians as a class were to be avoided as they were deemed likely to be easily swayed by the defense.[17]

In wily tactics, Burns solicited double agents, including Jim Cullen,

who managed Ruef's office; a supervisor's chauffeur; and "Mrs. R.,"
who posed as a society woman and cultivated the wives of Ruef's associates (the boss was single).[18] Working undercover, agent Charles
Oliver gained the confidence of one "GHC," a funeral parlor owner
and Ruef supporter, by convincing him that he, Oliver, had a key to
Burns's desk and could therefore obtain information about the investigation that would benefit Ruef.[19] Of course, Burns had devised the
story in the hope of extracting evidence of graft common in funeral
parlor licensing. Burns was not the only one engaged in the cloak-
and-dagger game. United Railroads, a target of the investigation, hired
the Helms Detective Agency of San Francisco to follow Burns and
check out persons on the jury lists. Burns was not deceived, managing
to lose his shadows and discover their employers.[20] Luther Brown, a
URR detective for the defense, succeeded in bribing Burns's secretary,
Rex Hamlin, who passed on prosecution secrets and reports on jurors.
Burns discovered the betrayal and raided United Railroad's offices,
arresting Brown and recovering the documents.[21]

In the end, Burns convinced Ruef to confess to the French Restaurant bribery charges and to testify in Schmitz's trial. Ruef negotiated
a deal that provided limited immunity from other charges and further
testimony (e.g., against the URR president, Patrick Calhoun) in exchange for his cooperation. Although Burns trumpeted his success in
national media,[22] Ruef and his cohorts escaped the full force of law.
The boss went to prison for four and one-half years, but the prosecution's case against other ring leaders fell apart. Further pursuit of the
graft cases lost public support. Always the gentleman, Abe Ruef accepted his prison sentence, wrote his memoirs, and took up the cause
of prison reform. From San Quinten he observed, "Here all men are
equal. . . . Here is a great opportunity to study sociology."[23]

Despite the compromised results, Burns achieved national recognition from the sensational investigation and trials. This was the heyday
of the Muckrakers, Roosevelt's metaphor for a phalanx of journalists
devoted to exposing the evils of poverty and exploitation including
Jacob Riis (*How the Other Half Lives*, 1890), Upton Sinclair (*The Jungle*,
1906), and Lincoln Steffens (*The Shame of the Cities*, 1904). Steffens
covered the San Francisco trials, finding in Burns the avatar of municipal reform. "To William J. Burns, the intriguer, we can do justice here.
A detective, he is crafty, but he certainly is a master of his craft. He
deals, and he double-deals; he must, for he has criminals to deal with,

but he is loyal to his clients, Mr. Spreckels and the good citizenship of San Francisco."[24]

Burns loved the attention, but more profoundly he understood the national mood and the propitious timing it presented to an entrepreneurial detective. In 1909, at age forty-eight, Burns left the Secret Service and founded the William J. Burns National Detective Agency in New York, capitalizing on a soaring reputation and a long list of influential friends acquired in twenty years of public service. In its initial months, the agency lured away from Pinkerton a lucrative contract with the American Bankers Association for guarding its 11,000 member banks.[25] One of Burns's old Secret Service colleagues had become head of the association's protective services division and decided the new Burns agency would deliver better results than Pinkerton. And so began the great interagency rivalry.

### Who Were the Private Detectives?

The agency founders were a small but distinctive group. Allan Pinkerton was a Scottish immigrant, working as a cooper (or barrel maker), before taking a short-lived job with the Chicago police and then starting his own private "police agency" in response to opportunities provided by the railroads. Burns was the son of an Irish immigrant tailor; William Baldwin had been the keeper of a small store; Gus Thiel, a civil war soldier; and Pinkerton employee James Wood, a Boston policeman. Most moved from municipal police forces to small private firms and then to their own start-up agencies, initially as sole proprietor/employee. Both Pinkerton and Burns had important career experience in government. A pattern emerges. These were men (and a very few women) from modest social origins, self-made entrepreneurs in the rapidly developing detective business—indeed, creators of that business.

If this describes the notable founders and agency owners, those acting as the "principal," or the "chief," as Allan Pinkerton liked to be called, who were the "operatives," the rank and file? Surprisingly, given the central place of the private detective in popular culture, very little evidence exists about who played this part in reality. There are plenty of stereotypes, ranging from the Sherlockian eccentric and master sleuth to the pedestrian "gumshoe" and criminal associate, but almost no evidence. Fortunately, some data are buried in the archives.

Much of this evidence comes from agency records that were either subpoenaed by investigating commissions or leaked by insiders sympathetic to reform efforts. Beginning with the large corporate agencies, detectives were divided into several tiers and occupational specialties. First is the "general operative," the conventional "op," the regularly employed person available for assignments that frequently required special abilities. "A good proportion of Agency general operatives should be capable of factory, mill and warehouse work in skilled or unskilled capacity, truck and bus chauffeurs, store clerks and porters, alert, active young men suitable for training into shadow operatives and those speaking foreign languages common to the territory." By contrast, the "special operative" is employed temporarily "for service as ticket takers and ticket sellers at fairs, exhibitions, etc. to protect valuable exhibits, guard payrolls, for assignments to private individuals and at private residences as protection against kidnapping . . . and other types of work." Sometimes the "secret operative" is used for jobs that require "a high degree of intelligence."[26] Typically, operatives of all varieties were assigned code names or numbers to conceal their identities and employers in field situations. Communications were directed to and returned from shadowy figures identified by initials, or, better yet, by initials and numbers like GT-99, Z-5 or W-62-R.

All of these "ops" were distinguished from a second and lower (by prestige and pay) tier consisting of patrolmen, guards, watchmen, and security personnel who were not proper detectives. These security personnel, nevertheless, constituted a large fraction of the industry's labor force, and employees frequently moved between the first and second tiers. Similarly, private businesses such as hotels and stores employed "house detectives" assigned to control prostitution and prevent shoplifting—second tier jobs at best. A distinct third tier consisted of strikebreakers, temporary enforcers recruited on short notice from the urban underclass, some with proven criminal records, who were dispatched from the cities by train to the sites of labor strikes. Strikebreakers had a deservedly opprobrious reputation and would scarcely be considered detectives, although they worked for detective agencies and were recruited and supervised by regular operatives.

A rare portrait of the detective business appears in Robert La Follette's famed US Senate investigation (on Violations of Free Speech and the Rights of Labor), within subpoenaed records of (among others) the Glen Bodell Detective Agency of Los Angeles. The records include a set of thirty-eight employment applications for detective positions in 1935. Prospective operatives answered a series of questions about standard personal information, education, and experience. The sample reflects the population of first-tier operatives at the height of the industry. Although we don't know which ones were ultimately hired, we can safely assume that these applicants reflect the detective demographic. They are all men, all white, in their 30s and 40s, mostly married, often with children. Educational attainment is low, almost none of the sample having gone beyond the primary grades. They hail from all over the United States, three were from abroad, and almost none were native to Los Angeles (as was typical of the city in those years). Nearly half belonged to voluntary organizations (fraternal lodges and veterans associations). Few owned any property other than an automobile and a gun. Most impressive, nearly all had experience in police or detective work, and some who had the latter had worked for familiar agencies (Nick Harris, Wheeler, Pacific States, Burns, Pyles, Pinkerton). They also listed detective experience with major corporations: Swift and Co., Safeway Stores, Paramount Studio. In sum, they were solid working-class men with reputable employment histories, family men with community attachments, not scum.[27]

The California sample is complemented by another rare find from Wisconsin. A state law dating from 1925 required that Wisconsin detective agencies apply for licenses and report information about their employees. In 1928 the Russell Agency, the state's largest industrial detective firm, provided data on twenty-four employees. According to the historian Darly Holter, "These records offer the only known profile of industrial detectives," true enough at the time Holter was writing. The group of twenty-four included only one woman. Most were young, 20s and 30s, and two-thirds of them were married. Unlike the Los Angeles sample, most were native to Wisconsin and neighboring states, and they were better educated, having reached high school and, a few, college. Like their California colleagues, most had experience in military, police, and labor espionage work. "The notion that labor spies [Holter's characterization of these agency employees] were nomadic or homeless itinerants is contradicted by the Russell sleuths. . . . Nor were they mysterious loners."[28]

The seeming contradiction these data pose for familiar depictions of the disreputable private eye is resolved in part by the timing of the surveys (1928 and 1935) and by confusion about who really was a detective. In the late nineteenth century, experienced private eyes and municipal police detectives did not exist, and many individuals recruited to the emerging trade had sketchy backgrounds. The actual "operatives" described in the surveys contrast markedly with guards and strikebreakers, although individuals could move from one category to the other. The story of bona fide strikebreakers, however, is unambiguous. According to the La Follette report, "The committee's record also demonstrates that the men available for strike work are generally socially maladjusted; they constitute a sort of underworld and many of them have criminal records or are professional criminals."[29] An ingenious study by the committee's staff revealed evidence the agencies were at pains to hide. Strikebreakers were recruited by word of mouth from the streets and boarding houses of big cities, especially New York, home to the perfidious Farley, Wadell-Mahon, and Bergoff agencies. "The results are astonishing. . . . Approximately one-third of the known strikebreakers have criminal or arrest records," mainly for alleged violence.[30] The lower ranks of the detective business may have deserved their unsavory reputation, but bone fide operatives came from the righteous working class.

### Women

The original Pinkerton agency policy manual says, "Female employees must not be employed permanently at any office [unless] an emergency makes it necessary."[31] The official position may be explained by a misguided effort to distinguish the professional agency from the practices of smaller independents in "domestic" cases, where women were used in exposing, even setting up, infidelities. Stated policy notwithstanding, women were assigned to many professional tasks ranging from undercover store clerks and Burns's "society ladies" to industrial work and female-run agencies.

The belief that private detectives were all men and that agencies employed women only in temporary or secretarial position is belied by the evidence. From the beginning women operatives worked in arenas inaccessible to men. Kate Warne, the first female private detective, was hired by Allan Pinkerton in 1856. "Warne convinced Pinkerton, who probably had an eye for females anyway, that women could be useful spies on trains. By 1860, Warne superintended a small number of women operatives in Chicago."[32] Although the major agencies avoided matrimonial work unless it paid well, smaller agencies relied on this business, the métier of female investigators. Mrs. Clara Thurnaur worked for the Edward Hall agency in Philadelphia: "The Thurnaur woman is one of the cleverest female operatives in the country. . . . Her chief forte was to gain the confidence of women and then let them tell her damaging testimony [for divorce proceedings financed by husbands]."[33]

Women detectives were prominent in department stores, on the lookout for shoplifters and union organizers.[34] In Chicago, "the department store millionaires of State Street and Milwaukee Avenue are paying huge sums to private detective agencies to spy upon and breakup every meeting of the recently organized department store clerks. . . . A woman who gave her name as 'Miss Stewart' was expelled from the [union] meeting after being forced to admit that she was the agent of a private detective outfit."[35] Beyond these sex-segregated jobs, women also did industrial work. Employer associations representing different kinds of industries provided private detectives as an essential service to their corporate members. Among the larger employer associations, "the spies of the National Metal Trades Association included two women, Mrs. D. D. Anastasis, Operative 568, and Bertha Rutter, Operative 619. The National Corporation Service employed 11 women among its active operatives apart from those doing office work."[36]

The remarkable Cora Strayer headed a Chicago agency specializing in the concerns of women. The agency advertised its date of establishment as 1890, although that may be a stretch since Strayer was just twenty-one and married (soon to be widowed) at the time. The first newspaper ads for her services appeared in 1902. The agency was located above a tavern at 5443 West Lake before moving south to 3104 Cottage Grove in 1905. The firm appealed to female clients with domestic issues but employed women and men, including George S. Holben, superintendent of the "criminal department." Intrigue unfolded when Holben, living with Cora in 1910, was murdered by Stephen Ayers, an ex-employee of the agency. Ayers claimed Cora had invited him to Chicago with a promise of marriage and a job. Cora denied any affair, claiming Ayers was unreliable. She was still managing the agency in 1914 when war with Mexico was threatened (or

LADIES

When in need of legal
or confidential advice
why not confer with
one of your own sex?

Established 1890

MISS CORA M. STRAYER'S
**Private Detective Agency**
GEO. S. HOLBEN, Supt. Criminal Dept.
3104 COTTAGE GROVE AVENUE
Telephone 2625-Douglas                              CHICAGO

Figure 2.3. *Chicago Tribune* advertisement for Cora M. Strayer's Private Detective Agency, founded in 1890 and specializing in women clients (Chicago City Directory, 1905).

provoked) by General Pershing's filibuster across the border. Self-appointed "Colonel Strayer" mustered thirty women in the First Volunteer Woman's Calvary Regiment, which was saved a trip to Mexico when the United States turned its attention to the developing war in Europe. Cora Strayer lived a life worthy of detective fiction.[37]

Miss Ethel B. Hanks, who became an "industrial investigator for the government," put the question of female employment in detective agencies to an actual test. She applied for jobs at eight prominent New York firms, including the Thiel Detective Service, the William J. Burns International Detective Agency, and the Corporations Auxiliary Company. "She reports that experience and point of view on the industrial situation seemed to be the only line of importance in considering an applicant's eligibility. . . . She was actually employed by the Thiel Agency to 'investigate stealing' by girl clerks in a Woolworth store."[38] Her observation about "point of view" suggests that the agencies were looking for operatives who shared their own animus toward the labor movement.

## Blacks

Another exception to any white-male monopoly of the industry was the black detective. Rarer yet than female ops, black operatives occupied very special niches. There were, of course, large numbers of "negro strikebreakers" beginning with the Ohio Coal Fields Strike of 1874 and continuing until the mid-1930s. Black recruits were drawn from southern mines and factories to replace striking European-American unionists, mainly in northern cities.[39] Yet black "scabs" (an epithet that meant nothing to black workers, who welcomed an industrial wage in places where the unions had excluded them) were a phenomenon apart from the lumpen battalions organized by strikebreaking agencies—none of them really "detectives." But a few did fit that description. The Railway Audit and Inspection Company (a large firm devoted to strikebreaking and industrial espionage) recommended to Fulton Bag and Cotton Mills of Atlanta "Isaac L. Jones (colored) operative #396, [who] has been able to do some very good work in St. Louis for the Curtis Manufacturing Company, in speeding up colored help by means of using propaganda. He is an Alabama negro and would be at home among the southern negroes. . . . This man could be used as a laborer and could be kept exclusively amongst the negroes."[40] Charles Siringo recalls working for Pinkerton on "the Haymarket riot case [with] dozens of men of all ages, colors and nationalities. Even Africa was represented in the person of a negro familiarly known as 'Black Jim.'"[41]

Fragmentary evidence confirms black-owned agencies, which appeared in growing middle-class neighborhoods of northern cities. Sheridan A. Bruseaux founded the Keystone National Detective Agency in Detroit, billed as the "pioneer and only colored licensed and bonded detective agency in the world"[42] Bruseaux was a 1913 University of Minnesota graduate and a veteran of the Secret Service who apparently served the black bourgeoisie, including world heavyweight boxing champion Joe Louis. Q. J. Gilmore combined his National Negro Detective Agency with his day job as traveling secretary of the Negro National League's Kansas City Monarchs baseball team (where Jackie Robinson would later start his professional career). His agency superintendent badge survives at Ben Harroll's P.I. Museum in San Diego, California. L. S. King operated the King

Detective, Photography and Fingerprinting Agency, advertised as "Cincinnati's Negro Detective Agency."[43]

In 1915 California introduced detective regulations that required agencies and their owners be licensed. Surviving "minutes books" of the licensing board list applicants by address, sponsoring persons (usually police), date, and license number approved. A detective agency license was granted to Samuel A. Marlow, "negro," of South Central Avenue, Los Angeles, on December 17, 1926.[44] The Los Angeles City Directory for 1927 lists a Samuel Marlowe [sic], also on South Central Avenue, who is a notary and very likely the same person. Central Avenue was the center of a flourishing black community in 1920s Los Angeles, distinguished by the upscale Dunbar Hotel and jazz clubs frequented by prominent African Americans from all over the country. Central Avenue commercial life was supported by members of the Brotherhood of Sleeping Car Porters on layovers from the Chicago–Los Angeles Pullman Car trains. In a surprising coincidence of fact and fiction, Los Angeles's Central Avenue is the setting for Walter Mosley's recent novels in which black private detective Easy Rawlings sets up shop in the late 1940s.[45] Whether by accident or intent, the coincidence makes good empirical sense. Like Detroit and Kansas City in the 1920s, Los Angeles supported a black middle class in which the services of an independent private detective would find a clientele.

### The Portrait

Who was the American private detective? The answer varies from the nineteenth-century assortment of individuals who invented or drifted into the business to the twentieth-century members of an established labor force. The pioneers were outsiders, often immigrants or their offspring, looking for opportunities of "careers open to talent" as the British phrase goes. They included business entrepreneurs—risk takers who were fortunate to encounter opportunities afforded by a growing economy and, particularly, the federally subsidized railroads. The industry and personnel changed in the late nineteenth and early twentieth centuries. It grew prodigiously and differentiated into corporate and small-business sectors. Big industrial firms specializing in business services and labor conflicts were the largest employers. Detectives in the main were white working-class men of humble origins and limited education, men with families and community ties looking for careers paying a living wage and even offering some excitement. Resourceful women and black men became detectives in response to similar incentives, albeit within clearly circumscribed limits. As a whole, they resembled the Continental Op of Dashiell Hammett's life and literary invention in one respect: they were working stiffs in a world of corporate power and small-business ambition. They possessed limited autonomy and little empathy for other workers, or at least for those who tried to organize. They had an ethic of their own, an individualistic Americanism that informed their lives and careers. In other respects, however, they were quite unlike the detective of contemporary fiction—not loners, outsiders, nor particularly romantic figures.

# 3

# AGENCY BUSINESS

## Service Providers

On December 22, 1917, managers of eight regional offices of the Sherman Detective Agency met at the Hotel Biltmore in New York City. President and general manager John F. Sherman called the meeting to reconsider the agency's public profile. Sherman began his career as an office boy with the James Wood Detective Agency of Boston and worked his way up to a partnership. He started his own firm in 1910, headquartered in Boston and branching out from the Northeast as far as Chicago and St. Louis. Now, after seven years of successful operation, Sherman proposed changing the firm's name to simply the Sherman Service. "The word 'detective' has never quite done justice to the full scope of our endeavors. . . . We have always rendered a service far beyond the mere 'detection and apprehension' which the word 'Detective' would imply. . . . Our services, in the main, are original, and include the removal of causes which result in crime—social exploitation—industrial unrest." The managers apparently agreed, as the agency immediately published a booklet extolling their advance in the field entitled *Industrial Society and the Human Element* under the Sherman Service imprimatur.[1]

In this document, Sherman explains "Why the World Needs Us," beginning with a swipe at the competition. The so-called detective agencies' "inefficiency, incapacity, non-secrecy, lack of finance, etc., has obtained a biased condition in many minds." Sherman presents his agency as a different animal all together, founded on a "new field . . . *the human element in industry*." He proposes that the key is to foster harmony in the relations between manufacturers and labor, which he deems an entirely achievable end. "Knowledge is the only remedy—

Capital must learn, Labor can be taught—Sherman Service is the teacher." Sherman notes that capital and labor have their respective shortcomings and suggests that some manufacturers are "over greedy [and] have in some instances neglected to give the same consideration and attention to the human element of their factory or mill as they have to their machinery . . . [but] the majority intend to be fair to their employees." In ecumenical tones, he declares, "I am not opposed to labor unions or associations which may be conducted along such lines as to bring a *closer understanding* between the two classes . . . but I am utterly opposed to any organization which under the guise of a labor union will endeavor to invoke legislation . . . or to practice such methods as unlawful maintaining of prices, boycotting, discrimination and other acts, which are clearly in violation of the laws." The Sherman Service promised to do what real detectives should do: "harmonize discordant conditions in industry, bringing a closer and happier relationship between employer and employe [*sic*]."[2]

The agency's new service consisted of two parts. The first, the Preventive Strike Service, is described with an actual case of a major corporation with thousands of employees in which strikes in four of its largest factories threatened to spread. Sherman was called upon to stop the contagion at a plant in the early stage of organization. The "method of operation" begins with four operatives, unknown to one another, mingling with the workers and cultivating the organizers, who turned out to be "a nucleus of Lithuanians, principally Socialists and Anarchists." With this intelligence, fifteen more operatives were dispatched to attend meetings "to lead the workers who did not care to vote for a strike, and to argue against any discordant subject." Another operative was sent "to mingle among the storekeepers and the wives and families of the employes, in order to cause them to see (by use of diplomatic argument) that it would be a great error on the part of the workers to strike—that the trouble was being fomented by agitators seeking personal gain." Success was facilitated by "swinging the wives and children over to reasons for harmony."[3]

Labor disputes already underway called for the Sherman Strike-Breaking Service, which resembled in its essentials the Preventive Strike Service. The case in point concerned workers in a "manufacturing house of national prominence [who] submitted demands for a fifty-four hour week and ten per cent wage increase." The "discordant" note was an appeal for *reduction* in the work week (from six ten-hour to six nine-hour days). The largely ethnic labor force included Italians, Poles, and Irish, among whom "six secret operatives, two for each nationality . . . were detailed to learn the inside conditions," that is, hired as spies in the factory. The objective was to divide the workers along nationality lines; "we [were] successful in splitting the union into three factions." In this case the strike was broken and harmony restored, although no mention is made of any gains for workers. On the contrary, afterward "the leaders of the strike were gradually discharged" and the "dis-unionizing of workers" was furthered.[4]

The Sherman Service functioned through a division of labor similar to other large agencies. Sherman's organizational chart is impressive, with three major departments, each embracing various subunits. The Financial Department, run by a comptroller and an office manager, included a cashier, a bookkeeper, and clerks. The Business Department was elaborate, comprising three subdivisions: the Statistical Department, the Stenographic Department, and the key Soliciting Department in charge of generating new business. The third major department, the Professional Department, also contained three subdivisions that covered the operational end of the business: the Criminal, Industrial, and Civil Departments, each with superintendents, supervisors, and operatives. Dangling from the organizational chart are the Employment and Legal Departments, which don't seem to fit in the tripartite design but probably had a lot to do with operations. Finally, absent from the organizational chart but pictured in full police-like uniform are some fifty members of the Sherman Special Police.[5]

The Industrial Department gets the most attention among the booklet's selling points for the agency, and certainly it accounted for the greatest share of the agency's earnings. Described exploits of the department are exclusively in the field of strike prevention and strikebreaking. The Criminal Department gets less attention. Several cases are described involving murder, theft, and arson. Credit for solving the cases goes to the agency's female operative, Ethel Gardner (No. 17). These examples of criminal work are sparse and singular by contrast to the abundant descriptions of industrial work drawn, one infers from broad experience. In each criminal case, the Sherman Service was called upon to assist the police or the state's attorney. There is no indication of who paid the agency in such cases or how much income they generated—probably not much as these were individual jobs contracted by public entities. Similarly, the Civil Department offered a variety of services with only modest income possibilities. Sherman operatives would shadow plaintiffs and defendants in tort actions, investigate jurors, search for concealed assets, surveil company employees off the job (especially those spending more than they made), expose married persons living dual lives (bigamists), and work undercover with retail clerks, checkers, and inspectors suspected of devising systems for stealing from their employers. A novel specialty provided "experienced shoppers for the assistance of department or other store managers who are desirous of knowing just exactly what their competitors have on sale."[6]

Like most businesses, detective agencies presented themselves in the best possible light with the advantage of appealing to the public's colorful notions about what they did. The presentation of self by detective agencies was seldom challenged by oversight committees, government regulators, or fact checkers, except when sensational conflicts precipitated public inquiries. The Sherman Service was caught in such an exposé.

The Great Steel Strike of 1919 occurred in a year roiled by the largest wave of work stoppages to date (over four thousand compared to several hundred in prewar years) and the virulent Red Scare aimed mainly at labor radicals.[7] Suffering from wartime restraint and inflation, steel workers seized the moment to press for wage increases, while steel manufacturers likewise saw an opportunity to crush the unions on the strength of the Red Scare. Although the strike in September shut down half the industry nationwide, it focused on Pittsburg and on Chicago, where the Sherman Service maintained a large office in the imposing Continental and Commercial Bank building. By now Sherman was advertising his firm as "Industrial Conciliators" who would provide clients with "representatives" (not to be confused with the earlier operatives or detectives) to help settle labor disputes. Sherman representatives weighed in on the turmoil in Chicago acting very much like the strikebreakers described in the 1917 promotional tract.

The strike caused such havoc across the nation that the reform-minded Interchurch World Movement (IWM) created a Commission of Inquiry composed of prominent church men and women, including a field staff of academics headed by Heber Blankenhorn of the American Bureau of Industrial Research, a privately funded study center. The commission issued a descriptive *Report on the Steel Strike of 1919* followed in 1921 by the critical *Public Opinion and the Steel*

*Strike.*[8] Evidence in the second volume includes a letter "intercepted" by the Chicago Federation of Labor written by Sherman's local office director H. V. Phillips to "representative" A 563 D. "We want you to stir up as much bad feeling as you possibly can between the Serbians and Italians. Spread data among the Serbians that the Italians are going back to work. Call up every question you can in reference to racial hatred between these two nationalities. . . . Daily maxim—sent out to every representative today." This and other evidence of incitement to violence led the state's attorney to raid Sherman's South LaSalle Street offices, "seizing fifty officers and employees and several truckloads of files and documents." Ironically, the state's attorney was tipped off by a defector from the ranks, Sherman operative No. 300—fair play, perhaps, since industry spies had attempted to infiltrate the commission. Quoted in the *Chicago Herald* on November 2, 1919, state's attorney Maclay Hoyne revealed that Phillips "gave instructions, not only verbally, but over the telephone and in writing, to commit violence. . . . Operatives advocated the destruction of property, aroused antagonism between different groups of strikers, and employed sluggers— all the time professing to be engaged in conciliating troublemakers." Director Phillips was indicted on charges of conspiracy to riot, insurrection, and murder. Although the grand jury upheld the indictment, Phillips had not been brought to trial when the second commission volume was published.[9]

The Sherman Detective Agency and the William J. Burns International Detective Agency began at the same time. Like Burns, Sherman had worked for one of the small, regional pioneering firms and then moved to the national level. Both were preeminent businessmen, entrepreneurs with a talent for salesmanship. Their agencies were set up as corporate enterprises with a division of labor and specialized services. The Pinkerton Agency had pioneered the model, although their monopoly was declining with the appearance of other large firms in the early twentieth century. Industrial work was the staple of all the new corporations, but the increasingly competitive business encouraged service differentiation. Some, like the Bergdoff Agency in New York, specialized in strikebreaking, while others, like Pinkerton, generally avoided it in favor of industrial espionage. Burns and Sherman did both. Most agencies developed security services, guards, and patrols. Sherman advertised a new service based on the "human element" and "labor conciliation," although it turned out not so new.

The public relations effort, nevertheless, clearly demonstrates agency competition for a new and improved model.

## Growth Industry

By the 1920s, detective agencies great and small were thriving. Estimates suggest an $80 million yearly business carried out by 230 firms, many with multiple branch offices and thousands of employees. These numbers are speculative and probably low. In 1915, the United States Commission on Industrial Relations compiled a list of 278 detective agency offices (243 subtracting subsidiaries) with addresses included, many on the East Coast (the work of Heber Blankenhorn for the commission).[10] The La Follette Committee attempted, with little success, to survey 700–800 agencies but published no list beyond the 218 firms identified in another investigation by the Cabot Fund in 1920.[11]

California began licensing detective agencies in 1915, initially under the State Board of Prison Directors.[12] By 1923, 246 licenses had been issued to bonded (for $2,000) agencies (not employees). Although not all of these were renewed year to year, others came along to increase the actual total. William J. Burns International Detective Agency of San Francisco received the second license issued, Morse Detective and Patrol Service third, W. A. Mundell International Detective Agency of San Francisco fourth, Pinkerton fifth, Thiel ninth, Kane of San Francisco tenth, and Nick Harris of Los Angeles fifteenth—a clear mix of national and local agencies alert to the advantages of state sanction. In 1935, there were 191 active licenses. Curiously, the California numbers nearly equal, and in some years exceed, the estimated national total for comparable years. The problem stems from the absence of any accurate national enumeration. The first US Census of Business to provide a separate category for detective agencies, in 1939, counted a mere 280. By 1946 the number was 603 and still on the rise.[13]

The mystery of how many detective agencies existed and exactly what they did stems as much from deliberate deception as it does from negligent oversight or careless recordkeeping. To the extent possible, agencies operated in secret. Passwords and codes shrouded their communications, both internal instructions to operatives and external reports to clients. Code words were given to clients for secret messages to the agency. The Railway Audit and Inspection Company

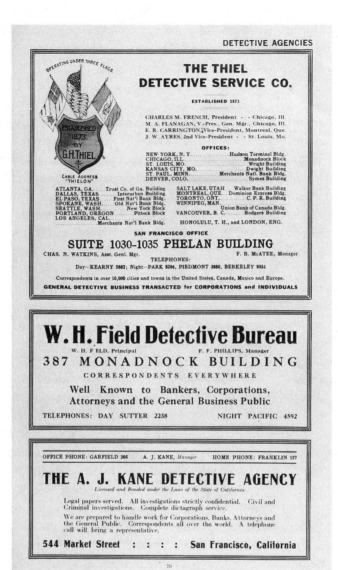

Figure 3.1. The San Francisco City Directory for 1920 advertises detective agencies licensed by the 1915 law and representing both local and national firms.

suggested that messages use the word *field* when they meant "furnish me with lady operative to check my conductors" or the word
*humor* for "we desire to break up the union on our lines," and many
more.[14] Reports sometimes ended with the injunction "destroy this
after reading." Typically, the agency produced two typed copies of
each operative report, one for themselves and one for the client. For
purposes of confidentiality, agency records were routinely destroyed
on the completion of the job. F. A. Tharp, manager of the Burns San
Francisco office, told investigators for a US Senate committee that he
destroyed material pertinent to an inquiry "in accordance with routine procedure."[15] Efforts to hide documents from government investigators were more blatant in cases where subpoenas were issued. The
Railway Audit and Inspection Company trashed barrels of evidence
documenting their industrial espionage practices. But resourceful investigators captured the trash bins and "reconstructed reports recovered from the Philadelphia office waste."[16] Burns yielded certain documents under subpoena and disposed of others, some of which were
also recovered and "compiled from waste material." Always seeking
the high road, Pinkerton was generally forthcoming.[17]

Paradoxically, a wealth of empirical evidence on how the industry
operated was generated in the very controversy over its methods and
its efforts to hide or selectively represent them. The richest source is
the set of reports, hearings, and exhibits published from 1937 to 1940
by a subcommittee of the US Senate Committee on Education and
Labor, the Violations of Free Speech and Rights of Labor—better
known as the La Follette Civil Liberties Committee after its chair-
man, Robert M. La Follette Jr.[18] The La Follette Committee focused
on industrial espionage and strikebreaking services by the five largest
agencies—Pinkerton, Burns, Railway Audit and Inspection Company,
Corporations Auxiliary Company, and National Corporation Service
(an employers' association that provided detectives to members)—
although the mountainous evidence covered many other agencies,
events, and lethal equipment sales (e.g., firearms, munitions, clubs,
tear gas).[19]

The business of major agencies was conducted through field offices.

> The field office is in the charge of a responsible official, variously des-
> ignated as a superintendent or office manager. If the office is a large
> one, the superintendent has under him a group of lesser officials,

men who have probably acted as spies, but whose function is now to hook [enlist an employee to spy on fellow workers], recruit, train and install spies in industrial plants, receive their reports, or arrange their reports, and in general to supervise their work. If the office is a small one, the superintendent, who is also required to be an experienced operative, may handle such matters himself. Stationed in the office is a clerical force whose function is to edit and copy the reports received for transmission to the client. The office generally has at its command a force of skilled operatives who may be sent from job to job. In addition is a group of occasional employees, known in the parlance of the trade as the "back-room boys" who are on hand for shadowing, guard work or the simpler forms of sleuthing, such as eavesdropping or dictaphone work. . . . The channels of authority are simple. In the larger firms the field office reports to the divisional office, in the charge of a divisional superintendent . . . coordinating the field offices [and] the larger clients. Above the divisional superintendent is the national office, the final directive force [which centralized information and dealt with major clients].[20]

Agency income derives from advantageous contractual arrangements. Rather than receiving a flat fee for performing a defined task or providing specific information, the agency "simply undertakes to furnish as many operatives as the employer requires, in return for a monthly payment, plus reimbursement of expenditures for each operative. The agency assumes no business risk." The monthly payment averaged $140–150 per operative, of which the operative received $60–70. Agents working undercover also generally received a wage from the employer as part of their cover. Agency profits swelled when additional industrial work, and the number of operatives deployed, increased while office overhead remained constant.

Although the large agencies offered a variety of services, the big earners were industrial and security work. Pinkerton financial statements divide annual income into "industrial" and "general" categories, where the former derives from work done by employees with a "secret designation" or those working under "strike conditions." The general category is not explained and, although it may have included services concerned with labor, the revealing fact is that 53 percent of income derived from industrial work in 1935 ($1,023,776 of the total $1,922,910). [21] Burns Agency data distinguish "undercover industrial" and "industrial guards" from "all business," showing industrial work as 33 percent of gross receipts. The top six agencies reported (perhaps underreported) employing nearly four thousand operatives engaged in industrial espionage in the mid-1930s, Pinkerton alone having 1,228. The big agencies were very big, with as many employees in other support functions spread over an average of twenty branch offices nationwide.[22]

Evidence of interagency competition comes from demand on field offices to generate more income, especially in the lucrative industrial field, where new threats were readily conjured. Agency bosses cajoled their regional managers to solicit more strike work. Writing to "all offices" in 1936, William S. Burns (now heading the agency as one of the "principals" with his brother Raymond) noted, "There has recently been and no doubt will continue to be considerable industrial unrest, and although this agency does not furnish strikebreakers, we do handle undercover and guard work. The principals feel that a number of the offices are not giving this potential business the proper attention. . . . This type of business is the most lucrative in our line."[23] Proactive efforts were needed: advertising, canvassing, and soliciting. The Burns Agency prepared tailored form letters urging the patronage of firms in a variety of industries (e.g., shipping, stevedoring, retail sales). The boilerplate offer to industrial companies reads, "Let us determine for you the loyal, or disloyal, status of your organization. . . . What percentage could be charged with theft; Disloyal Propaganda; Careless and Indifference; Collusion between Employees and Outside Criminals; and divulging of Plant Secrets by Employees; Strife and Jealousies between Departments; Incompetent and Arrogant Foremen; [etc.]." Agency representatives were told to canvass prospective firms, to explain the potential client's need for the proffered service and to report these contacts to the main office. Burns agent E. C. Davis of the San Francisco office reported meeting with Rosenberg Brothers Fruit Packers: "In discussing our service with [General Manager] Mr. Green I gave him information regarding certain activities of Communist organizers contacting the employees in their Fresno plant."[24] Such methods were standard practice. The Glen Bodell Agency of Los Angeles mailed copies of a booklet entitled "Communism's Iron Grip on the CIO" with their solicitations. Bodell wrote the Interstate Aircraft & Engineering Corporation, "We have heard through a confidential source that there may be some difficulty in your plant in the future." Interstate Engineering politely replied, saying the "statement is without foundation."[25] Indeed, canvassing appears to have had little success and mainly served to grind regional managers, some of whom responded, "It has practically been impossible to get any labor work as there has not been any labor agitation in this section."[26]

Elsewhere the alleged communist threat was embraced with opportunistic fervor. The agricultural labor force had scarcely been touched by detective agencies during the period of industrial conflict. Yet fierce battles roiled in California, from the Wheatland Riots of 1913 to the Cotton and Cannery strikes of the 1930s. The Salinas Lettuce Strike of 1936 used a tactic of preemptory strikebreaking with a new "third party" technique. The trouble began in the summer of 1936 as lettuce growers anticipated difficulty in pending contract negotiations with packing-shed workers organized in the Fruit and Vegetable Workers Union, an affiliate of the centrist American Federation of Labor. Field workers in California were mainly of Mexican and Filipino descent while packers were native Anglos, many of whom had arrived during the Dustbowl migration. The drumbeat of communist menace began with manufactured news from state and local farmers' associations. The mood darkened as the Grower-Shipper Vegetable Association hired guards and detectives supplied with a store of weapons. A Citizens' Association of the Salinas Valley was created to mobilize public opinion using the "third party" gambit of appearing as an independent grassroots organization to publicize communism's threat to the American Way. In fact, the Citizens' Association was a creature of the growers in league with the Industrial Association of San Francisco.

Preparations demonstrated the growers' intent. Colonel Harry Sanborn of the State Army Reserve was brought in to lend his experience at organizing citizen armies in earlier labor conflicts. Sanborn hired Kathryn Cree, an acquaintance from their mutual work with the Industrial Association. Cree took over the coordination of the Grower-Shipper Vegetable Association and the Citizens' Association beginning with employment of Charles N. Watkins Detective Service of Oakland and Glen E. Bodell Industrial Detectives of Los Angeles (which billed the Grower-Shipper Vegetable Association for the services of ninety-seven men). The armed forces prepared for confrontation. The Grower-Shipper group was at the center of an alliance with employer associations statewide, local and state law enforcement, and the faux Citizens' Association with vigilantes deputized by the Salinas police chief.

The packing-shed workers struck in May over grower use of non-union labor, some of whom had been strikebreakers in other disputes. The strike was quickly settled in the union's favor, adding to grower conviction that the advance of labor needed to be stopped. As contract negotiations came due in September, a lockout was imposed. Union workers began picketing the ice plant where lettuce was kept awaiting shipment. The conflict broke out on September 16, when a phalanx of fifty men swinging clubs and police launching tear gas canisters attacked the union pickets at the ice company before moving on to destroy the Central Labor Union headquarters. The Watkins men made arrests as police looked on and thugs patrolled the streets. The whole operation was run from the downtown Hotel Jeffery by Colonel Sanborn, Salinas Police Chief Griffin, Monterey County Sheriff Abbott, California Highway Patrol Chief Cato, and citizen liaison Kathryn Cree.

Gratuitous violence and grower-shipper sponsorship of the widely reported "Battle of Salinas" soon brought disgrace on the town. Newspaper reports exposed provocations by guards and detectives. The La Follette Committee mounted a thorough-going investigation. University of California, Berkeley economists Clark Kerr and Paul Taylor wrote a meticulous account of Salinas events in light of California's agricultural labor problem. John Steinbeck grieved for his hometown. Hollywood celebrities (including Humphrey Bogart, who played Sam Spade in *The Maltese Falcon* film five years later) contributed to the union strike fund. Paul Smith wrote a trenchant series of articles in the *San Francisco Chronicle* that played off Sinclair Lewis's antifascist novel *It Can't Happen Here* with his own title, "It Did Happen in Salinas." Yet despite revealed unlawful actions and legitimate social criticism, the Fruit and Vegetable Workers Union was routed, defeated in subsequent contract talks and banished from the fields for the next thirty years.[27] Detective agencies had become mercenary partners of police, industry, farmers, and phony citizens' associations.

### Crime Fighters or Counterspies?

The great myth of detective agencies of the time is that they fought crime. The popular memoirs of Pinkerton, Furlong, McWatters, and

Burns (and, of course, Vidocq) all present their protagonists as crime fighters—no doubt because a union buster or labor spy would have less appeal to mass audiences. The truth is, very little detective work had to do with crime, except perhaps in cases where labor organizing was treated as a crime. Describing "detectives who detect," former District Attorney Arthur Train explains, "the largest part of the work for which detectives are employed is not in the detection of crime and criminals, but simply watching people."[28] The fact is nicely demonstrated in an examination of Pinkerton financial records.

Morris Friedman achieved fame on a par with his detective colleagues when he quit his position as private stenographer to celebrity Pinkerton James McPartland. Like Charles Siringo, Friedman rebelled against Pinkertons' "underhanded mode of operation [and] gross abuse of public trust," most recently, he argued, in the kidnapping and frame up of Western Federation of Miners officials for the 1905 assassination of ex-Idaho Governor Frank Steuenberg.[29] Friedman left the job with a trove of documents in his possession, including financial statements, which were soon published in his book *The Pinkerton Labor Spy*.[30]

Adding up office and operating expenses, for rent and "janitress," office boy and manager, the annual cost of doing business was $43,758. Although weeks often went by without a single criminal operation, Friedman poses a hypothetical example in which five cases per week, each using five operatives, would generate $10,920. "If the Denver office handled Criminal Detective Operations exclusively, the net annual loss would be $32,838" (i.e., hypothetical criminal work earnings less annual expenses). In fact, however, the office generated an annual profit of $34,866 (therefore, before $43,758 in expenses, a gross earnings total of $78,624). Friedman's calculation demonstrates that even a generous estimate of criminal work earnings contributes a small share of profit ($10,920 of $78,624). Yet, to foster the crime fighter image, whenever a criminal was captured, "a careful report of the case [was] written up, and given to the press for the edification of those who glory in detective exploits."[31] Yet Friedman's well-publicized exposé, and many that followed from the likes of Charles Siringo and Arthur Train, also informed public opinion about detectives and their agencies. Professional hyperbole was challenged by reformist criticism.

Routinely, the business developed far beyond crime to encompass a growing number of services and client types, which prompted a scramble to attract clients from rival firms. Apropos of interagency competition, Pinkertons kept tabs on their rivals, saving for their files various letterheads, logos, and descriptions. A synopsis of information about the Thiel Detective Service Company itemizes their headquarters in Chicago and their thirteen branch offices (nine in the United States, three in Canada, and one in Mexico), and identifies the Seattle manager, his address, and his office and home phone numbers. Quoting from Thiel publicity, the document reveals a great deal about services and claims of the modern corporate detective agency:

> We transact business with precision and dispatch in every quarter of the United States, Canada and Mexico. Our operatives are of known integrity and ability . . . proficient in every language, trade and profession . . . operatives for mines, ranches, lumber mills and transportation companies . . . services especially valuable to lawyers, to prosecuting attorneys, to lawyers who have not time to personally secure evidence in intricate cases, or to find witnesses . . . to bankers and others who have suffered losses through forgery, robbery, embezzlement [and on to mine owners, lumbermen, fire insurance companies, and merchants].[32]

However inflated such claims may be, they indicate the wide range of detective agency clients and ambitions. The fact that agencies were thriving at the time suggests they had successfully penetrated a great many areas of public and private life.

The proliferation of detective agencies inevitably led to widespread knowledge of their activities and methods. Intrigue practiced by agencies was no secret to their subjects, targets or victims. Labor organizers, in particular, were well aware of informers in their midst and sometimes called them out in public gatherings: "If the bosses and their spies are listening, know this . . ." Unions took precautions to exclude informers from secret meetings and to root out spies in the workplace who sowed distrust among workers. Rising to the threat, unions retaliated. "Emil Rieve, president of the hosiery workers' federation, told a Senate subcommittee Thursday that his union was loaded with labor spies. Reports on every meeting, Rieve said, went to employers through private detective agencies. Asked by Senator La Follette how he knew this, Rieve replied that the union had been forced to 'fight fire with fire'—to hire spies of its own to spy on the spies."[33]

F. W. Stockman, St. Louis District Manager of Railway Audit & Inspection Company (RA&I), wrote to C. E. White, Manager of Fulton Bag and Cotton Mills Company of Atlanta, reporting on a threat to the firm that RA&I was equipped to eliminate. "It has come to our notice that the International Association of Machinists has organized a private detective agency called the ACTIVE DETECTIVE AGENCY" with an office on Broadway in New York City and a license (#895) issued by the comptroller of the State of New York. The new agency was interviewing prospective agents about their experience of labor spying, "what companies they worked for, and how they did their work. . . . We understand it is the purpose of this bureau to try to get some of their employees into every [detective] agency in the United States in order to get a line on the methods, and if possible, to gain the names of a good many of the clients." Crying foul, the letter continues, "They have even gone so far as to put a number of men into plants pretending they were non-union men."[34] Given the reported address and state license number, the Active Detective Agency was evidently real, although their success at placing informers within the traditional agencies is unknown, and perhaps unlikely. No evidence of double agents has come to light in extensive studies of the industry. There were, to be sure, operatives who defected from the conventional agencies for money, favors, personal disputes, fears of prosecution, and reasons of principle. None of these were known to be in the employ of labor-sponsored agencies. The warning letter to Fulton Bag and Cotton Mills, like other threat advisories, was clearly an effort to solicit business—and detective agencies were all about business.

In a final irony, the railroad bosses who helped launch the detective business to spy on workers later turned the private eye on their fellow managers. "The Southern Pacific was partial to detectives. When in 1896 antimonopolists elected the Populist Adolf Sutro as mayor of San Francisco, [SP president] Collis Huntington denounced him [and] put a detective on Sutro, hoping to uncover enough dirt to discredit him. He spent the railroad's money for nothing. Far more often Southern Pacific men employed detectives to follow other Southern Pacific men."[35] A general superintendent used detectives to undermine a rival manager and then actually had Huntington and his nephew followed.

Like a great deal of labor espionage, these investigations were fruitless and ill-advised, especially when the subject of surveillance learned about it and retaliated. Such casual employment of private detectives is further evidence of how pervasive the business had become.

## The Independents

Although industrial work was the principal income source of detective agencies, it was not the only one. Associations of bankers, jewelers, and railways provided Burns with a handsome income for protecting property and nabbing swindlers. Smaller agencies overlapped in some of these commercial areas and catered to department stores, hotels, street railways, insurance companies, and private individuals troubled by fraud or matrimonial problems—few of which made good copy unless scandal or celebrity clients were involved. Day-to-day work, watching people, seldom appears in surviving agency records. In rare instances, however, we can reconstruct the life of representative independent agencies.

Miss Cora Stayer's Chicago agency specialized in domestic matters and women clients. In a 1907 case, Stayer was hired by a Mrs. Campbell to investigate a Mrs. Harris who, Campbell alleged, was writing fake letters for purposes of blackmail, accusing her of an illicit affair with Dr. Harris, Mrs. Harris's husband. Cora befriended Mrs. Harris, got her drunk to the point of passing out, and stole the letters. The letters, however, led to further investigation that proved the affair was real, that the adulterous Mrs. Campbell intended to use the detective to discredit the wife's charges. It turned out that Dr. Harris had performed an abortion on Mrs. Campbell, raising the question of his paternity. That suspicion was furthered when Mr. Campbell entered the drama and killed Dr. Harris. In a less tragic but more publicized case, Stayer uncovered a love triangle involving Chicago socialite Jack Russell (real name), Mrs. Russell (a former opera singer), and show girl Miss Marion Carroll. Cora Stayer and her sleuths uncovered the affair by following Russell, although the reports do not show how it ended or who paid her fee.[36]

James R. Woods left the Boston police force in 1879 to establish his pioneering agency with several partners in the early years. Initially, the work consisted of assisting police in criminal cases as a hired consultant. His son James took over the firm in 1908 and expanded its professional services. The younger Woods was a good publicist, writing articles about the agency's exploits for the New England magazine *Startling Detective Adventures*. In "We Solved the Riddle of Vermont's Strange Love Crime," he narrates how he and Miss Eleanor Evers, "clever operative and expert stenographer," exposed another philandering doctor who had poisoned his wife. In fact, by time the article was written in 1934, the firm was devoted entirely to services for lawyers, insurance companies, and department stores.[37]

Nick Harris founded the detective agency bearing his name in 1906 and managed it for nearly forty years before it passed to his heirs, who are still operating in Los Angeles today. Harris, son of a Chicago newspaper editor, followed in his father's trade as crime reporter before a short stint with the Los Angeles Police Department. Enterprising from the start, he married well, to Mary Martin, daughter of a prominent Southern California oilman. The young agency benefitted from Harris's ties to the police and sheriff's departments, which at the time sought assistance from private investigators. Most of Harris's criminal cases were acquired in this way, with the police in charge and the detective advising. Famous among these adventures was the kidnapping of Hollywood matron Gladys Witherell in 1921. The police expected a ransom demand and waited by the telephone. Working with four police officers, Harris was posted at the family home monitoring calls, one of which police traced to a phone booth, where they found the culprit still negotiating the ransom.

Splashy advertisements for Nick Harris Detectives appeared regularly in Los Angeles newspapers. A 1911 ad advised the potential client, "should you require the services of a reliable private detective, you will know where to come. Our male and female agents are honest. . . . Shadowing [is] a feature of this office."[38] Their normal trade involved varied personal and business problems. A couple who owned a café and gas station in Bakersfield north of Los Angeles had been victimized by a local protection racket. Harris and a few of his operatives took over and ran the business for several weeks, waiting for the extortionists to show up. They never did, perhaps suspecting a trap. The case ended badly when the business owners sued Harris for profits lost to the failed operation.[39]

Similar difficulties arose from within the agency. If operations sometimes disappointed, so did operatives assigned to cases. A San Bernardino couple named Reder hired the Harris Agency to recover money they had given to a psychologist who was also promoting a phony land deal. The Harris agent assigned to the case failed to get their money back but nevertheless sent the victims a large bill before resigning from the agency. The Reders complained to the State Board of Prison Directors, which licensed and regulated California detective agencies, and the board judged that the Reders had been mistreated. Eventually, Nick Harris agreed, or at least complied, settling the case for a reduced fee.[40]

And there were well-publicized successes. One of Harris's female agents employed by the Broadway department store apprehended a shoplifter who had been working the neighborhood during the Christmas shopping season.[41] The agency welcomed divorce work. Film actress Jocelyn Lee won child custody and $100 a week alimony after a Harris detective raided a party where her film-director husband was found in a "compromising situation" with another woman.[42] Vice raids could be tricky; it was never certain who might be caught up in the sweep. Harris investigators on a stakeout tipped off police, who raided a prostitution parlor at the Orange Hotel in Los Angeles. A week later, two of their own operatives were nabbed in a similar bust at San Francisco's Hotel Clayton.[43]

The Harris Agency prospered, moving to better offices in the downtown Pantages Theatre building while Nick expanded his portfolio of services. The agency took on family and financial counseling. Large ads in the Los Angeles Times offered an invitation: "Let's Talk it Over—Are you worried over family or business troubles?"[44] They could help recover money owed, stop business leaks, and verify or disprove suspicions about potentially dishonest associates. Sincere, amiable, and able, Nick Harris was becoming a prominent figure in Los Angeles business and society. He considered himself an expert on crime, a subject he learned most about from his days as a journalist and crime reporter. He gave public lectures to church groups and the Chamber of Commerce on his signature theme, "Why Crime Doesn't Pay." He could also enlighten audiences on the roots of crime, which he believed were a lack of discipline taught in the home. His lectures led to a regular radio program recounting lurid crimes like "The Bluebeard Case" and "The Saving of Chio San—a Chinese Slave Girl Story."[45] Announcements about forthcoming lectures or radio shows appeared regularly in the press.

Figure 3.2. Nick Harris and Henry Hull (driving) showing off the Professional Detective School truck mounted with an oversized model of the Nick Harris Official Police Whistle, ca. 1935 (San Diego History Center).

Nick's advice to consumers knew no limits. An ardent Hudson (automobile) owner, he recommended the 1926 model for its fuel efficiency in newspaper feature stories and advertisements.[46] Another ad included Harris in a group of "Men So Prominent You Cannot Doubt Them" who urged the use of Coso Volcanic Iron Water for acid stomach, torpid liver, and rheumatism.[47] By way of crime fighting, he "invented" the Nick Harris Official Police Whistle, designed especially for the safety of women who might find themselves out alone at night or at home alone and desiring additional burglar protection. (The whistle was available in "all" drug, auto supply, grocery, and department stores or by mailing a coupon to Nick Harris Detectives with $1, or $5 for six). The "internationally known French dancer and screen actress" Miss Fontaine Larue credited the Harris Police Whistle with

saving her from robbery and assault, appearing with Nick in a newspaper photo advertisement (offering a special price in quantities to
firms who wanted to supply employees).[48]

Harris's proudest business innovation was the Nick Harris Professional Detective School, which offered a mail-order course for
training to the next generation of sleuths. He outfitted a truck with
the school's name artistically decorating the side panels and a giant
version of his police whistle on top. Detective schools were a growing business nationally, promising career opportunities in a variety
of specialties. Harris's skills, not least those in public relations, led to
his selection as president of the Southern California Association of
Detective Agencies and the International Detective Association. Such
achievements were extraordinary, and by all accounts Harris was
liked and respected (although his 1929 Los Angeles mayoral campaign
flopped). Yet, his business and public career offer a unique portrait of
how the independent agencies worked.

And Nick Harris was a writer—a former newspaper reporter graduated to genre author of true-crime chronicles. In 1923 he published
*In the Shadows: Thirty Detective Stories Showing Why Crime Doesn't
Pay*, [49] stories derived less from his actual detective work than from
his days as a crime-beat reporter or police adjunct. Stylistically, the
stories evoke a feeling of Pinkerton's tales, complete with ink-drawing
illustrations. The popular genre built on early works by Andrew For-
rester, George McWatters, and Thomas Furlong, and grew with William J. Burns and now Nick Harris—one of the few who did not use
a ghostwriter. True crime stories were not always true, as the Mollie
Maguire tales showed, and, equally important, they were not really
stories of detective work. Burns never wrote about strikebreakers or
jury fixing, just as Harris did not mention Bakersfield café proprietors
or philandering film directors in his storybook. The detective business
was business, whether at the level of great national corporations or entrepreneurial local firms. Publicity attracted business and "detective
stories" made good publicity.

### The Industry in Sum

Private detective agencies were big business and small business. The
large agencies were corporations with offices throughout the country

and thousands of clients ranging from major American corporations such as General Motors in manufacturing to Montgomery Ward in commerce and Warner Brothers in entertainment. In the halcyon years their work was mainly industrial, aimed at labor organizing, the most lucrative of a variety of services. Hundreds of employees— operatives, managers, and clerical staff—occupied positions in a complex division of labor. Annual earnings registered in the many millions. Yet the industry was also divided roughly between large corporations and small independents, between national and local firms, with some middle ground where large firms might contract services with a local agency in areas beyond their reach. The independents were far more numerous, possibly thousands nationwide, although efforts at enumeration were inexact. Independents worked the territory of local commercial establishments and personal services. They maintained storefront offices and a staff consisting of the owner and two or three operatives at best. Many were one-person operations that employed part-time help by the job. The standard prejudice held that the independents were prone to unscrupulous characters, the "gumshoe" with an "office in the hat"—a prejudice that stemmed from business rivalry. Data from the California licensing board suggest that agency abuses bore no relation to size.

Despite differences between corporate and independent agencies, it is fitting to speak of a private detective industry. The business at all levels expanded dramatically from the 1870s to the 1930s in response to an environment of growing industry and commerce. Some of their clients were similar and many sought similar services in the general area of surveillance. Very little of their work involved bona fide crime. All of the agencies were part of a highly competitive business. Offices were enjoined by their superiors to get out and solicit business, especially business with high profit margins. New product lines were fashioned and promoted—a growing communist threat, proprietary information potential clients should have, security services, technological innovations (wiretaps and Dictaphones), multilingual ops. Nick Harris excelled among independents in the development of new products and services: counseling, a detective school, whistles. Small agencies practiced specialties like women's issues, legal problems, domestic disputes, and insurance work. A good measure of competitiveness is the attention these agencies gave to public relations. All advertised in various media, from newspapers to the lecture circuit (Burns and Harris in particular regularly addressed business groups).

A series of detective memoirs doubled as agency publicity and true crime stories. Many of the better-known operatives and agencies published books and magazine articles that blended fiction styles with stylized facts. Shrewd operators like Wood and Harris exploited the public's taste with tales of their crime fighting despite their minimal involvement with such low-profit work. Pinkerton and Burns reimagined their exploits in more positive and dramatic light. Genre lines blurred as memoir bled into true crime and true crime segued to fiction. The detective agency became a fixture in the world of American business and, as a result, in the American imagination.

# 4

# DETECTIVES AT WORK

## Thiel and the Miners

In 1971, the Wells Fargo Banking Museum of Los Angeles purchased an antique safe once belonging to the Yellow Aster Mining and Milling Company of Randsburg, California, a mining camp in the Mojave Desert. The safe had been kept unopened for thirty years in a shack owned by the retired foreman, who salvaged company property after the played-out mine closed. When the foreman took ill, the safe was rescued from the collapsing camp ruins by a friend, who lugged it home, hoping to feature it in a trading post he planned to build. Instead he sold it to Wells Fargo, whose museum curators finally unlocked its surprising contents. Here they discovered an El Dorado of company records, including reports and invoices from the Thiel Detective Agency of San Francisco describing how their operatives infiltrated Randsburg during a prolonged miners' strike that began in 1903.

The Yellow Aster Mine was discovered in 1895 by three prospectors whose expectations of riches ran so high they named the burgeoning mining camp after the South African rand. Their hopes were not unreasonable. Randsburg's productive gold mines attracted a population of fifteen hundred souls: miners, their families, merchants, trades people—and detectives. The centerpiece of the camp was the rich Yellow Aster mine surrounded by number of small claims staked out by independent owners and prospectors. The early 1900s were trying times for hard rock miners and the Western Federation of Miners (WFM). Mine owners turned to new refining methods, which led to wage reductions and sparked the great Colorado Mine Wars of Cripple Creek and Ludlow. The Yellow Aster was by far the largest employer in Randsburg and set the wage standard for the region. When it, too, reduced wages, from $4 to $3 per day, three hundred miners struck on June 10, 1903. The owners held firm, led by Dr. Rose Burcham, the remarkable physician whose medical practice subsidized her husband's successful prospecting and who now held an ownership stake in the mine. Dr. Burcham and her partners decided to resist the strikers' demands for restoration of the four-dollar day. They hired the Thiel Agency to infiltrate the miners' ranks and report on any organizing activity.

By August 1903, three full-time Thiel operatives were in Randsburg, at work separately "cultivating strikers" and "investigating," according to billing statements submitted to the mine owners. Itemized entries show that each detective received $6 per day in wages and subsistence, including $1.50 for hotel lodgings and three meals at 90¢ each. Operative SR went to work as a miner at $3 per day. In one month his colleague DGM received $62 for "expenses at saloons with union men." Eight additional operatives were employed for varying lengths of time, assigned to "recruiting and escorting" replacement workers. The "scabs" (replacement workers) were unemployed coal miners from Joplin, Missouri. In four separate groups varying in number from 19 to 33 and totaling 110, they arrived by train during August and September. Expenses in addition to the salaries of operatives who escorted the Joplin men were substantial — $45 each for the three-day Joplin–Randsburg train journey plus "meals en route" (75¢/meal, $6.75/man for the trip). Thiel also charged for advertising job openings in Missouri to recruit replacement workers. The agency billed Yellow Aster a total of $7,277 for the months of August through October. For the next four years, at least one operative remained in Randsburg posing as a miner looking for work but secretly sending daily reports to agency offices in San Francisco and Los Angeles.[1]

During the strike, Thiel detectives consistently downplayed union efforts to mobilize their own ranks and to dissuade replacement workers from going to work at $3 per day. The operative reported, "The men arrived from Joplin this A.M. [and] appear to be well dressed and appear to be fairly well supplied with money." Speaking for the union, Mike Dolan "gave them a great talking to, and all at once one of the Missourians said that $3.00 a day looked pretty good to him 'union or no union.'" Strikers persevered, inviting the newcomers to a

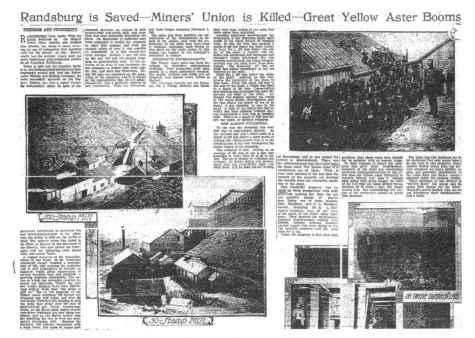

Figure 4.1. The *Los Angeles Times* of November 1, 1903, gleefully announces the defeat of the miners' strike at Randsburg, California.

free dance and union meeting, but the operative doubted they would get results. The Thiel man reported being "in good standing with all the men who are working" and that "it will be a hard job to get them to have meetings or organize [because I associate] with them every night until two or three in the morning, and on such occasions the boys get drunk and tell all they know, but have never been heard to say they would organize, as they don't take any stock in union matters whatever."[2]

The strikers were running out of persuasive appeals to the scabs. Strike leaders called on a show of solidarity from the community. "Billy Nelson, the president of the union, went to Miss Fay, the Madam of the sporting house, which is situated about fifty feet away from the cook house, and asked her to use her influence in getting the Missourians to leave the employ of the Yellow Aster company. The Madam, however, refused to take any part in such action."[3] The union men faced an uphill struggle. The initial strike call was observed by most miners, including many WFM members. The union orga-

nized dances, parades, a relief fund, a co-op store, and the Miners
Union Restaurant.[4] Their cause was just—protesting a precipitous
cut in wages with no opportunity for negotiation. Yet, by November
the major battle was lost. The WFM was tied down in the Colorado
mining wars, unable to send help to a small local in the California
desert. Most miners returned to the Yellow Aster, the only mine to
strike, although some continued the action against the company for
the next fifteen years. The miners had grit. At Randsburg they were
defeated by a potent combination of intransigent owners, hungry
strikebreakers, and seasoned detectives. The Yellow Aster was a small
case of a national struggle to recover profits in the mining industry by
destroying the WFM. The great detective agencies were hired for the
job. Only a stroke of historical good fortune preserved the operative
reports describing their work at Randsburg.

## The Op Report

The fundamental document of early detective work is the operative
report, the firsthand written observations of the field operative, typically provided daily. These "op reports" are highly stylized, following
a format that called for the operative's code name or number, the date
and times of the activities described, names of subjects surveilled
(when possible), places of the action and a factual account of what
happened. The ops' reports went directly to the agency's office where
supervisors reviewed, polished, edited, and embellished the first draft
before typed copies went to the client and into the office case file.
Successive drafts certainly colored the reports but did not usually obscure the operative's voice or details of the work. Consequently, the
best primary sources on the concrete activities of early detectives are
the operative report, in those fortunate instances where they survive.

Their survival, of course, was precarious, and vast quantities were
destroyed, as typically required by agency policy. Company records
of the agencies are not to be found, except in the unusual case of
Pinkerton files at the Library of Congress, and even those are just
partial remnants. Nevertheless, by stealth, chance, and diligence, a
representative number of operative reports survive. In some cases,
records were subpoenaed or recovered from attempts to avoid subpoena. Sometimes they were inadvertently preserved, as in the Yellow

Aster case, or buried in archived records of unlikely enterprises such as a World's Fair.[5] Although he probably lived to regret it, the general manager of the Pittsburg Steel Company freely turned over "600 reports by under-cover men [spies] together with blacklists" to representatives from the Interchurch World Movement Commission who were investigating labor espionage in the Steel Strike of 1919. [6] And sometimes incriminating documents were purloined from company offices by a sympathetic employee and given to labor groups.

The op report is a document that requires judicious interpretation. Far from raw data, it is the product of various authors and intentions. Operatives received instructions on how to prepare their reports, what to include, and how to get the information: "Time arriving on property . . . all conversations overheard . . . radical and disloyal employees . . . grumbling about work . . . after working hours mingle with the men and gather all information possible concerning the welfare of the employes and their families."[7] The op's report went first to the home office for improvement. Morris Friedman, the former Pinkerton stenographer, explains, "It is one of the principal duties of the executive office to revise reports of the operatives preparatory to their being typewritten and forwarded to the different clients, as many reports, particularly those received from secret operatives, are, owing to the neglected or limited education of the writers, almost unintelligible." More important, "there is something deeper in the revision of a report."[8] Reports forwarded to the client stressed the seriousness of the situation, the acumen of operatives, the malefactors in their midst, and "the necessity of continuing the services of the operative if he [the client] would safeguard his interests from the aggressions of a union and protect his person and property from criminal conspiracies."[9] One field operative found that the "office men" were often dissatisfied with his uneventful chronicles, so he saved up "juicy" information "to pad out otherwise dull reports."[10] Operative S-32 told the Interchurch Commission, "Most of these reports are actually framed up."[11]

The op report constituted something more than transmission of information. It provided a form of proof from the operative to the front office and from the agency to the client that work was being done—work that neither the office nor the client could observe directly. A lot rode on the credibility of the op report and its practical value. For researchers, the operative's report is a palimpsest through which several layers of action are discernable. Despite predictable editorial bias, it conveys information about the detective's craft and surroundings.

## Working Conditions

From its earliest days, detective work has had unique features. Above all, it is in most instances covert work, surveillance unbeknownst to the parties under scrutiny. The observer's presence, identity, and purpose typically are concealed. This central condition implies several additional characteristics. Observing others unawares usually means working in public places or using hidden surveillance tools (listening devices, cameras) in private places. Shadowing is an essential skill. The detective's identity must be disguised, often by assuming a false but plausible identity, or "cover." Maintaining a cover means vigilance and risk of discovery. The operative has to be something of an actor, fitting unobtrusively with the subjects and scene.

### *Place*

Place is the first consideration for detective work. The detective needs to discover those places in which the activities of interest occur and then arrange access to them. Embellishments to op reports left descriptions of the places in which activity occurred relatively unaffected. The work was often done in public places where the op could remain inconspicuous—saloons, hotel lobbies, trains, or the streets. An operative working the textile mills for Railway Audit and Inspection Company (RA&I) reported, "Spent most of Saturday hanging around the stores and barber shops near Puritan Mill. . . . Saturday evening I went to a ball game near Tolar-Hart Mill and talked to some of the help from that mill and from Faytex Mill." Burns agency investigator C-24 working for the Capstan Glass Company of Pittsburg discovered that "among the places we have found where men and radicals meet [are] the St. James Cafe and the European Hotel under the bridge leading to the West Side. . . . Women of ill repute meet in both places and a number of United miners meet here."[12] Sometimes the operative was out of luck: "Sunday is rather dull around here. There is not a central place where many of the mill workers assemble."[13]

The Marshall Detective Service of Kansas City, Missouri, sent Operative No. 18 to a midwestern grain mill to investigate a strike, the agency's specialty.

> Mr. Marshall took me by automobile to Illinois, and left me about one-half mile from the village of O'Fallon, to which I walked. I stopped by the flour mill and asked a man for a job. He informed me there was not much chance as there was a strike on at present. . . . I went up town and loafed around the bar rooms and park, also the street corners, visiting with who ever I could get to talk to me. . . . In a small town like this it is rather difficult to communicate with [the] manager of a plant that is in trouble without creating suspicion to say nothing about being in town without a valid or reasonable excuse.[14]

In most cases, however, the action occurred in factories, union meeting halls, or private homes that required access gained in unsuspected ways, typically through a job arranged between the agency and the employer being targeted by the strike.

### Managing Identity

The greatest challenge detectives face is to protect their true identity and purpose; to deceive, while simultaneously gathering information in ways that do not arouse suspicion and may even require trust. Where possible, operatives were selected for job skills that would allow them to join the ranks of those they surveilled: as factory workers, miners, union members. Agencies recruited with newspaper want ads that specified an occupation and little more. "MACHINISTS— Young, single, well-educated, willing to travel, confidential. Y-624"[15] The applicant in this instance was hired and dubbed GT-99, an enduring moniker that later graced his memoirs. He spoke German, which helped in the midwestern factory towns where he worked. Taking up the job, he proved his competence, socialized with his fellows, even joined the union glee club and played banjo. His serious work was to promote company policy among the workers and discourage union activity. Ironically, he accomplished this by joining the union and then urging moderation when "hot heads" spoke up in meetings. Amiable and levelheaded, GT-99 eventually was elected to union leadership positions, which allowed more active, if delicate, sabotage.

He claimed to have destroyed one local by stealing its treasury and blaming the crime on other officials. For cover he took up real estate sales as a sideline, work that gave him access to the workers' wives and families, whom he advised on such dire consequences of strikes as the loss of their homes.

Writing reports was essential to the field operative's work but it could also be risky. Factory hands who spent a lot of time writing and making trips to the post office raised suspicions. As GT-99 recalls in his memoirs, "Every night when I got home I sat down to write. . . . My landlady was a splendid woman, but she was curious about my continual typing. . . . I would tell her the reason. This was my first job away from home and my folks worried. . . . Later I claimed to be writing stories and typing, without much success, to sell them to magazines and newspapers. I also had to get a post-office box." Others were not so clever. "One of us would get exposed every so often, or 'turned up' as we called it."[16] An operative who reported by telephone made regular trips to a nearby town to avoid detection of his frequent conversations from a public phone. He was also secretary of the union and well known to people who observed his movements. "Some of the men began to note the daily trips and a few followed No. 5 and noticed that he talked a great deal over the telephone. . . . The men began to suspect there was something wrong, and in order to satisfy themselves invaded the operative's room . . . where they found more evidence than they needed."[17] Unions were well aware of "finks" in their midst, sometimes acknowledging that they knew they were being spied on and hoped their message would be conveyed to the bosses, at other times resorting to some foreign language, which they believed a spy would not understand.

As in spy work generally, small inconsistencies could lead to discovery. Operatives had to be alert to how effective their cover appeared to others. Operative 281, working for RA&I in a textile mill, was an experienced weaver, although he had been assigned a less-skilled job in an area of the mill where union activity might be more likely to occur. "Quite a number of the help have been asking me why I stay here on a shuttle filling job when I can weave. I must see Mr. Harrell about a job that pays more so these questions will stop."[18]

Assumed identities varied widely in content and plausibility. Operative 73 of the RA&I, while working on the General Textile Strike of 1934, "assumed the role of a bible salesman [and] canvassed among the strikers, watched their union halls, and kept on the lookout for the flying squadron."[19] The guise worked for a while until 73 was assigned to a strike led by a radical preacher who challenged his scriptural credentials and sent him packing. A San Francisco train spotter began selling "Chinese lottery tickets" to explain his frequent appearance on streetcars, where he was observing the conductors.[20] Assumed identities sometimes fail to elicit useful results. Dashiell Hammett, in "Memoirs of a Private Detective," described an occasion in which, "wishing to get some information from members of the W.C.T.U. in an Oregon city, I introduced myself as the secretary of the Butte Civic Purity League. One of them read me a long discourse on the erotic effects of cigarettes upon young girls. Subsequent experience proved this trip worthless."[21]

## Shadow and Ruse

Perhaps the most mundane detective job is shadowing suspects in the hope they will lead to new information. The work can be logistically difficult, tedious, and often fruitless. Hammett, who was good at it, explains, "A trained detective shadowing a subject does not ordinarily leap from doorway to doorway and does not hide behind trees and poles. He knows no harm is done if the subject sees him now and then. . . . A man whom I was shadowing went out into the country for a walk one Sunday afternoon and lost his bearings completely. I had to direct him back to the city."[22] Most shadowing is similarly uneventful and testifies to the observation that detective work is generally tedious. Burns agency investigator 44, working on a case of Chinese labor smuggling in Boston, picked up the trail of J. A. McCabe at the US Investigation Bureau where he worked. (It is unclear whether McCabe was suspected of collaborating with the smuggling operation, although that might explain why 44 followed him.)

> At 12:15 p.m. subject (McCabe) left the office of the Immigration Bureau in company with operative 59 and proceeded up State Street to Exchange Street, where he entered Cottrell's restaurant and had lunch. From there he proceeded to Devonshire St., where he entered the Post Office at 1:40 p.m. entering on the Water St. side. As he hurried through the corridor, I just missed going up on the same elevator. [McCabe returned to work from 2:00 to 5:50 p.m.]

Subject proceeded along Atlantic Ave. and entered the fish market under Plakias restaurant where he purchased some fish. Coming out he entered the Rowes Wharf Elevated station and boarded a train, remaining on same until arriving at Dudley St. Here he got out and waited for the next train and went to Forest Hills station [where] he changed and boarded a surface car on which he remained until reaching Northbourne Road. Getting off here, he entered #306 Hyde Park Ave which is on the corner of Northbourne Road, at 6:35 p.m. Remaining in this vicinity until 8:30 p.m. I did not see subject leave the house, and discontinued at that time.[23]

Agent C-7, a woman, continued to surveil McCabe, taking a rented room in the neighborhood. Meanwhile, Investigator D-4 was developing a ruse that might lead to the source of Chinese smuggling and how aliens were absorbed into the local labor force. D-4 would pose as a businessman who, with a partner, planned to open a Chinese restaurant. To find the right rental location he began to pursue Chin Shue, a café and store owner familiar with the business.

> I then went back to #79 [Chin Shue's office] and talked with the Chinamen about cafes and Oriental goods, until Chin Shue came. He asked me how much I wanted to lay out on the cafe and I told him ten or fifteen thousand dollars. I asked him if he would furnish me with Chinese help and he said he would. I asked him if he would import men from China or if he would furnish men from here. He said 'from here,' from China would not do, as they must be smart and speak English. I told him I thought of going into the laundry business at one time and asked him if the Chinamen working in his laundries learned the business here, or did he import green help. He said they were all educated in the business here. We talked on that strain, but I received no information of importance.[24]

The dialogue suggests that Chin Shue suspected what the questions were after if not the identity and purpose of the operative. Chin Shue was not about to explain where his employees came from, and the Oriental café ruse appeared no more effective than the shadowing.

Shadowing can take many forms and allows for extensive application. Groups involved in social protest beyond the labor movement were shadowed at the behest of government bodies. Surveillance activities normally associated with police or the FBI were assigned to private detective agencies when the case had more to do with political objectives than law enforcement. The Pyles National Detective Agency of Los Angeles was hired by the city's Department of Water and Power to investigate citizens of California's Eastern Sierra communities who were fighting the expropriation of their water supply. In 1905, the city's public water and power agency announced plans for an aqueduct that would channel a manmade river from the Eastern Sierra 230 miles south to an urban area where further development was constrained by the arid climate and meager water resources. Over the objection of Eastern Sierra communities, but with the blessing of Teddy Roosevelt, the city built its own concrete river, leaving Owens Valley towns, farms, springs, and lakes parched. With their livelihood threatened, the small commercial towns and agricultural interests organized to petition for a water-sharing agreement. As the city stonewalled any such negotiation, a resistance movement gathered with growing determination to seek "popular justice." The aqueduct was dynamited a dozen times beginning in early 1924, and when its flood gates were taken over in November of that year by a group of insurgents, the event soon grew into a large community celebration. For five days, Owens Valley citizens controlled the Los Angeles lifeline until decamping on a promise of good-faith negotiations.

The city's first response was to stop the resistance movement, although they had no idea who the rebels were or what they were planning. A force of detectives from the Pyles Agency, armed guards and investigators to protect the aqueduct and identify its saboteurs, was sent to Owens Valley by the carload. Hundreds of miles of canals and above-ground pipelines could hardly be protected from night raiders who kept up the bombing offensive in the vast spaces that guards and searchlights did not reach. Pyles operatives hung around the towns taking down names of citizens who attended public rallies, names just as readily obtained from local newspaper accounts. Unsuccessful negotiations were held in Los Angeles as the detectives surveilled the hotels where valley representatives stayed during talks with city officials. Identities of the bombers were no secret to locals. A group of them came forward in a county legal proceeding that was dismissed in the climate of public support. No one was hurt and no one grieved over the property damage. The detectives, in short, were ineffective, although the agency did submit a report to the Department of Water and Power and to the local district attorney. The city wanted to suppress the rebellion but lacked police power in the jurisdiction, so they sought the services of private detectives. But there was little detectives could do with a citizens' movement that had no secrets, enjoyed moral support, and broke no laws that anyone wanted to enforce.[25]

## *Joining In*

Chicago movie theater owner Balaban & Katz hired the Burns Agency to investigate union sympathy among its ushers. The job called for "an exceptionally high type investigator . . . college men, not necessarily graduates, however, but men of an unusual integrity and of an exceptional appearance . . . neat and good-looking." Evidently, R-38 fit the bill, as he was hired and began mixing with his fellow ushers: "I entered the theatre and proceeded to the locker room. Mr. Smith told me that I would begin work on Friday. He told me several things about the show business and also about himself. I soon learned that he was a fraternity brother of mine so doubtless I shall receive complete information from our conversation. He outfitted me with a complete uniform and told me to report tomorrow at 4:40 p.m." But R-38's initial impression proved overly optimistic. The next day, a fellow usher told him that "he and everyone else are keeping their grievances to themselves because 'you never can tell who you're talking to.'" Sizing up the situation in his next report to headquarters, the operative wrote, "I have come to the conclusion that little can be found out from the men individually while they are in the theatre, since they are exceedingly mute talking of their personal beliefs and dislikes."[26]

Some off-duty socializing was required:

> While changing my clothes in the locker room I carried on a conversation with Mr. Bykonin and suggested that as long as he lived north I would wait for him and we would go home together, to which he said "yes." After leaving the theatre, we stopped in a Tavern where I bought him some refreshments and talked with him for a few minutes. After leaving the tavern we boarded an L train at Clark and Lake Streets. On the train he asked me to have dinner at his home, saying he had just moved into a new place with two other fellows and as there would be several other fellows there for dinner we should be able to have some fun. We arrived at his place about

6:30 p.m. and had dinner about 8:00 p.m. Shortly after most of the fellows left for a masquerade dance on the west side. At this time I made the discovery that I was associating with a bunch of perverts. The fellows who went to the dance were dressed as girls and seemed to carry out their part to perfection.

Despite his surprise, if it really was, R-38 pursued the guise. "Finding myself alone with Mr. Bykonin, I suggested that we buy some refreshments and have a quiet party. He seemed to like the idea so I obtained some refreshments."[27]

"Perverts" or not, R-38 joined in the fun and soon succeeded in his mission.

I learned through indirect questioning the following things. He told me they were trying to organize the ushers in the outlying theatres and if they were successful they would then start on the downtown theatres. He appears to have connections with several assistant managers of different theatres. However he did not divulge any information on this point. I think that by contacting him frequently, I will be able to gather quite a bit of important information. He invited me to spend the night there, saying we could go direct from there to work the next day, which I did, putting in a very hectic night.[28]

No details about the hectic night were offered.

### People Watching

Among its many endeavors, the Pinkerton National Detective Agency specialized in security for large public events — racing meets, fairs, exhibitions. One of the greatest of these was the Panama and Pacific International Exposition of 1915 in San Francisco. Congress and the president, with the help of lobbyists, have the authority to designate the sites and themes of US "world's" fairs. The 1915 fete was conceived officially to celebrate completion of the Panama Canal. Locally its high purpose was to mark ostentatiously the re-emergence of San Francisco from the 1906 earthquake and fire, and, more recently, from the graft trials. Unity was the theme, unity of the country realized by the Panama Canal connecting more directly both coasts, and unity of the city in a compact of clean government, big business, and organized labor. Vast sums were raised for the purchase of property and construction on 635 acres on the city's north shore, at what became the Marina District (created partly with landfill generated from the exposition). Architecturally, various courts and "palaces" mixed Romanesque, classical, rococo, and utilitarian styles—all made of plaster and intended for demolition at the fair's end. Special trains were set up to provide spectators with free transportation from all over the city. For ten months, from February through November, large crowds turned out to view exhibits in a variety of theme palaces devoted to food products, education and social economy, agriculture, liberal arts, manufacturing, and fine arts (the Fine Arts Palace being the only one that survives to the present). Many of these aimed at social uplift, notably the exhibit titled "Race Betterment." Entertainment found in "The Zone," the midway adjacent to the palaces, featured concessions and amusements, including a working model of the Panama Canal and themed areas such as the Chinese Village, Toyland, Japan Beautiful, and the Irish Village.[29]

All was watched over by the Pinkerton undercover team of women and men assigned to strategic positions. There were "Special operatives for continuous service ($50/week each), Special investigation and expert criminal operatives for spasmodic or occasional service ($8/day each) and Uniformed patrolmen or watchmen ($3.50/day, spasmodic or $100/month continuous)." The total cost of Pinkerton services is difficult to calculate from scattered invoices, but it was substantial: twenty-seven detectives for the final week in November cost $1,050, another week in April cost $1,272 (the exposition ran for 41 weeks), though neither figure included other types of operatives or patrolmen.[30]

The observations of a dozen woman operatives are combined in a series of collective reports, doubtless assembled in the agency office. These are, nevertheless, firsthand commentaries written with such candor that their originality may be safely assumed. The documents show that women operatives worked exclusively as cashiers and ticket takers, surveilling other money handlers for evidence of theft. Although no dishonest employees were discovered, the women registered extensive complaints about their supervisors, bosses who did not know that these cashiers were really Pinkerton spies. The complaints consistently addressed working conditions: long hours without breaks, accusations that they were stealing when cash drawers

Figure 4.2. The Panama and Pacific International Exposition, San Francisco, 1915. South Garden, Calder's Fountain, and Festival Hall.

were short, personal restrictions. "A new order was issued to the effect that the girls were not allowed to be in the company of any male friend when on the zone either when on duty or off duty. This caused some sarcastic remarks as they all claim this is taking away their privileges as they have a right to go with their gentlemen-friends."[31] Free uniforms were promised but the cashiers ended up being charged for the required dress. Layoffs without explanation were a common grievance. "Mrs. Coyle discharged 35 cashiers today. One of the cashiers asked why she was letting them off, and her answer was, 'You are too old and not good-looking.' (If they were counting on looks in her position, she would not last long!)."[32] The consistency of the women's reports is noteworthy. The wrongdoing they discovered and sought to change concerned the treatment of cashiers by management rather than any theft or dereliction by their fellow workers.

Reports from the male detectives tell a different story. To be sure, the men were not assigned to tedious cashier work, but rather were employed as tradesmen. One investigation concerned "electricians' malicious interference," which was probably a dispute over work rules.

Another investigated without success the author of threatening letters to management. But the focus was on potential labor trouble. In fact, the exposition had been built by union labor and the San Francisco Building Trades Council was a sponsor. Operative 168 pursued the labor question with an electrician named Flynn, who the op thought might be a union spy given that he dressed well and had money. (Perhaps he was another op.) His report says that Flynn explained, "There is no ill-feeling existing between any members of his union and the Exposition Company; that union men had built the entire exposition, and all the officials seemed to be partial to the unions." Apparently 168 was not convinced. Two nights later he fell into discussion with Flynn about the famous *Los Angeles Times* bombing, "the [convicted] McNamara Brothers, and their work of destruction, but Flynn does not believe in that class of securing justice for the workers"—that is, in violence. Not satisfied with the answer, the operative tried to bait Flynn with a hypothetical:

> I then asked him if he wouldn't think himself justified in going out there to the Fair Grounds and cutting wires, destroying electrical apparatus which would work a hardship on the present men . . . but he said that he did not think that it was the proper thing to do; he could not see where he would gain by it. . . . He is a great man for quoting Payne, Ingersoll, Voltaire and the Great German Philosopher, Heckel [*sic*] saying he is a free thinker.[33]

Overall, it seems exposition management spent a lot of money on the Pinkertons, who provided them only with evidence of their own failings—plus the thoughts of some honest women and the odd free thinker.

## Work Ethic

For the most part, the early detectives believed in their work, or at least justified it as necessary. Pinkerton and Burns considered themselves working men with sympathies for 'honest American labor.' Their job was to rid society of the dishonest and self-serving element, which had duped the guileless working stiff. GT-99 admired the Irish in his factory, "real machinists," although he went on to say, "My hat is off to the bunch of bogtrotters."[34] The generation of GT-99 saw themselves as foils of sabotage, Communism, and alien enemies—as upstanding Americans. Such claims might be pure facade, like the hypocrisy of the Sherman Service. Yet many detectives, people like Cora Strayer or Nick Harris, believed their work benefitted society. One operative in a textile mill suggested "a little increase in wages [would] give the workers a better spirit toward their work."[35] An undercover detective who initially was told that his reports on the B. F. Goodrich Company went to the government for defense purposes later discovered that in fact he was being surreptitiously employed as a spy by the National Corporation Service. From that time forward, he began writing reports that exposed hazardous working conditions such as overheating and poor ventilation. "I wanted to hold the job, because I was afraid someone hostile to Labor would supplant me. . . . I was very much determined to help better the conditions of my fellow employees, even though I was being paid to spy on them."[36]

Defections from detective ranks were not uncommon. In the most celebrated instance, Charles Siringo took Pinkerton company secrets and turned them into popular books that celebrated the honest working person.[37] In less publicized, and possibly more effective, ways the clients of detective agencies raised questions about the effectiveness of operatives and their work ethic. Were they worth the money? Did their labor produce useful or counterproductive results? After receiving op reports containing inaccurate information, the Pillsbury Flour Mills Company wrote to the Marshall Service in September 1920: "We think we have given a sufficient length of time for your man to have obtained a little information. . . . Up to the present he has succeeded in doing nothing of any value whatever. We can get information of greater value at very much less expense. . . . [We] desire that you withdraw your man."[38] Similarly, Kuppenheimer Brothers clothing manufacturers of Chicago marked "the futility of espionage," the failure of the "spy's report to contain any information of value."[39]

There was also a real downside to infiltrating spies into any work setting, as they were likely to be detected and corrode morale. Fulton Bag and Cotton Mills of Atlanta suffered labor problems stemming from agents of RA&I. "What experience we have had in the past with service such as you refer to has not proven very satisfactory, and we have dealt with two different companies. We have felt that operatives of this kind . . . really have a tendency to stir up strife and give unnecessary trouble from that standpoint, feeling that their job depends on trouble always brewing."[40] The question of efficacy hung over detective work, affecting operatives and employers alike.

## Crime Solving

On occasion, private detectives of the time worked on actual criminal cases. That was unusual for two compelling reasons. First, crime was police business, especially after a national police bureau was created and municipal forces added detective divisions. Second, paying clients seldom supported criminal investigations (train robbers were mostly gone) except in cases of insurance and bank fraud or employee theft— almost never murder, as detective fiction would have it. The exception was real crime, even murder, committed by labor. Among such cases none was more sensational than the bombing of the *Los Angeles Times* building in 1910 that killed twenty-one people—described in the aftermath as "the crime of the century" (at least so far).[41]

Owned by the wealthy and politically powerful Chandler family, the *Los Angeles Times* was fiercely antilabor in a fiercely open-shop town. The newspaper was seen correctly as hostile to labor unions and, therefore, a prime target for those in the labor movement given to violent methods. The suitcase bomb that exploded at 1 a.m. on October 1 devastated the *Times* building and extinguished the lives of reporters and pressmen working to get out the newspaper's regular morning edition. Two more bombs, which were discovered before detonation or failed to explode, were found at the homes of *Times* owner Harrison Gray Otis and the secretary of the influential Merchants and Manufacturers Association—sworn enemies of labor.

On the same day, Burns was traveling by train to San Francisco but promptly rerouted to Los Angeles intending to sell his services to the city. Owing perhaps to Burns's vaunted reputation and doubtless to his salesmanship, Los Angeles mayor George Alexander hired him to solve the crime. In a coincidence that became key to breaking the case, the first investigation handled by the Chicago office of the William J. Burns International Detective Agency (founded in the previous year) was the bombing of a railroad bridge in Indiana where the Bridge and Structural Steel Workers Union was involved in an organizing struggle. Burns saw a connection between the events, both in the character of the crime and the materials used to build the bomb found in the *Times* building wreckage. From the outset, Burns saw the hand of John J.

Figure 4.3. The *Los Angeles Times* building after a bomb destroyed much of its operation, killing twenty-one people on October 1, 1910.

McNamara, secretary of the Bridge and Structural Steel Workers, in the deed. Burns alone conceived the solution. His job was to prove it.[42]

The investigation that followed exhibits the detailed methods and maneuvers of criminal detective work. The explosive device and powder constituting the bomb were traced to their manufacturers and eventually to a San Francisco area company that sold dynamite. Names and descriptions of the purchasers were elicited. Raymond Burns, William Burns's son and partner in the firm, worked the San Francisco connection, tracing the purchasers to local addresses and associates. Friends of the alleged purchasers of dynamite had connections with the utopian Home Colony near Tacoma, Washington—described by the senior Burns as "the nest of Anarchy in the United States." At this stage, Burns operatives got creative. They rented a house within surveilling distance of the colony and posed as land surveyors to explain their walking and looking about the area—hoping that no one in the community knew the details of surveying. They befriended the locals and went to great lengths to obtain a photo of their camera-shy prime suspect, the man believed to have purchased the dynamite for the bombers. This identification, in turn, led them to "arrest" (though literally to kidnap) the suspect and return to Indiana, where Burns coerced a confession. The man they had been trailing, who was using an alias, turned out to be James McNamara, brother of John, the union secretary. James's confession implicated his brother, who was also detained until an official arrest could be effected—all procedures that violated laws governing habeas corpus and rights of the accused.

A widely publicized trial was scheduled in Los Angeles pitting Clarence Darrow for the defense against the mercurial Earl Rogers of Los Angeles acting as special prosecutor. Bad blood between Burns and Rogers stemmed from the latter's defense work in the San Francisco graft trials, which mitigated the punishment of those involved in the corruption Burns had worked hard to uncover. But the "trial of the century" was averted when Darrow convinced the McNamaras on the strength of the evidence to plead guilty in order to avoid the death penalty.[43] The guilty plea outraged organized labor, which was convinced that the McNamaras were framed and that Darrow had betrayed the workers' cause. In the end, however, it was Burns who won, for justice he said, not against honest workers whom he admired.

The McNamara case further vaunted Burns's reputation as the American Sherlock, but it also created a potential problem. Up to now, Burns had been a crusader for progressive causes—municipal reform, official corruption. Now it appeared he had sold out. Burns relished the publicity but worried that his image as a reformer might be tarnished. His rejoinder appeared in the 1913 publication of *The Masked War*, at once a fast-paced account of the investigation and a bloated paean to William J. Burns. The title rested on the premise that the real war is "a war of Anarchy against the established form of government of this country [which is] masked under the cause of labor." In avuncular tones, Burns advises, "It will be well for honest, clean-living working men with a family, a craft and a spark of patriotism in them to read the reports of my operatives as they gradually unfold the story of anarchism."[44]

Back to business, Burns expected to earn a handsome fee for solving the McNamara case. His team ran up a bill of $8,000 under the terms of his hire by Mayor Alexander. Public outrage over the murder of innocents led to offers of rewards for apprehending the culprits: $10,000 by the state, $10,000 by the city, and $5,000 from the county of Los Angeles. Burns knew that he had faced opposition all along in the city from his nemesis Rogers but also from Otis, who despised everything about the San Francisco trials. As a result, Burns was not paid for his successful efforts. On February 11, 1913, he wrote to the great progressive governor of California, Hiram Johnson, asking for help. "I am writing to earnestly urge your assistance and cooperation in securing for me from the Legislature the reward of $10,000 offered by them for the arrest and conviction of the persons responsible for blowing up the Los Angeles Times Building." He alleged that "Earl Rogers and others at Los Angeles, including the Grand Jury stopped Mayor Alexander from paying me." Burns claimed to have borrowed $18,000 to fund the operation and now "needed the money badly." Evidently his cordial letter produced no prompt result as it was followed by a telegram on March 24 with a blunt repetition of his request, to which he added, "Unless I can get your co-operation and assistance I will have to abandon the effort."[45] Whether Burns ever got paid for the job is a mystery. But he profited in reputation and from royalties from *The Masked War* and a spate of magazine articles in *McClure's* during this period. Burns and several acolytes told his story with imagination and panache approaching fiction.

## Storytellers

Detective work is hard work—long hours at tedious assignments for modest reward and little real excitement. The early detectives worked mainly in public places where the activities of their quarry could be watched, noted, and reported. The detective dealt with the ever-present risk of exposure, being "turned up," cover blown. That risk shaped the detectives' conduct and demeanor. False identities had to be maintained, confidences established and held, potentially revealing acts avoided. And despite these constraints the detective needed to produce information useful to bosses and clients—even if it was made up. If surveillance dominated the detective's daily routine, a good deal of time was devoted to writing reports and seeing to their delivery. The job involved very little criminal investigation and none of the glory seized by a celebrity boss like Burns, when there was any glory to be had. The job also entailed exposure to unscrupulous methods common to the industry. Operatives dealt with them in varied ways: some defected and exposed wrongdoing, some used their covert positions for good, but most thought their work useful and justified their actions as a service to society, to Americanism. With all its limitations, many liked the work. Those who wrote about it identified with honest American workers—like themselves.

The op report is the best evidence of what early detectives actually did on the job. Reports passed through several hands, where the operative's original text was sometimes and to some extent edited to make the op and agency look good to the client, to demonstrate the need for continued employment. Consequently, much in the documentary record of detective work is a product of creative storytelling. Morris Friedman, who at one time authored Pinkerton op reports, described them as "realistic art."[46] They were composed from boilerplate outlines provided by the agency. Ops in the field knew that the message destined for bosses and clients should emphasize the gravity of the problem and the effectiveness of their work. Editors in the office corrected grammar and spelling, and improved on the drama. Former detective Howard McLellan explains, "Like the beginning of a successful short story, the successful report must have strong elements of suspense."[47] There is fabrication in these reports, but there is also a good deal of fact that cannot help but be revealed: about places where action occurs, the agent's purpose, associates, risks, sympathies, and, indeed, even constraints which infuse the narrative.

Op reports written for purposeful readers are evidence of how detectives told stories. Like the French pardon letters examined by Natalie Davis, they are "fiction in the archives." Detectives' reports provide evidence of "what they thought a good story was, how they accounted for motive, and how through narrative they made sense of the unexpected and built coherence into immediate experience."[48] The commercial books of Pinkerton, Burns, and GT-99 concocted op reports to add realism to the text, judging from their florid narrative style that contrasts sharply with the more pedestrian, though storied, primary sources. In the gray area between documentary evidence and fiction, a style was improvised that would infuse the cultural imagining of the private eye.

After twenty years in the business, GT-99 retired to a peaceful Canadian farm "to make use of my only remaining talent. I've written from six to ten million words of copy in the past twenty odd years, and it should have taught me something about the art of story-telling."[49] The op reports that recall the voice and describe the action of the working detective are fictions, but fictions in the fertile historiographic sense of testimony produced in response to real situations.

# 5

# CRIMES OF DETECTIVES

## The Case of the San Francisco Parade Bomb

The Preparedness Day parade began forming early on the warm Saturday morning of July 22, 1916. Promoted as the greatest demonstration of patriotism in San Francisco's history, the line of march would stretch along Market Street for nearly two miles, from the Ferry building to City Hall. Thornwell Mullally, parade organizer and director of the city's United Railroads (URR) was grand marshal, heading the file on horseback. Next, on foot, came Mayor James Rolph and a covey of judges (standing in for delayed Governor Hiram Johnson), followed by an ensemble of 115 local and state organizations including the Down Town Association, Street Railroads, Women's Division, Building Industry, Knights of Columbus, Moose, Architects, Olympic Club, Boat Builders, Plumbers, and the Indo-Tibeto-Chinese College Yogi. Market Street was decked out in patriotic bunting, and "gay dress" was recommended for participants, who carried flags of all sizes while marching to the accompaniment of brass bands. Scarcely noticed for their absence were members of the San Francisco Labor Council and the Socialist Party, who organized an alternative manifestation called Union against Militarism.

The parade stepped off at 1:30 p.m. as successive divisions flowed into Market Street from the Embarcadero and immediate side streets. Eleventh in the order of march, gathered along Steuart Street just one block from the Embarcadero, was the Grand Army of the Republic, their Women's Auxiliary, the Sons of the American Revolution, and Spanish War Veterans. As spectators watched them move to the corner of Steuart and Market at 2:06 p.m., a powerful bomb exploded, leveling the crowd and silencing the street for what seemed an eternity before screams of the shocked and wounded began to rise. Placed against the brick wall of the Ferry Exchange Saloon, the bomb exploded directly into the Steuart Street crowd with a force that toppled vehicles and horses, scattering debris and body parts as far as the roofs of nearby buildings. As chaos descended on Steuart and Market, the head of the parade passing the Eilers Music Company building at 975 Market continued unaware of the tragedy nine blocks behind. Police on the beat and survivors began ministering to the shocked and wounded. Their calls for emergency services broadcast within the hour described how the city's greatest patriotic demonstration had turned into its worst crime. Ten people died in the explosion and forty-four were injured. The Preparedness Day bomb shaped San Francisco's politics and reputation for years to come.[1]

The events that played out in San Francisco reflected a controversy that polarized the nation. A Preparedness Movement urged by former president Teddy Roosevelt and Army Chief of Staff General Leonard Wood warned that the nation's military readiness was inadequate to the growing threat from Germany, which had already launched into World War I, and from Pancho Villa's incursions along the Mexican border. A stronger armed force and universal military service would toughen the country's flabby fitness and serve the additional purpose of forcibly integrating recent waves of immigrants into a patriotic Americanized society. President Woodrow Wilson's initial resistance to militarism was compromised when a German U-boat sank the passenger ship *Lusitania* in May 1915. Yet the Preparedness Movement became the Preparedness Controversy as progressives like social worker Jane Addams of Hull House and biologist David Starr Jordan, president of Stanford University, rallied the peace movement and a multifaceted opposition to World War I. Simplifying the controversy, Republican elites, bankers, and industrialists (of steel and munitions) squared off against progressives and labor. Wilson acquiesced, appealing for public expressions of support for preparedness with parades such as those staged in New York in May and Seattle in June, 1916.[2]

San Francisco mirrored the national controversy, and then some. Proponents of a preparedness demonstration came from the Chamber of Commerce, various men's clubs, veterans' organizations, and high society, embodied in the Women's Section of the Navy League. Opponents included the San Francisco Labor Council, the city's progressive coalition—headed by industrialist Rudolph Spreckels and editor Fremont Older—suffragettes, and socialists, represented in the person of Emma Goldman. Preparedness advocates held the upper hand, wrapping themselves and Market Street in the flag. Patriotism fit the interests of bankers, merchants, and the politically powerful United Railroads, whose director also headed the parade organizing committee.

Each side mobilized supporters prior to parade day. Two weeks earlier, the Chamber of Commerce met in emergency session prompted by a series of strikes; "more than 2000 irate businessmen gathered to demand action."[3] The result was formation of the Law and Order Committee, pledged to the open shop, and $600,000 in funding from chamber members. Two days before the parade, antipreparedness forces held a mass meeting at the Dreamland Skating Rink to denounce the event and the militarism it represented, which they saw as the design of corrupt munitions makers. "Preparedness means militarism and militarism means tyranny. . . . [It] is an exploitation of labor . . . designed [not] merely to raise the price of Bethlehem steel stock but aimed against the workingmen of the country."[4] Militarism struck an ominous chord with unionists who had seen federal and state militia troops used violently to break strikes. The Irish, San Francisco's largest nationality group, despised military force such as deployed by the British against Ireland's Easter Rising just four months earlier.

Against the San Francisco backdrop, a set of parallel events became entangled with the bombing and subsequent efforts to assign blame. Thomas Mooney, an unemployed iron molder, decided to try his hand at labor organizing. Mooney's last job was as a laborer for the Panama-Pacific International Exposition, whose ultimate boss was the ubiquitous executive director, Thornwell Mullally. In a further coincidence, Mooney's new objective was organizing the street car conductors of United Railroads. Although not a member of the citywide carmen's union, Mooney's plan was to rally unionists from other companies and at least a few URR workers to stage a wildcat strike. United Railroads was much reformed since the days of its involvement in the graft trials of 1907–9, although it remained staunchly anti-union. As Mooney began leafletting the car barns, URR hired Thiel Detective Agency operatives to shadow the agitator.

In the early hours of Sunday, June 11, the city's power-line towers at the top of San Bruno Mountain, which supplied United Railroads electrical streetcars, were destroyed by dynamite. Naturally, Mooney and his confederates were suspected, although no evidence connected them or anyone else to the deed. Rumors flew, placing responsibility on everyone from anarchist saboteurs to agents provocateurs.[5] Detectives were quick to pounce. Ex-Pinkerton Martin Swanson, working for a new agency called Public Utilities Protective Bureau, suspected Mooney. Swanson attempted unsuccessfully to bribe two witnesses for testimony about Mooney's alleged role in the tower bomb. Swanson had a history with Mooney and with the use of unscrupulous methods for framing suspects. Nevertheless, the tower bomb case, like the carmen's organizing effort, went nowhere. The wildcat strike was a flop, managing only to tie up downtown traffic at rush hour on July 14. Eight days later all these developments converged with the tragedy at Steuart and Market Streets.

In the immediate aftermath of the explosion, the crime scene commanded the city's attention. The wounded and dead were carried away and bloody sidewalks hosed down. Police, parade officials, and curious bystanders swarmed over the scene in a confusion that surely destroyed evidence, not least by ghoulish souvenir hunters. More deliberately, police swept up debris and disposed of it against proper forensic procedure. Later, disagreement would arise over exactly what type of bomb it was. A set of photographs taken that afternoon shows District Attorney Charles Fickert and Frederick Colburn, banker and president of the Chamber of Commerce, with three others who appear to be digging in the site of the explosion. They later claimed to have found embedded in the wall various bullets, presumably contained in the bomb and miraculously unexploded. Oddly, no actual bomb components were found. Before and after photos show the result of their work: an enlarged sidewalk crater and wall indentation. Author Curt Gentry entitles the photographs "Searching for Evidence or Destroying It?"[6]

A conspiracy began to unfold from the day of the fatal bomb, or perhaps sooner. Fickert met with Swanson that evening and appointed the detective to the district attorney's office, where he was given complete access in the months that followed. Swanson focused immediately on Mooney. Anyone who would dynamite electrical towers would also bomb a parade, or so he surmised, and he proceeded to manufacture supporting evidence. No other suspects or explanations were pursued by Swanson or, therefore, by the district attorney, who eagerly embraced the theory of Mooney's involvement.

An explanation of how the district attorney's office and Swanson developed the case requires a step back in time to 1913 and San Francisco's tumultuous labor scene. Pacific Gas and Electric (PG&E), California's vast public utility, was experiencing labor unrest in the form of strikes and sabotage to company property: "one of the most serious [conflicts] in the history of the American light and power industry [including] 770 depredations against company property, eighteen of them with dynamite."[7] PG&E hired the Pinkerton Agency and its key operative at the time, Martin Swanson, to help solve their labor problem. In search of likely suspects, Swanson took an interest in Warren Billings, a drifter and IWW supporter en route to join Pancho Villa in Mexico who had decided instead to settle in San Francisco. Billings went to work in a shoe factory and began passing intelligence to the union that was striking the company at the time. Billings moved on to support the San Francisco Labor Council in the PG&E strike, where he made the casual acquaintance of Tom Mooney. Billings had been canvassing PG&E facilities, at the same time stealing dynamite from quarries and construction sites with fairly obvious intentions. He was paid by a union official to transport explosives by train to Sacramento, a crime in California. It was a setup. PG&E detectives who arranged the transport were trawling for labor militants who might reveal others in the network. Billings was righteously arrested and sweated to name his associates in the strike movement, which he refused to do.

Mooney by this time saw that things were getting hot for strike sympathizers and decided to lay low. A fishing trip seemed like a good idea, and he set off from Vallejo with two fellow radicals in a leaky boat laden with supplies. As none knew how to sail, they were unable to navigate the Carquinez Strait into San Pablo Bay and were washed ashore at Richmond. A tip from an unknown source brought down the Richmond Police, with a crew of private detectives led by the dogged Martin Swanson close behind. In the beached skiff, detectives claimed to have discovered a menacing arsenal: a rifle, a revolver, a shotgun, ammunition for all, dry cell batteries, an alarm clock, a 500-foot spool of wire, and tools—but no dynamite. How the boat could have floated with all this and three hapless sailors aboard was not explained. Nor was it clear what crime justified the arrest since the suspects had not transported actual explosives, only guns and dynamite caps, allegedly.

Three separate trials in Martinez, Contra Costa County, exposed the prosecution's machinations and finally acquitted Mooney and his co-defendants, thanks to the county's independent district attorney and scrappy newspaper editor. "[T]he Martinez affair [was] a rehearsal for the final frame-up" in San Francisco three years later.[8]

On July 26, 1916, after four days of consideration but little real investigation, Fickert and Swanson began making arrests. First was Warren Billings, now on parole from his prison sentence for transporting explosives. Next came Israel Weinberg, a San Francisco jitney driver and friend of the Mooneys. (Tom's wife, Rena, was Weinberg's daughter's piano teacher.) The central focus on Mooney became clear when Swanson and several police broke into Rena Mooney's music studio, where the couple lived. "Among the material recovered from her studio in the raid last night was a notebook containing records of the explosives stolen from quarries in the bay region and of structures dynamited in and around San Francisco." (Woe be to the bomber who keeps records of stolen explosives and dynamited structures.) Another raid of the home of Mrs. Belle Lavin, Billings's landlady, produced "a quantity of steel-jacketed bullets, slugs and other missiles identical to those found in the bomb that was exploded during the preparedness parade."[9] Belle Lavin ran the rooming house where two figures in the Los Angeles McNamara case had stayed, which probably explained her being targeted. Tom and Rena Mooney had left town for the Russian River after the bombing and were unaware of the raids and arrests until they read in the newspaper that they were targets of the investigation. Hearing the news, Tom called San Francisco police to report his location and intention to return by train from Guerneville directly. Police met the train and took him into custody, where he would remain for the next twenty-two years, despite a protracted legal struggle that demonstrated his innocence.

Mooney, his wife, Billings, and the others arrested were framed — framed on a charge of murder by the guardians of law enforcement: the district attorney, police, and private detectives working closely with officials, the Chamber of Commerce and the Law and Order Committee. A photograph by Wade Hamilton that shows the couple watching the parade from the roof of the Eilers Building five minutes before the explosion and a mile away was never allowed into evidence at trial. Two book-length studies and two government-sponsored reports document the travesty.[10] Details of the train of legal injustice

Figure 5.1. Amateur photo showing Tom and Rena Mooney (right) on the roof of their building at 975 Market Street watching the Preparedness Day Parade at 2:01 p.m., according to a jeweler's clock on the street. (Bancroft Library)

are well researched and need not be rehearsed here. Tried separately, the cases of Mooney and Billings (the others were dropped) dragged through the courts despite proof of perjured testimony and oblivious to public protests by the Tom Mooney Molders' Defense Committee and labor organizations across the country and across the Atlantic in Europe and Russia. The same antilabor elements in business and government that convicted the pair blocked all attempts to void their convictions and get new trials. Mooney's pardon and release from prison came twenty-two years later only after progressive governor Culbert Olson acknowledged the injustice in January 1939. Eight months after that, Billings was released for time served, not pardoned.

The most puzzling aspect of the Preparedness Day parade bomb case is the absence of any attempt to solve it. For whatever reasons, the police had no intention of looking beyond Mooney and his associates. The frame-up was so blatant, the press coverage so sensational, and the partisans so vocal that the actual deed faded in the consciousness of adversaries focused on the case for and against Mooney and Billings. Selected witnesses on the parade route claimed to have seen someone carrying a suitcase or someone on the roof of the Ferry Exchange Saloon at Market and Steuart. Fragmentary recollections pictured a device dropped from the roof or a suitcase left on the side street. Several agreed they had seen a "dark-skinned man." But all that was unexamined speculation. It was left to reporters and latter-day authors to ask the question ignored by law enforcement: If Mooney and Billings were innocent, as they certainly were, who was guilty? "Whose bomb?" as Curt Gentry asked in 1967.[11]

Three theories were suggested: labor reprisal, German sabotage, and establishment plot—workers, spies, and bosses. Labor militancy was the conventional supposition which provided a context that could explain the actions of Mooney and Billings or any of their radical fellows. The Chamber of Commerce and the Downtown Association had been pounding this theme for months, which gave the original impetus to the parade celebration. Real anarchists were available for accusation. Emma Goldman was in town on a lecture tour and attended the antiparade rally two days before the bombing. Her friend and colleague, Alexander Berkman (who had actually attempted to assassinate Henry Clay Frick of Homestead fame), had been resident in San Francisco for the past year publishing a radical newspaper called, most unfortunately, the *Blast*. Sabotage by dynamite and other means was common in the PG&E strike. And, of course, the Wobbly menace was ever present in those years, San Francisco being well represented by cells of the International Workers of the World. The Law and Order Committee was already advocating passage of a draconian Criminal Syndicalism Law in the state legislature, aimed primarily at the IWW, which passed in 1919.[12] The notion that labor in one guise or another did the bombing was almost an article of faith. But the theory had one disconcerting problem: there was no evidence for it whatsoever.

German sabotage offered a more fertile hypothesis. Incidents of alleged German sabotage targeting infrastructure works and industrial facilities occurred episodically from 1914 onward. Sinking of the British passenger ship *Lusitania* (which was also carrying arms), killing 120 people, including Americans, in May 1915 heightened awareness of the threat. Just eight days after the San Francisco bomb, the Black Tom Island munitions plant in New Jersey was destroyed in a spectacular explosion, the largest in American history. Although definitive proof and arrests never materialized, the deed was traced to two suspects known to have been in the area at the time, German nationals Kurt Jahnke and Lothar Witzke. A shadowy figure, Jahnke also appeared in San Francisco in 1914, associating with the German consul, Franz von Bopp, himself suspected of local acts of sabotage. Jahnke had joined the US Marines in 1909 and was eventually stationed at the Mare Island Naval Shipyard on San Francisco Bay (the site of a saboteur's bomb in 1917). After military service, he became involved in arms trafficking and sabotage, including attacks on US factories.

The intrigue runs deep. Robert Spence's meticulous study of Jahnke's career discovered, "By the time war erupted in Europe, Jahnke had entered into the somewhat more settled profession of private detective. By early 1916 he had worked for the Pinkerton, Cleary, and Morse detective agencies in San Francisco. . . . Much of his work, particularly for the Morse Agency, involved guarding ships, docks, and warehouses."[13] The Pinkerton connection was probably arranged by Jahnke's Marine Corps sergeant, Martin Swanson. The sabotage theory of the bombing begins with these fairly well-known circumstances. But then it turns to speculation. Spence believes that Jahnke, either on his own or on instructions from von Bopp, intended to plant a bomb on board one of the British ships docked in San Francisco Bay on the morning of July 22. Assuming that the bomb was in a suitcase (rather than dropped from above, as some witnesses re-

ported), Spence thinks Jahnke and Weitz were headed for the Embarcadero port when their headway was blocked by the parade crowds.
"Either by design or necessity, the men abandoned the case at the spot
and slipped away."[14] Gentry's review of several theories agrees that
this is the most likely.

Yet it strains credulity. Certainly, German sabotage was a fact and
Jahnke was up to no good in San Francisco. But German sabotage had
been purposefully and expertly aimed at war matériel—munitions,
ships, and military facilities—not people. The idea that a lethal time
bomb would be abandoned in a crowd by an otherwise wily spy
makes no sense. Nor is it plausible that someone carrying a bomb
would plunge into a well-publicized and well-attended event in the
first place when various alternative routes to the bay were at hand.
Someone wanting to abandon a suitcase bomb, moreover, had the bay
available just one block from Steuart Street. It is something of a puzzle
why the German sabotage theory attracted such circumspect analysts
as Spence and Gentry. One possibility is that the dense account suggests something devious "must" have been going on. But, Spence also
hints at another scenario: "Whether Jahnke arranged the bombing
to further Swanson's scheme [of framing Mooney] or was merely an
accomplice is uncertain, but there can be little doubt that Jahnke was
the man behind the blast."[15]

That possibility leads to the third, establishment plot theory. The
central premise suggesting an official plot holds that the events before
and after the explosion are all of a piece. The argument proposes that
the bomb was planted with the specific intention of implicating labor
and permanently destroying its credibility with the public. The campaign for "Law and Order" had been launched with substantial fund-
ing and virulent opposition to labor. The open shop movement was
in full swing and would reign through to the Red Scare of 1919–20.[16]
A successful plot needed a fall guy and Tom Mooney served the purpose admirably—a pesky agitator with no organized labor credentials,
a member of the Iron Molders Union but a nuisance to the moderate
San Francisco Labor Council. Mooney's bravado made him a visible
target of private detectives looking to justify their hire by catching
villains, even if they had to be framed with planted evidence.

In Mooney's defense, claims of an official plot were advanced early
on by supporters in radical labor circles but readily silenced by the
weight of publicity, sensationalism, and manufactured evidence. The

great progressive editor Fremont Older protested against Fickert's investigative tactics and the denial of due process, but he also thought for a long time that Mooney and Billings were guilty. The strongest argument against an establishment plot was sheer disbelief that anyone would deliberately do such a thing. Yet, planted bombs intended to discredit the labor movement were a familiar tactic known on occasion to have killed innocents.[17] It is likely that the bombers did not intend the loss of life, that they miscalculated. The idea may have been to create an incident, a small explosion on a side street producing mild property damage and public outrage at those who had opposed the patriotic demonstration in the first place.

Collusion between District Attorney Charles Fickert and Martin Swanson was deep and devious. As the Mooney-Billings case proved, Fickert was ambitious, ruthless, and reasonably stupid. A federal investigation of his office in 1918 revealed a host of indiscretions, from soliciting false witnesses to arranging assignations with prostitutes at city expense. When his roughshod treatment of suspects and encouragement of perjured testimony against Mooney became evident, a recall election effort was mounted in the spring of 1917. Fickert campaigned to hold his office with the claim that he represented law and order; after all, he had broken the parade-bomb case. Late on December 17, the night before the recall election, a bomb exploded on the back porch of the governor's mansion in Sacramento. The bomb was small and carefully placed so as to avoid injury. But news of the bombing was quickly flashed to newspapers. "The next morning San Franciscans read that an attempt had been made to assassinate the Governor [and they] turned out heavily at the polls to defeat the recall."[18] Given the timing and context, the Sacramento bomblet was an obvious plant, yet Sacramento police reflexively turned to the IWW as the perpetrators. A San Francisco reporter learned that the mansion's night watchman might have been involved, along with a prominent detective: "Not long before the night when the dynamiting took place, the watchman and Martin Swanson . . . were seen together in Sacramento."[19]

Cold cases are difficult to solve and the case of the San Francisco Preparedness Day parade bomb is a classic example. One hundred years later, witnesses, evidence, and even interest are gone. The proven frame-up and cover-up did their job. But theories persist, hypothesized explanations that may be evaluated as more and less

Figure 5.2. Anton Refrieger mural depicting the Preparedness Day bombing, from a series painted in 1937 in San Francisco's Rincon Postal Annex Building near the corner of Market and Steuart Streets.

plausible on the evidence. In this instance, the labor reprisal theory lacks any supporting evidence. The German sabotage theory takes in a number of antecedent facts and enjoys the support of respectable analysts. Sabotage, German and otherwise, was certainly happening, some of it the work of agents who were in San Francisco on July 22, 1916. Circumstantial support, however, doesn't go the distance. The civilian parade target and abandoned bomb notion defy reason. The establishment plot theory, unpalatable as it may be, nevertheless conforms to the broader sociological landscape. Planted bombs were sometimes employed by labor and by private detectives. Precautions to avoid injury were not always successful, or even taken. Swanson had previously planted explosive materials in another, unsuccessful effort to frame Mooney. Skullduggery pervaded San Francisco's political culture at the time with a strong and officially embraced motivation to crush labor in general. And the ground-level agents for this work were willing and ready in the presence of Martin Swanson and his network of private detectives. Indeed, collusion of business, officialdom, and detectives was an established institutional arrangement. The establishment plot hypothesis is the most plausible, though ultimately unproven.

## The Common Frame-up

It was not uncommon for private detectives and their more aggressive agency employers to operate at the margins of legality, readily crossing over to manifestly criminal acts in pursuit of results. In a highly competitive business, results, real or concocted, were at a premium. The legal climate was tolerant and the laws sometimes ambiguous in their application. Recklessness was easily justified in pursuit of supposed enemies of the American way. Until expressly proscribed and sanctioned, the detectives enjoyed wide latitudes of conduct.

The frame-up was a standard tactic. Supposition that the San Francisco parade bombing was a scheme concocted by city officials and their Law and Order sponsors gains circumstantial plausibility when placed in the larger context of American class struggles. Bombs were used in a variety of settings by pro- and antilabor groups—and even by rebellious citizens. Planting bombs to discredit labor was a familiar subterfuge. During the Lawrence, Massachusetts, Textile Strike of 1912, the president of the American Woolen Company and his assistants were convicted of planting a bomb, which police recovered on a tip from a supposed union conspirator. Later it was revealed that William Wood, president of the company, had arranged the scheme, although his prominence and philanthropic work won him an acquittal. In August 1914, the New York City Police placed two bombs in St. Patrick's Cathedral, which were then attributed to anarchists. The devices were "fizzlers" that avoided damage to the shrine but served to convict two patsies to long prison sentences.[20] During the great Cripple Creek (Colorado) Miners' Strike of 1903, the Independence railroad depot was bombed, killing thirteen strikebreakers. Later it was revealed that Pinkerton operatives had planted the explosives in an outrage they intended to blame on the Western Federation of Miners.[21] A private detective named Emmerson working for the Merchants, Manufacturers, and Employers Association of Stockton, California, was arrested for stealing dynamite from the Santa Fe Railroad. Tom Mooney was among those who uncovered Emmerson's plan to cause an explosion implicating labor.[22]

As the Emmerson case demonstrates, the frame-up by means of manufactured evidence and false witness was the modus operandi of many agencies—not only the notorious ones. The case of the Modesto

Boys arose during a West Coast strike against Standard Oil by tanker ship operators in April 1935. A group of eleven men from the Joint Tanker Strike Committee piled into two cars heading from California's East Bay to the Central Valley town of Patterson, intending to reconnoiter a contingent of strikebreakers billeted at the Del Puerto Hotel. Implied in the act was some form of intimidation to discourage the strikebreakers, although their plan never materialized. Among their ranks were two undercover detectives, one from the Independent Detective and Patrol Service of Oakland, California, and one employed by Standard Oil. (The company was a client of the Burns Agency at the time.)[23] The spies had infiltrated the strike committee and their present assignment was to engineer a frame-up. Alerted earlier by the detectives, police and oil company guards stopped the cars on the highway and produced blackjacks, fuses, and dynamite, which, they claimed, were found in one of the cars. A Modesto, California, jury was unconvinced. They rejected a charge of conspiracy to bomb the hotel but agreed on the lesser offense of transporting explosives. Eight of the Modesto Boys went to prison for terms up to five years.[24]

A telling piece of evidence suggesting that the frame-up was a common practice of detective agencies comes from an advertisement by Nick Harris Detectives that appeared in the *Los Angeles Times*. The ad promised, "Our male and female agents are honest and their testimony will be sworn in court if necessary. We resort to no frame ups."[25] The pledge not to do something implies that others did do it and that prospective clients from the general public would know and appreciate the distinction. Interagency competition worked both ways, with Nick Harris appealing to the more respectable side of the business.

### Crimes of Violence

Detective agencies bear a deserved reputation for the use of violence; deserved because it applied to all of the major national agencies at some time and to others throughout their history. By far the greatest incidence of violence occurred in the practice of strikebreaking and with the many firms specializing in that work. The La Follette Senate investigation in the late 1930s reported, "Detective agencies that figured repeatedly in the industrial disputes of the decades of the twentieth century were the Thiel agency of St. Louis, and the Ascher, Bergoff, William J. Burns, and Wadell-Mahon agencies of New York."[26] Later Baldwin-Felts, Railway Audit and Inspection Company (RA&I), and many more joined their ranks. Strikebreaking as a general practice typically involved the importation of scabs to operate or simply occupy the facility under strike. The more notorious strikebreaking agencies, particularly RA&I, came to wreak havoc by literally breaking equipment and bones. "These strikebreaking jobs . . . were remarkable for the bad character of the men shipped and employed and for the violence and bloodshed attending their employment."[27]

Agency operatives sometimes provoked violence as a means of discrediting labor. "Violence is started in a number of ways. Trouble is created in open meetings. Street operatives pose as strikers and start slugging. Charges of injury by strikers are faked."[28] In one Pennsylvania steel strike, an RA&I man joined the picket line posing as a Communist Party militant in solidarity with the union. His job was to inform RA&I of the propitious moment to attack the pickets on the pretext that they were communist subversives, not legitimate unionists. Once unleashed, the violence was indiscriminate, affecting both the pickets and the operative:

> The Railway Audit and Inspection office, however, failed to inform him and as a consequence, he, with all the other pickets were caught unawares when the attack was launched. In the attack [he] claims that he was badly beaten; in fact, he was so bruised from clubbing and kicks and his lungs were so badly affected by gas that he was forced to stay in the hospital nearly 3 weeks. The picket line, of course, was completely crushed, he said, and the strike broken.[29]

The Baldwin-Felts Detective Agency, based in Virginia, rivaled RA&I in the systematic use of violence to break strikes. Beginning in railroad protection work, they later specialized in labor disputes in the West Virginia coal mines. The agency had earned a fierce reputation in a decade of conflicts leading up to the Matewan Massacre in May 1920. Baldwin-Felts detectives came to Matewan to evict striking miners' families from their homes, leading to a gun battle with townspeople that killed three of their number and seven detectives, including two Felts brothers. In retaliation, the agency assassinated the local sheriff, who led the resistance to the eviction.[30] Matewan became yet another symbol of industrial violence.

The La Follette Committee investigation describes "two separate vested interests in violence. The agency's interest in violence, and by the same token that of the strikebreaker's, is that it will prolong and embitter the fight so that a stronger guard will be called out and more money expended through the agency. The employers interest in violence is that it shall be attributed to the workers, bring discredit to them, thus alienating public sympathy for their cause."[31]

Violent strikebreaking and the detective agencies specializing in this work are closely associated with the development of municipal railways in American cities from the 1890s to the 1930s. As cities grew and early suburbs spread, streetcars became essential features of urban life. That innovation, in turn, fostered both local carmen's unions, many of them affiliated with the Amalgamated Association of Street and Electric Railway Employees of America (AASEREA), and a new line of work for detective agencies with train spotters assigned to surveil conductors who collected fares. Streetcar railways also gave labor a new strategic resource—the potential to shut down much of a city's commercial activity with a well-timed strike, particularly a general strike. Trolly lines ran through working-class neighborhoods and the carmen enjoyed riders' sympathy. Taken together, these developments explain a wave of streetcar strikes in the early decades of the twentieth century—Brooklyn (1895), Cleveland (1899), St. Louis (1900), Chicago (1903), Pittsburg/McKees Rocks (1909), Philadelphia (1910), Indianapolis (1913), Wilkes-Barre (1915), New York (1916), New Orleans (1929), and more. Many of these conflicts involved deaths and extensive injuries to carmen, strikebreakers, and bystanders.[32] Theodore Dreiser wrote of his own experience in the 1900 Toledo, Ohio, strike in *Sister Carrie*. William Kennedy's award-winning novel *Ironweed* presents a vivid account of the 1901 Albany, New York, trolley strike and its devastating effect on the lives of working people.

The major strikebreaking agencies developed a standard organizational structure. Well-known owners managed the firms through a few permanent employees in charge of recruitment and logistics. The labor force was hired on a temporary basis, by the job, even though jobs came along steadily. They were divided into three groups: strikebreakers, guards, and street operators ("strike missionaries"). Street operators mingled in the community, disparaging the strike effort among families and merchants. Strikebreakers were further divided into "nobles" (the elite leg-breakers) and "finks" (foot soldiers). Often referred to as an "army," strikebreakers were recruited from the urban lumpen proletariat, casual and unskilled men from the streets of New York, Chicago, or Philadelphia. These "armies" were raised on short notice, transported across the country if needed, and set up in temporary barracks at the site of the strike, often in the streetcar barns, barricaded against the carmen. Strikebreakers were paid a daily wage (typically $4) exceeding the carmen's pay, and they were provisioned by the agency, which supplied the troops from a company store run for profit. Gambling occupied the men during idle hours and provided the agency with an additional profitable concession. Available records show that strikebreaking was a most lucrative business. The Brooklyn Rapid Transit Company spent over $2 million on strike expenses in 1922 with Bergoff Brothers and Wadell, Inc. collecting $712 thousand of that total, Washington Detective Bureau, $306 thousand, Archer Detective Agency, $175 thousand, and so on, all for "furnishing miscellaneous labor."[33]

James Farley began his career as a streetcar policeman in 1895 and worked his way through the ranks of railroading to become "king of the strikebreakers" by the time of his retirement in 1922. He seemed to enjoy violence and was known to lead his nobles in attacks intended to disperse and discourage strikers. Farley's notoriety derived in part from the San Francisco Streetcar Strike of 1907, which was the nation's deadliest and most publicized. Thirty-one people were killed and 1,150 injured, mostly civilian sympathizers and passengers in each category. The strike occurred during a period of turmoil in San Francisco. Recovery from the 1906 earthquake and fire was underway in what amounted to a rebuilding of the city. The influential United Railroads (URR) used the occasion to modernize the system by replacing the old cable cars (except on steep hills, where they remain to this day) with overhead-wire electrical power. The fatal bribe of $200,000 from URR president Patrick Calhoun to Mayor Ruef, which precipitated the graft trials, served to nullify a local ordinance against overhead wires, thus allowing the modernization project to move forward. Meanwhile, URR platform men suffering from reconstruction-induced inflation determined to win a wage increase and an eight-hour day (reduced from the prevailing ten hours). The local union of platform men (later joined by the carmen) secured a charter to become Division 205 of the AASEREA, a move that added muscle to

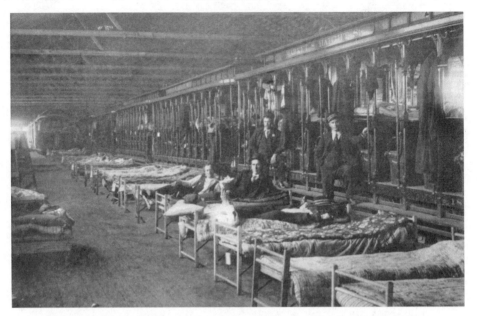

Figure 5.3. San Francisco streetcar strike of 1907. Streetcar barns and the cars themselves were converted to dormitories housing "Farleyite" strikebreakers. (Bay Area Electric Railroad Association)

the campaign. Negotiations begun in May 1906 produced meager concessions to the union and incentives to strike. In May 1907, Calhoun contracted with Farley for 400 strikebreakers who were promptly imported from the East and installed in the URR streetcar barns. On May 5, Division 205 went out on strike.[34]

In a rare eyewitness account entitled "The Violent Art of Strikebreaking," journalist John Craige observes, "Strikebreaking is nowadays a profession, and strikebreakers are a class, distinct and strongly marked."[35] Often they shared common employers, jobs where they lived together, criminal records, and grisly nicknames like "Blackjack Jerome." Farley was called "Potato Face," though probably not to his face. And they knew their job, as "Frenchy Joe" explains: "You give me twenty-five good guards with clubs and guns and put 'em in wagons, and a couple of stool-pigeons with guns to run through the crowds and fire at the wagons to give us a chance to start, and we'd go through all the crowds in this town in a day."[36] In the San Francisco strike, nobles carried clubs to beat back carmen who surrounded the barns trying to prevent any streetcars from operating. A special closed car designed to transport race horses was loaded with riflemen, who fired into the crowd. Strikers, too, armed themselves, with clubs and stones, which proved no match for the guns carried by riot police and strikebreakers attempting to run the trolleys.

In an effort to profile the occupation as a whole, the La Follette Committee compiled from their records a list of 150 strikebreakers and then checked their criminal records. Although the survey was hampered by pseudonyms and incomplete sources, they nevertheless discovered an "astonishing . . . one-third of the strikebreakers have criminal arrest records."[37]

Jim Farley retired from the strikebreaking business a rich man, with an estimated net worth of $10 million. The San Francisco strike alone reportedly yielded a $700 thousand profit. The promise of riches attracted a number of new entrepreneurs and agencies to the business around 1900. Best known was Pearl L. Bergoff, the "Red Demon" from New York City, who exceeded even Farley in reputation, wealth, and infamy. Bergoff began his career as a train spotter for the Brooklyn Heights Railroad and later worked as a "tracer" for installment-credit businesses, finding people who had moved to a different address without notifying their creditors. Moving up the social scale, he worked for a prominent lawyer preparing evidence for divorce cases, a job that led indirectly to involvement in one of the great scandals of the era, when he was chosen as bodyguard to Stanford White. White was a famous New York architect and infamous philanderer with a taste for young women other than his wife. He enjoyed an affair with actress Evelyn Nesbit, who, much later, married wealthy (and allegedly unstable) Harry Thaw. Bergoff was attending another event when, in a fit of jealousy, Thaw shot and killed White at the Madison Square Garden rooftop theater in 1906. The whole affair is memorialized in E. L. Doctorow's novel *Ragtime* (later adapted as a Broadway musical and a film).

Bergoff left the matrimonial business that year and founded the Vigilant Detective Agency. He worked as a private investigator for the district attorney on Thaw's murder trial and wrote a "diary" of the case published in the New York *World*. Work for the public prosecutor paid insufficiently for Bergoff's growing ambition, especially as he came to understand the profits in strikebreaking exhibited by Farley and other agencies. Playing on the publicity generated by his diary, the agency was renamed "Bergoff Detective Bureau, Shadowing, Locating, Investigators and Serving Legal Papers," and soon emended to include "Labor Adjusters."[38] His first contract was to break a strike by New York City street cleaners. Bergoff went on to become a symbol of provocative labor violence, including the lethal Standard and Tidewater Oil strikes at Beyonne, New Jersey, in 1909, where, according to the US Commission on Industrial Relations, "These men shot without provocation at anyone and everyone who came within sight and the killing of at least three strikers in Bayonne and the wounding of many more is directly chargeable to these guards."[39] Profits were substantial. Bergoff noted that "a hundred thousand [dollar] job was an everyday job in the good old days."[40] In 1920 the agency earned $2 million.

Farley, Bergoff, Archer, RA&I, and others were specialists in a violent business that grew increasingly distasteful to the public and to the more established agencies. Pinkertons mostly got out of the business in the interest of their reputation as professionals. Over time, Burns shied away from strike work but made exceptions for profitable jobs like the 1936 New York elevator strike when he furnished 600 regular finks, "recruited from the streets in the same fashion as the guards supplied by the Railway, Audit and Inspection Co., the Sherwood Detective Agency, and the Bergoff Service Bureau, in the same strike."[41]

Violent methods were ingrained in strikebreaking and conventional detective work. A standard practice was to obtain information by coercion, beating suspects for a confession or simply for a lead. William A. Mundell owned the Mundell International Detective Agency of San Francisco and also did special jobs for Burns. Mundell and a deputy named Cradlebaugh were given the job of rounding up anyone involved in California's tragic Wheatland Riot of agricultural laborers in 1913 who might have information about the deaths of two law enforcement officers in the riot. The detectives managed to corner two itinerant workers camping near Guerneville, California, far from the site of the troubles. The suspects were detained (illegally) and moved from one jurisdiction to another over several days to avoid having to file charges. According to Mundell, suspect Alfred Nelson attempted to escape his hotel confinement in the East Bay town of Martinez. To prevent the escape, Cradlebaugh was said to have struck Nelson with an open hand, causing him to fall and hit his head. Out of frustration, perhaps, the detectives deposited Nelson in the Contra Costa County jail in Martinez, which was under the jurisdiction of District Attorney A. B. McKenzie. McKenzie learned that Burns detectives had beaten a man and left him in the county's custody. McKenzie then asked the sheriffs "to bring the man to my office. . . . When he came into my office he had a cut on the left side of his head probably 2 to 3 inches long. His eye was black; he had two bruises on his left cheek; and his lip was swollen and somewhat bruised. I afterwards learned from the physician who examined him that he was black and blue all over the shoulders and the leg, and I think somewhere else. The man had a wild and haunted look in his eye, and seemed to be very much afraid."[42] McKenzie indicted Cradlebaugh, who was convicted of assault and served a one year prison term.

Dramatic cases alone do not prove the claim that private detectives routinely employed abusive, violent, even lethal methods. But a good deal of anecdotal and documentary evidence does suggest a pattern. The California Bureau of Prisons that supervised the detective licensing process entertained citizen complaints about malpractice. Alleged crimes or malfeasance could be brought before the licensing board by affidavit for a determination of whether an agent's conduct deserved sanction. Detective agency owners required a license and, although employees were not licensed, the agency was responsible for their behavior. The bureau's minute books record common instances in which detectives were either cleared, admonished, or, on occasion, had their agencies' licenses revoked for violent acts. Illustratively, John Jerome, holder of California State Detective License 219, was judged "a vicious person of ill repute who has ordered and caused his employees to commit criminal assault on peaceful American citizens . . . resulting in murder and permitting him to continue operating a detective agency would be a dastardly outrage."[43] Two Burns agency operatives were arrested in San Francisco on assault charges when a client, whom they had led to an assignation of his wife's, stabbed her lover. As it happened, one of the operatives had a criminal record, and the whole affair jeopardized the agency's right to do business in the state.[44]

Detective agencies traded in the tools of violence: pistols, rifles, machine guns, night sticks, gas, hand grenades, and gas masks. "The munitions dealer-detective agency connection of longest standing and greatest importance is that between Federal Laboratories, Inc. and the Railway Audit and Inspection Co.—a marriage of the two foremost exponents of their respective brands of anti-unionism."[45] The two companies shared board members, personal friends, and a substantial sales–purchase relationship; one they went to lengths to conceal from investigators. Federal Laboratories was the source of "tear and sickening gas" that RA&I used in strikebreaking campaigns against the New Orleans Street Railway Company (1929) and Lake Charles Longshoremen (1935). They sold the Thompson submachine guns employed in the West Point (textile) Manufacturing Company strike of 1934. The La Follette Committee, once again, performed an amazing feat of data collection using subpoenaed invoices to tally company purchases of tear and sickening gas and equipment. The purchases from detective agencies and their affiliates were divided in two groups, large ($1,000 or more) and small ($300–$1,000). Eighty of the country's major corporations were included in the first category and another 115 in the second. In addition to gas, the same companies maintained arsenals of guns, documented in photographs demonstrating their variety and use in labor conflicts.[46]

### Eavesdropping and Wiretapping

Snooping, legal and otherwise, is the métier of private detectives. A good deal of surveillance and prying can be done without any invasion of privacy as legally defined. In the early twentieth century, the law on surveillance was vague and seldom invoked. Burns and Pinkerton both recognized eavesdropping as a legitimate technique, and Burns went further to point out that electronic surveillance was a common resort of government investigations, including his own in the Boss Reuf case. Following the San Francisco Preparedness Day parade bomb and the transparent schemes of DA Fickert and Detective Swanson to frame Mooney, the US Labor Department employed John Densmore to bug Fickert's office. Outrageous revelations recorded on a hidden dictaphone and published in full in the newspaper provided Mooney's defense lawyers and the public with convincing evidence of the frame-up. In the Martinez case, Detectives Mundell and Cradlebaugh spied on jailed suspects in connection with the Wheatland riot. Asked by investigators of the US Commission on Industrial Relations, "Did you also put in that jail a dictograph?" Mundell answered, "Two of them."[47]

Within two decades of the telephone's invention in 1876, law enforcement agencies were tapping phone conversations for alleged criminal investigations in the absence of any legal constraint. World

War I occasioned authorization of federal wiretapping as a temporary security measure. Electronic surveillance of bootleggers was permitted in the 1920s, although the Radio Act of 1927 made it illegal to divulge information acquired from radio messages. As time and technology moved on, surveillance methods were steadily proscribed. By 1930, forty-one states had outlawed wiretapping, and the federal government followed suit with the 1934 Communications Act. Prior to enactment of these laws, nongovernmental eavesdropping and wiretapping were considered nefarious activities subject to prosecution under related statues having to do with illegal entry or, in New York, revealing the contents of private documents.

In 1915, banker J. P. Morgan hired the William J. Burns International Detective Agency to explore potential leaks about the involvement of Morgan interests in supplying munitions to Britain and France prior to US entry into World War I. Suspicion centered on New York City law firm Seymour and Seymour for reasons that remain unclear. Burns maintained later that Seymour was involved in a "monstrous plot" to reveal information about the supply of munitions for the allied war effort to Germany's ambassador in the United States. The suspicion was never confirmed (and denied by Seymour and the ambassador), although the Seymour firm had recently negotiated a large munitions contract, possibly for a competitor of J. P. Morgan. Pursuing the case for Morgan, Burns agents planted a dictaphone in an office adjoining the Seymour premises and drilled a hole in the wall for better reception. Subsequently, a former employee of the Burns agency revealed the wiretapping scheme to New York's district attorney, who persuaded an initially reluctant Frederick Seymour to press charges of illegal entry and copying private papers.

Burns went directly to the district attorney saying that it was true he had placed a dictaphone in the Seymour offices but explained, "There is nothing wrong in using a dictaphone so long as it is being used in the detection of a crime."[48] Asked what crime he was investigating, Burns replied that the evidence was not yet in shape to present, but when he proved to his own satisfaction that a crime had been committed he would present the case to the district attorney. Evidently he saw no inconsistency in his wiretapping when no crime had actually been detected, only a suspicion thereof, which would justify any act that he, Burns, deemed appropriate. A trial found him guilty of surreptitiously entering the law office and making and publishing copies of private papers. The court imposed a fined of $100, saying, "We feel that no detective, no private detective, has any right to enter a place of business to get information of his own," but also allowing that Burns had "the best of motives."[49]

The case revealed more going on behind the scenes. The district attorney would not have urged Seymour on several occasions to press charges without his own motives. When the news broke initially, Peter J. Brady of the Allied Printing Trades Council presented evidence of a "list of wires" to the district attorney showing "that employers of labor hired private detectives to spy on labor organizations and that these detectives, acting in connivance with the police officials, were permitted to tap telephone wires."[50] In addition to pressure from organized labor, there is evidence to suppose that the Pinkerton Agency was helping to build the case in an effort to discredit their competitor. Burns believed that information had been transmitted to the district attorney by "a rival detective agency, in the hope that such revelation would tend to block and impair the efficiency of Burns activities."[51] The serious threat to his agency's efficiency lay not in the paltry wiretapping charge, but in the possibility that their state license to operate a private detective agency in New York could be revoked if professional misconduct were proven.

Burns was a clever man and his suspicion of professional jealousy was not without foundation. The Pinkerton Agency had been keeping a file on the freewheeling methods of their rival for some time, and the wiretapping case seemed to provide an opening. The "former employee of the Burns agency" who reported the dictaphone eavesdropping to the district attorney may have been working for Pinkerton. In any event, someone was passing Burns's private correspondence to Pinkerton. The collection of Pinkerton Agency papers in the Library of Congress contains a letter from Burns to the Anderson Electric Corporation written on June 6, 1917, not long after the guilty verdict in the Seymour case. Burns wrote, "We have used your secret service appliances as you know in considerable quantities. We are glad to state that they have given us excellent satisfaction. . . . We have used your instruments in a number of important cases." The endorsement alone is no secret as Burns publicly declared his belief in the legality of listening devices, even when the law disagreed. A handwritten comment on the copy of the letter reads: "Note: nearly 100 of the Anderson Secret Service apparatus are used by this famous organization." The comment was obviously added to the copy that went into the Pinkerton spy file on Burns in anticipation of some future unfriendly use.[52]

## Troublemaking

Beyond the realm of manifest crime, private detectives often made trouble for others. In fairness, detectives sometimes did good, as we shall see, and sometimes justifiably faced labor thugs and white-collar malefactors. For the moment, however, the subject is mischief—how the detective's modus operandi did harm to innocents. In labor relations, agencies and field operatives sowed distrust. Employers were told that their workers were union agitators, anarchists, and communists plotting to undermine company morale when no such evidence existed. Spies placed in factories were instructed to foster mistrust and suspicion. Racism served their purposes when one group of workers could be turned against another with planted rumors—blacks will take your jobs, "huns" will gain better positions than "dagos" or "bog trotters." The Sherman Service bragged of "splitting the union into three [ethnic] factions." Operatives routinely passed along to company managers the names of alleged agitators, particularly those leaders who resisted being used. Such activists often lost their jobs and were blacklisted with other employers.

Sherman believed in "covering every environment in the living and working conditions of the employees . . . calling attention [of store-keepers to] the fact that money would be lost should their customers be out on strike, working upon the relatives and friends of the employees"[53] The Sherwood agency of New York suggested that "the way to win a strike was to organize community sentiment" by setting up a Citizens' Welfare Committee. "They sent men from door to door to get citizens to sign their membership slips, and if possible to get them to contribute to advertisements which would be run over the name of the so-called citizens welfare organization saying good things about the company."[54] The trade name for these operatives was "missionaries," used without irony.

Larger national agencies had the power to influence, even corrupt, local law enforcement. A. B. McKenzie, the independent district attorney of Contra Costa County, told the US Commission on Industrial Relations,

In my opinion a great many public officials are overawed by a private detective agency. They lose their moral courage. Most men have some things about their private lives, or some things that they have been doing on the sly, that they don't care for the public to know. And for that reason I think that there are very few of them who care to run up against a powerful private detective agency. And for that reason they have had rather the whip hand. And they have been accustomed to calling down and going roughshod over public officials. That has been the policy of those people in this state. And in fact with this particular [Burns] agency . . . they claimed that I was crooked, because I had dismissed a case; and that they were going to show me, and told me that they represented the American Bankers' Association, and that they would stand me on my head. . . . And I talked back to them pretty vigorously myself.[55]

Regrettably, few public officials had McKenzie's moxie.

Vested interests of detectives in industrial violence identified by the La Follette Committee extended to other forms of injustice, intimidation, and crime. Just as violence exacerbated labor conflict, justifying further use of detective services, so too did frame-ups, eavesdropping, and troublemaking produce marketable results. Criminal and duplicitous methods were standard practice of private detectives, the evil in "necessary evil." The explanation is clear; crime paid. Strikebreaking by violent means if necessary was the most profitable line of detective agency work. The rates charged to the client were high and the profit margin wide, given no overhead (the client paid transportation and housing). Agency expenses were reduced on occasion by abandoning the "finks" without pay after the job, as Bergdoff was accused of doing. Farley and Bergdoff were considered "kings" in the business, not least for the fortunes they amassed. But strikebreaking was risky work that could lead to an unsavory reputation or even an agency's demise, the ultimate fate of Bergdoff and of Baldwin-Felts. In the competitive and constrained detective business, the result was specialization; a few identifiable firms devoted largely to strikebreaking and many others shying away from it to offer more professional services. However professional these services were advertised to be, agencies commonly resorted to methods verging on crime in effort to show results that outdid their competitors. Burns epitomized the audacious agent with predictable results, profit, and public censure. Others like Nick Harris advertised probity and there was a market for that, too. During its bullish years the business operated in a marketplace governed by competition and the needs of employers, with few legal constraints.

## Dirty Work

The crimes of private detectives fit the general problem that sociologist Everett Hughes describes as "good people and dirty work"—how society deals with deplorable, yet tolerable activities in its midst.[56] The examples Hughes discusses—Nazi concentration camps and American lynch mobs—may seem a stretch from detective violence and intimidation. By definition, however, dirty work covers a spectrum of instructively comparable social practices. Hughes described typical reactions to dirty work as denial and silencing on one hand and invention of fictions on the other. Detective crimes received similar treatment. They were silenced with perjured testimony and destroyed evidence. More extensively, they were fictionalized in boastful memoirs and mystery-story entertainments. Indeed, these responses to dirty work go beyond Hughes's original insight by illuminating how the initial problem may foster a new occupational ideology, how the act of justifying a practice can be elaborated into legend.

The case of the private detective sheds light on certain broader dynamics of dirty work. Who does it? The evidence suggests that recruits to the detective business come from society's outsiders: immigrants, the working class, and the less educated who lack the credentials for more esteemed jobs, as well as entrepreneurs with the wit to exploit a new occupational niche. How is the work shielded from public criticism or exposed to sanctions? Detective crimes were excused for many years despite sensational revelations like Homestead, protected by the power of business and industry until successfully challenged by reformers in and out of government when the Depression swung public opinion in labor's favor. What comes of challenges by moral entrepreneurs dedicated to the elimination of dirty work? The regulation of detective agencies following scandals played a part in the industry's transformation, but only a part, alongside the changing economy. Tom Mooney languished in prison for twenty years after the frame-up was exposed. By contrast, Richard Nixon's "dirty tricks" ended in forced resignation owing to leaks, defections, revelations, luck, aggressive investigators, Senate hearings, and the resulting public opprobrium. Going a step further, Argentina's "dirty war" was exposed and sanctioned following the overthrow of a culpable military regime and a return to democracy. The lesson seems to be that eliminating dirty work requires a major shift in the distribution of political power. As concept and analytic strategy, "dirty work" illuminates a great deal about the detective business, and society's business.

The verities of dirty work operate in contemporary society. One thinks of the acknowledged evils of sweatshops in which young women and children are exploited mercilessly in dangerous factory conditions for beggars' wages. Certainly this is reprehensible, but then again, as the story goes, the practice results in low prices for consumers and jobs for the otherwise unemployable. Of late American citizens have been presented with undeniable evidence that their government practices torture in violation of purported ideals and international law. Disgraceful, yes, but some claim, without good evidence, that the practice keeps us safe. Denial, cover-up, and justifying fiction regularly follow exposé. Dirty work is very much with us today; its identification opens up a field of analysis that not only exposes the sources of societal crimes but explains the myths created to justify them.

Early detective work was unavoidably associated with shady business. That recognized fact, in turn, led to the characteristic denial and mythologizing of the industry's reputation for malfeasance. In a competitive industry, considerable effort was devoted to crafting an image that would appeal to a select clientele. Much that is written and believed about detectives stems from this conundrum.

# 6

# INVESTIGATION
# AND REFORM

## The State

From its beginnings in Gilded Age America, the private detective industry developed relatively immune from legal restraint and governmental regulation. That was how corporate clients wanted it, and the weak state of the nineteenth century provided the necessary supportive environment. As the industry's abusive practices grew in tandem with progressive reform movements of the early twentieth century, pressure mounted for investigation and state intervention into the contentious arena of industrial relations. The Anti-Pinkerton law instituted after Homestead was an early, mild, and ineffectual expression of official concern. Little more was done in the next three to four decades until industrial violence was finally recognized as a social problem. The change was due to Progressivism as a social and governmental reform movement, notably through the advent of a stronger state with new institutions intended to regulate industry and commerce.

Beginning with the Commission on Industrial Relations established in 1912, a series of private and public investigations began piling up documentary evidence of industrial malfeasance in general and specifically of how private detectives played a central role as agents of corporate power. Effective regulation was long in coming and subject to conflicting interests in the political process. Nevertheless, a movement was set in motion that would change fundamentally the detective business. When change came, it was as much a result of forces operating within the business as it was a product of direct state intervention. Yet the state was a pervasive force operating at many levels through a regulatory regime affecting capital, labor, and public opinion. Key among forces that set this transformation in motion was a series of investigations that not only revealed to policymakers the workings of detective agencies but also produced a great fund of evidence from which this history can be recovered.

## The Investigator

Heber Blankenhorn, a small, bespectacled, balding man with an odd name (his friends called him by the equally odd nickname "Blank"), probably did more to document the workings of private detective agencies than anyone of the era from Pinkerton to Hammett. Born in 1884, Blankenhorn graduated from Wooster College (Ohio) in 1905, earned a master's degree in literature at Columbia University in 1910, then went to work for the *New York Evening Sun* as a reporter specializing in labor matters. New York City in the first decade of the twentieth century had some of the nation's worst industrial conditions, notably among immigrant garment workers. In the Triangle Shirtwaist Factory fire of 1911, 146 people (mostly young Jewish and Italian women) died trying to escape a fire on the ninth floor, where doors were locked. Blankenhorn witnessed these events, became assistant editor, and devoted himself to publicizing the condition of the working class, as did a host of other progressive reformers including fellow New York newsman Jacob Riis and Lincoln Steffens. Frances Perkins, future Secretary of Labor, headed a New York City Committee on Public Safety after the Triangle Fire. As a group they advocated improved working conditions and a shorter workweek (fifty-four hours rather than the prevailing standard of sixty).

During World War I, Blankenhorn served in the US Army's psychological warfare unit preparing propaganda leaflets dropped from the air on German troops and civilians. Later he wrote an account of the experience entitled *Adventures in Propaganda: Letters from an Intelligence Officer in France*.[1] Quite by accident, in the course of his army work he stumbled on military intelligence files dealing with labor unions and corporate spying, material collected by the army on the premise that unions were a potential threat the war effort. He soon turned the discovery to good use. At war's end he embarked on a career in research on the factors affecting public opinion about labor problems and progressive reform.[2]

Blankenhorn's initial investigative work was on the staff of the nonprofit Bureau of Industrial Research, which had just been hired to conduct a study of the Steel Strike of 1919 for the Interchurch World Movement (IWM). The IWM was an alliance of Protestant Church leaders, part of the broader social gospel reform movement dedicated to raising the working-class living standard. The IWM Commission of Inquiry funded the study, which took place over six months, from October 1919 to March 1920. The highly qualified staff of field investigators included academics and journalists with experience in government, the War Department, foundations, churches, and the US Commission on Industrial Relations. They interviewed five hundred steel workers and took testimony from corporate and union leaders. Although the strike was nationwide, intensive study focused on the Pittsburg area (including Youngstown and Johnstown, Ohio) and United States Steel Corporation. Blankenhorn masterminded the research and wrote much of the two-volume study published by the commission. His army experience provided familiarity with corporate attitudes toward unions. He knew what to look for, and he knew things that soon came as a rude shock to the commission and its sponsors.

The first volume, *Report on the Steel Strike of 1919*, reached a number of conclusions that contradicted the claims of US Steel and the prevailing opinion shaped by the press. The workers were new immigrants, mainly Slavs (Serbs and Croatians) along with Czechs, Austrian Poles, Russians, and smaller numbers from the Balkans and the Mediterranean. Wages were well below a living standard. A series of "Christian Findings" demonstrated that the major grievances were excessive hours (an average work week of 68.7 hours), a militaristic "boss system," and no right to organize. Exercising strict discipline, the company denied that workers had any real grievances and reported exaggerated wage rates. The strike, they claimed, was a mischievous scheme of Bolshevik agitators, a widely accepted view until the commission published its results. Steel workers, the report showed, were paid well below the "American standard of living. . . . For many years this was so in the industry; decency, or comfort, just out of reach, for two-thirds of the workers. Therefore many strikers, who looked blank at mention of 'Bolshevism' and who knew little even of the A.F. of L., insisted on talking a great deal about wages to this committee's investigators."[3] Among a series of recommendations centered on wages, hours, and representation, the report identified the need for "a vast extension of house building" by the community and the company.[4]

Figure 6.1. Heber Blankenhorn, author and organizer of the major investigations of private detective agencies including the La Follette Committee on Violations of Free Speech and Rights Labor, shown here during his World War II experience working with the US Army. (Walter P. Reuther Library, Archives of Labor and Urban Affairs, Wayne State University)

In the second volume, *Public Opinion and the Steel Strike*, Blankenhorn's direction is even more evident. Overall, it is a rich sociological analysis on a par with the great community studies of the time. Chapters authored by individual members of the research staff deal with "undercover men" (private detectives, mainly from the Sherman Service), newspapers and their coverage in the Pittsburg area, "the mind of the immigrant communities," welfare work by US Steel, and the Pittsburg churches, and a summary by Blankenhorn discusses the study's impact. Although the investigation was intended to influence policies of the federal government and the steel companies, its main contribution was to scholarship rather than public affairs.

Initially, US Steel attempted to block publication of the commission's findings. Detectives were put to work spying on the IWM and the commission. An anonymous "special report" given to the president of US Steel inaccurately claimed that the organizations were staffed by "reds," "radicals," "members of the IWW," and the National Civil Liberties League. "None of these people should be told anything at all, nor should they be allowed to get any information from the mills in any manner."[5] The report published in July 1920 was delivered to the White House with a letter to President Wilson. Major newspapers and members of Congress received copies with the central recommendation that the federal government investigate the condition of labor, their rights to organize, and the role of "labor detective agencies."[6] For several days, the report received prominent coverage in the national press but soon was relegated to labor journals alone. President Wilson, shortly thereafter disabled by a stroke, did not reply. W. B. Wilson, the Secretary of Labor, expressed his agreement with the commission's results but explained that he could not mount a federal investigation without congressional authorization. Congress did not move. In later years, Blankenhorn acknowledged that the investigation had no constructive effect on policy or industrial practice.

The IWM also fared badly. The commission represented a landmark in American church–labor relations and copies of the published report reached clergy around the country. Business and industrial interests, however, condemned the work and blamed the IWM for straying from its religious mission, for stirring up trouble. Contributions to the nonprofit fell as debts mounted. The organization was disbanded in 1921, its work for social justice unattended for the next thirty years until the National Council of Churches organized with similar goals. Yet the Interchurch World Movement's study of the steel strike and Blankenhorn's early experience provided a foundation for a series of more consequential investigations to follow.

### Early Investigations: Cabot and Walsh

The next step in privately funded investigations of detective agency practices concerning labor was launched by Richard Cabot, a physician, educator, and social work pioneer who received his MD from Harvard Medical School in 1892. A friend of Ralph Waldo Emerson, he studied with William James, taught for thirty years at his alma mater, and wrote the first of his many books on blood diseases, all before turning to the field of social ethics as the result of his experience in WW I. More books, professorships, and public service followed. Although there is no direct link, Cabot probably knew about the IWM, given their congruent interests. Indeed, the later years of Cabot's career were devoted to applying ethics to human problems. With money inherited by his wife, Elizabeth Dwight, the couple established the Cabot Fund for studies of social issues. Despite an auspicious beginning, however, the investigation apparently met obstacles en route to the public.

"Following the publication of the Report on the Interchurch World Movement Commission investigating the steel strike of 1919, Dr. Richard Cabot, professor of social ethics at Harvard University, financed [a] private investigation conducted by Sidney Howard and Robert W. Dunn on the nature and scope of [labor] espionage. A preliminary confidential report was submitted in October 1920, consisting of four large sections of typewritten script. This report was never published."[7] In an appendix to the La Follette Committee hearings, the Cabot Report is described in detail. The 650-page document contained four volumes divided into eight parts, including Part II, The Detective Agencies; Part III, Methods and Tactics; Part V, The Detective and Violence; and Part VIII, Espionage and the Law. The contents are described in short statements, for example: "A trenchant analysis of espionage tactics here covers 18 pages, ranging through means of recruiting spies, their training, requisites of operating and reporting and favorable points of approach for the spy . . . almost a complete manual of spy operation." In total, the Cabot Report is characterized as "the most complete study of its subject yet made . . . a range and scope of documentary evidence unmatched by any other public or private investigation."[8] The sad fact, however, is that the Cabot Report seems to have disappeared. It is nowhere in the records of the La Follette Committee in the National Archives and not included in the extensive Cabot Papers held by Harvard University Library Archives. The fate of its "four large sections" is a mystery.

Yet, the essence of the report was made public in two forms. First, Blankenhorn knew it well and incorporated its topical framework and some of its contents in the La Follette Committee's many published volumes. Second, Sidney Howard and Robert Dunn published some results of the investigation in the *New Republic* (where Howard was a staff writer) in 1921 and in the more complete 1924 book *The Labor Spy*.[9] Howard went on to become a playwright, winning a Pulitzer Prize in 1925 and two Academy Awards for screenplays (one for *Gone with the Wind*). The social networks connecting these authors are important as a reflection of the American progressive reform movement of the era and the social climate in which the critique of anti-union and private detective practices developed.

In the history of federal investigations, the Commission on Industrial Relations looms large. Created in 1912 by President Wilson in the midst of a rash of violence, the investigation was charged with uncovering the roots of industrial unrest. Kansas City attorney Frank Walsh was chosen to head the commission based on his reputation for progressive civic work and Democratic Party service. Walsh attracted such talent in the field of labor economics as University of Wisconsin professor John Rogers Commons to take the investigation in a more radical direction. The fieldwork took place over five months, in fourteen cities (from New York to South Dakota and Seattle), and investigators interviewed 740 witnesses representing employers and labor (from Andrew Carnegie to Mother Jones). The encyclopedic "Final Report and Testimony" published in 1916 filled eleven printed volumes and provoked two minority reports (one by Commons, who felt the majority Walsh version was too political). Generally, the Walsh Report demonstrated the "deplorable" condition of working people, their low wages and decreasing share of national income since 1890, and rates of working-class child mortality three times that of the population average. The report posited that industrial unrest, in turn, resulted from inequality of wealth and income, unemployment, injustice before the law, and denial of the right to organize. These generalizations were underpinned by extensive testimony and documentary evidence. The first, overview volume ran more than one thousand pages.

By contrast to the Interchurch Commission and Cabot investigations, the Walsh Report gave less attention to detective agencies as a separate topic. Strikebreaking was discussed in the context of major conflicts. But the commission had learned enough to condemn "the endless crimes committed by the so-called detective agencies" and to recommend to Congress that such agencies "be compelled to take out a Federal license, with regulations to insure the character of their employees and the limitation of their activities to the bona fide business of detecting crime, or that such agencies be utterly abolished."[10] Nothing of the sort followed. Division within the commission blunted some of its message, and Congress was in no mood to defend labor. Walsh was denounced by industry, and the *New York Times* called him

a "passionate Red." Meanwhile, events in Europe occupied the nation
with preparedness, war production, and the manpower draft. Wages
began to increase with full employment. Officially at least, the War
Labor Board supported union representation and collective bargaining. "After a turbulent career, the U.S. Commission on Industrial Relations receded into history. Its surviving records drifted into the dead
files of various archives. Scholars occasionally picked at some portion
of the voluminous published *Testimony* as an aid to their research on
some special topic."[11]

Yet the "mouldy fate"[12] of the report also included a less apparent
diffusion of evidence and experience. Staffers in the commission's Research Division went on to publish influential works. Walsh continued
his advocacy of labor issues, successfully representing the National
Women's Trade Union League and the Tom Mooney Molders' Defense
Committee. The unpublished records of the commission's Research
Division include a list of 278 detective agencies, most of them in the
East and Midwest, albeit without explanation of how the list was assembled.[13] But this enumeration informed a follow-up list included in
the Cabot Report, which in turn was updated by Blankenhorn for the
La Follette Committee.[14] These investigations built on one another,
just as some of the investigators moved from one effort to the next,
bringing their experience along.

### From NLRB to the La Follette Committee

The Great Depression and New Deal administration of the 1930s
provided the watershed of reform in labor relations leading to a fundamental transformation of the detective business. At its heart the
change was embodied in the establishment of labor's right to organize unions at the workplace and to bargain collectively over wages
and working conditions. To a large extent, that ended the career of
the labor spy. The change resulted from multiple factors: the labor
movement itself, dawning corporate liberalism, New Deal legislation,
and a public now supporting reform. Intertwined among these forces
was the accumulating evidence of the commissions investigating corporate labor and detective agency practices. That evidence informed
legislators, public opinion, and the historical record. There was a direct, if multistranded, connection between the researchers, the investigations, and the changing shape of the detective business.

Figure 6.2. President Roosevelt signing the Social Security Act with Secretary of Labor Frances Perkins (behind FDR), Senator Robert La Follette Jr. (on her right, light suit), and Senator Robert F. Wagner (on La Follette's right, dark suit).

Following the collapse of the Interchurch Commission and the Bureau of Industrial Research in 1924, Heber Blankenhorn returned to journalism and to Europe, where he reported on labor and the rise of fascism. Finding new hope for American labor with Franklin Roosevelt's election, he came home to a public relations job with the National Labor Board (NLB), a creation of the National Industrial Recovery Act (NIRA) of 1933. The NLB sought to enforce new statutes protecting the right of workers to organize unions, a charge made difficult by employer resistance and constitutional challenges to the NIRA. Obstructionism in the midst of continuing depression prompted Senator Robert F. Wagner (New York), with Blankenhorn's assistance, to propose a legislative successor to the NIRA that would win court approval. The upshot was the National Labor Relations Act (NLRA) of 1935, better known as the Wagner Act, which authorized the National Labor Relations Board (NLRB) to carry on the work of its predecessor.

From his staff position on the new board, Blankenhorn began lobbying for a comprehensive congressional investigation of labor–employer relations that would reinvigorate the pursuits of earlier and largely ineffective commissions. Blankenhorn writes, "I had had the plan in mind for years and laid it before the new NLRB. . . . They were skeptical[,] not believing that 'starting a Senate investigation was Board business.' They finally said that if I thought I could do it I could try."[15] He consulted with his "old chief," Wagner, who thought it was a good idea but declined heading it. Wagner suggested Robert M. La Follette Jr. of Wisconsin ("Young Bob," as he was distinguished from his famous governor, senator, and Progressive Party presidential candidate father) would be a good choice: "Ideal [Wagner said]. I'll talk to him. Bob needs something of this kind to get re-elected."[16]

Blankenhorn wrote a diplomatic letter to La Follette that began, "Dear Bob: I need a word of advice." Intending to offer persuasion rather than actually seek advice, he praised the senator for his support of the Wagner Act. With some urgency he went on to say, "I predicted to the Board that a by-product of the Act would be increased activities on the part of undercover agencies, in the way of espionage and disruption of unions. . . . As you know, we have never in twenty years had a Senatorial investigation, despite many demands of this system. How can we get it?"[17] Although La Follette initially thought he would lose rather than gain Wisconsin votes by chairing such a committee, he saw a way to merge labor issues with his pursuit of civil liberties legislation and eventually agreed to head the inquiry into "Violations of Free Speech and Rights of Labor" (as it was officially titled). Later he would win reelection for his stand on both counts.

Blankenhorn was the inspiration, architect, and administrator of the La Follette Investigation. "As committee planner I drew up preliminary plans in 26 of the committee's 27 investigations in 4 years."[18] Of course, he already knew about the skullduggery of industrial corporations from his work in Army Intelligence and the Interchurch Commission. He knew the identity of hundreds of private detective agencies, which were now sent questionnaires and subpoenas. In short, he knew where to look and what to look for. He brought dozens of NLRB staffers to work for the committee, and he brought a passion for labor and for research to his team. Buoyed by insurgent unionism, the committee "struck directly at the latent fascism in American capitalism."[19] Committee Secretary Robert Wohlforth later wrote to Blankenhorn of the investigation's esprit de corps, "My god we had our nerve in those days! We didn't care who we took on. . . . And there wouldn't have been any of it without you."[20]

There were, of course, countless others who made the movement possible: labor activists, committee staffers, and the resourceful field investigators who tracked down evidence hidden in trash. Many played a part. CIO leader Walter Reuther believed that "more than any other single person, Eddie Levinson was responsible for the creation of the La Follette Senate Civil Liberties Committee."[21] Jerold Auerbach's history of the committee suggests that Levinson's book *I Break Strikes* did for strikebreaking what Upton Sinclair's *The Jungle* had done for the meatpacking industry. And Sidney Howard's book *The Labor Spy* seeded much that followed. But in the end, this was a reform movement that uniquely centered on a congressional investigation, its architect Blankenhorn, and its portentous results.

Committee hearings held across the country over four years and published in ninety-four volumes constituted the most extensive congressional investigation up to that time. In addition to copious material on detective agencies, strikebreaking, munitions, and corporate labor practices, the committee investigated a plethora of subjects including employer's associations, citizens' committees, farm labor, farmers' alliances, migrant labor, Harlan County, Little Steel, Private Police Systems, Chicago's Memorial Day Massacre, and many more. The committee's publications and archival records continue to provide an unrivaled source on the history of American labor and employers, on public and private policing, and on the work of public servants.

With all that, however, neither the La Follette Committee nor the NLRA succeeded in their ambition to bring peace and stability to industrial relations under a regime of collective bargaining, supervised by the NLRB. In March 1939, La Follette introduced a bill in the Senate (S. 1970) that would eliminate repressive labor practices documented by the committee (espionage, strikebreaking, use of munitions and gas). Secretary of Labor Frances Perkins endorsed the bill as the embodiment of New Deal labor policy. Then the opposition gathered in Congress, supported by the National Association of Manufacturers, the US Chamber of Commerce, and the American Legion. As World War II appeared on the horizon, the public mood shifted to security and opposition to any restraints on defense manufacturing. The bill was fatally amended in the Senate and died without a vote in the House.[22]

Jared Auerbach's study of the period concludes, "The La Follette Committee's legislative failure should not dim the luster of its earlier investigative achievements." It helped legitimate unions and collective bargaining so "workers could use their own resources to terminate anti-labor practices. As a means of protecting workers' civil liberties, union power loomed as a more effective weapon than oppressive-labor-practices legislation."[23] On reflection, Blankenhorn believed his efforts to eliminate the "nefarious under-cover system," first attempted with the Interchurch Commission and given a second chance in the Senate committee, succeeded in the long term. "Today [1952] the main body of that business is pretty well destroyed."[24]

### Wagner and the Detectives: Laws and Licenses

At the time, private detectives feared the result that Blankenhorn later announced. Many agencies believed the Wagner Act struck at the heart of their business. The Act prohibited "unfair labor practices," meaning interference with employees' rights to form unions of their own choosing and to bargain collectively, just as it prohibited employers from discouraging unions, discriminating against anyone involved in union activity, and refusing to bargain collectively with employee representatives. The NLRB could supervise union elections and sanction violations of the act. From the detective agencies' standpoint, the law meant that they could no longer prevent or frustrate worker organizing in any way, which had been the purpose of espionage and strikebreaking.

Initially, some lobbied to defeat the Senate bill. An Indiana member of the National Metal Trades Association reported, "Today I am addressing a joint meeting of all the civic clubs of Evansville, some five hundred people, and I shall do everything I can to get these people stirred into action over the Wagner bill. . . . I think our senators and representatives will receive several hundred protests from employees of this company."[25] Another member in Massachusetts thought the "vicious bills being considered in Washington" ultimately injured ordinary working people, like those in his open shop, whose letters to Congress would be effective, "since Senators and so forth, know the that the strength of the voting public rests in the average man."[26] In a more antagonistic vein, the Metal Trades Association commissioner wrote to La Follette Committee Secretary Robert Wohlforth, noting that the relative importance of the association's "purely defensive services, such as employee surveillance and strikebreaking" in 1936 had declined to a mere 4 percent, while at the same time lamenting "the now prevailing attitude of the federal government and a number of state governments that employers are not entitled to protect themselves and their employees against the aggressions of labor unions." Reluctantly, the association had decided to discontinue "all undercover or surveillance service, all furnishing of guards, and all furnishing of employees to take the place of strikers."[27]

For the first time, agencies came together to oppose the new laws. Proposed legislation in Massachusetts and Vermont provoked "a meeting of the detective agencies of Boston, at the Bradford Hotel . . . to determine what action is going to be taken to off-set this bill."[28] Three months later, a more insistent appeal read, "Notice of Emergency Meeting Under the Auspices of the International Detective Association . . . to be held this FRIDAY evening, APRIL 10, 1936 at 8 P.M. SHARP . . . [at] the HOTEL DIXIE 241 WEST 42nd STREET, NEW YORK CITY (Times Square), and we insist that each and every agency principal make it his or her business to attend."[29] Specifically, the meeting intended to offer amendments to a proposed New York law on detective licensing. Agency principals, not their representatives, were urged to attend. Credentials would be checked at the door—to prevent espionage.

W. Sherman Burns worried about labor's efforts "to force laws" through Congress and state legislatures, which "would put restrictions on the agencies that would likely force them out of the industrial field."[30] But the avuncular Pinkertons led the major agencies in high-mindedness. At a special meeting of the board of directors on April 29, 1937, Robert A. Pinkerton stated "that, in his opinion, public sentiment generally was condemning many practices in employer-employee relations," and he endorsed as company policy a Senate resolution which declared "that the so-called industrial spy system breeds fear, suspicion and animosity, tends to cause strikes and industrial warfare and is contrary to sound public policy."[31]

Another federal law, the Byrnes Act of 1936, aimed directly at strikebreaking by preventing interstate transport of persons for the purpose of interfering with peaceful picketing. The legislation was ineffective, given arguable claims about the "purpose" of guards and operatives sent to an industrial site. But it did signal a general mood. A dozen years earlier, *The Outlook* magazine polled its readers on the question of whether there should be federal licensing of private detectives: 49 percent agreed, only 12 percent disagreed, and 39 percent ignored the question. One suspects the approval rating increased in the following years (although these magazine readers were probably a progressive sample of the population, given that 62 percent supported equal rights for women in the same 1924 survey).[32]

State governments began to adopt or extend their regulation of private detective agencies, mainly through licensing requirements. Wisconsin pioneered the field, initially with meager efforts in 1909 that were successively modified in a weak but successful law of 1919 and a more comprehensive measure in 1925, which became the national standard. With strong support from the Milwaukee Federation of Labor and a socialist city government, the Wisconsin law required that both detective agencies and individual operatives be licensed and bonded. License applications also required a fee and approval by city police and fire commissions. Employer associations opposed the legislation and, once it passed, resisted its authority. Pinkerton and Corporations Auxiliary challenged it in court but lost. The Russell Agency, Wisconsin's largest private detective firm, moved their offices to White Fish Bay, Wisconsin, which had no police or fire commission and, thus, no approval process. Pinkerton closed the Milwaukee office and left the state, explaining that registration of individual operatives made their business (espionage) impossible "because the men would be exposed."[33]

The La Follette Committee reviewed the status of licensing laws in states where they were in effect in 1939. "The growing realization in recent years of a need of comprehensive regulation of the detective-agency business has resulted in statutes in certain states that mark an advance." [34] Five states had laws with different provisions. Wisconsin's had been the strongest up to that time, although New York enacted the nation's "most effective" regulation in 1938, incorporating all of the licensing requirements from Wisconsin plus "sweeping prohibition of the strikebreaking business"[35]—and that despite opposition from the International Detectives Association. Massachusetts, Illinois, and California had licensing laws requiring fees, bonds, and approval of agencies, but not of individuals. In 1913, a law proposed in California would have included agency owner-operatives and employed detectives, assessed $500 and $100, respectively. "Captain William Field, Pinkerton superintendent in California, with other prominent detective managers were at the hearing, opposing the provision whereby operatives have to register and also opposing the amount of

DIRECTORS
GEO A. VAN SMITH President
JNO. G. MATTOS JR.  WILL F. MORRISH
THOMAS M. GANNON  JULIAN H. ALCO

ED. H. WHYTE
LICENSE CLERK

OFFICE OF
State Board of Prison Directors
OF THE STATE OF CALIFORNIA
ROOM 6, FERRY BUILDING
SAN FRANCISCO, CAL.

*ORIGINAL*

The State Board of Prison Directors of the State of California has this day

received from_____

_____

TEN DOLLARS_____$10.00

in payment of the annual License Fee for the year

SEPTEMBER 1, 19_____, TO SEPTEMBER 1, 19_____

in connection with License No._____ TO ENGAGE IN PRIVATE DETECTIVE BUSINESS IN
THE STATE OF CALIFORNIA heretofore issued to the aforesaid by the State Board of Prison
Directors of the State of California, pursuant to the provisions of the Statute of the State of California
entitled,"An act to license and regulate the business of private detectives and private detective agencies"
approved June 7, 1915.

STATE BOARD OF PRISON DIRECTORS

By_____

*License Clerk*

Figure 6.3. Application for a private detective's license in California, 1915. (California State Archives)

the license."[36] They succeeded, in part. But the public weighed in with "a flood of complaints" to the Los Angeles Public Safety Committee, citing "abominable abuses" by private detectives and residence patrols.[37] California's relatively mild law passed in 1915 predated some of the more comprehensive measures in other states and set a precedent by requiring references from local law enforcement officials and a public complaint process administered by the State Board of Prison Directors. The board was known to deny and revoke licenses in cases of misconduct. Records of the board, in fact, list by name, address, and references many of the state's private detectives in one-person agencies. In the same year, the California legislature passed an anti-spotter (train and streetcar) bill with the support of labor councils and railroad brotherhoods. The bill required "spies" to confront employees charged with theft, which corrected anonymous allegations.[38]

How effective were these laws? The La Follette Committee lamented a pattern of noncompliance, the lack of teeth in the Byrnes Act, and the limited number of states with regulation. "Large parts of the country, such as Southern States, where both industry and the detective agencies are expanding, lack regulatory measures."[39] But they also observed that actual incidences of strikebreaking were declining. Within months of the passage of the New York law in May 1938, the state license of the notorious Bergoff Detective Service was revoked. Ironically, it was not the agency's violent methods that caused the action, but failure to pay its own strikebreakers left stranded in Georgia.[40] License revocation became a tool for constraining some of the egregious practices that prevailed undercover for years.

Some private detectives believed the growing number of state laws would significantly affect, if not doom their industry. Glen Bodell worried that the "Wisconsin Labor Bill" being introduced in the California Legislature meant "few agencies will be able to exist." But he liked the idea of a $1,000-per-year license fee, which "would eliminate the majority of the wildcatters and they are numerous here now."[41] Bodell thought that the industry would benefit from some competitive housecleaning. But it was not necessarily true that smaller firms were the more troublesome. James Wood Jr., son of the founder of New England's first detective agency, relates how "in 1919, we (Private Detectives of Mass.) were instrumental in having a bill passed whereby we obtain our licenses from the Commission of Public Safety." The new law raised the license fee (to $100 for individuals and $200 for corporations, per year), increased the required bond (to $5,000), and required that licensees demonstrate experience. Ethics clauses insured confidentiality and truthful reporting. "We have done everything to safeguard the interests of our clients [through] hard work of two or three of the leading Private Detective Agencies in Boston."[42] The agency's professionalism is explained, no doubt, by common decency as well as by its clientele, which included lawyers, insurance companies, and department stores ("Detectives Furnished for Weddings, Banquets, Receptions, Etc." according to their ad). James Wood Sr. earned a reputation for recovering Italian immigrant children forced to become "padrone slaves." The detective business was many things.

Times were changing. The redoubtable GT-99 spoke for the business end of the business. "There was a senatorial investigation, several of them in fact. Labor, and the New Deal and the heir to the Progressive Party rode roughshod over industrial espionage from one end of the docket to the other. I am glad I got out when I did."[43]

### The Fall of Burns

Roughshod was a better description of the methods of William J. Burns. Through intimidation, strikebreaking, deception, wiretapping, and jury tampering, Burns patented many of the tactics that brought discredit to the industry. He was not alone and the objects of his attentions, whether labor or sundry malefactors, were not without sin. But Burns not only crossed the line of propriety, he defended his right to do so based mainly on his own belief that the overstep was justified because he was doing it. Referring to attacks on the IWW, Richard Frost argues, "It was unquestionably the Burns Agency's conduct in 1913 that precipitated the regulatory legislation, such as it was, passed in the next [California] legislature."[44]

Along with his powerful agency and progressive friends, Burns accumulated equally determined enemies, both in the labor movement and among business interests affected by his zealous pursuit of municipal corruption. And worse, his own detective colleagues came to resent his work, whether out of probity, jealousy, or financial competition. The Pinkerton Agency led the rivalry, actually investigating Burns (as he did in return) and keeping a file of potentially damaging evidence of misconduct. Pinkerton discovered, for example, which Burns operatives had been convicted of crimes, not only in their past (which Burns acknowledged) but during their period of employment (which the agency denied). The file is replete with incidents of alleged improper conduct within the agency: a Burns operative named Count von Brunswick who manufactured evidence to convict a Wisconsin factory worker of planting a bomb; a female agent who lied to an Illinois woman about her husband's alleged paternity in the pregnancy of an agency client; an operative in Louisiana who stole jewelry during his own investigation.[45] Much of this activity was fairly routine for freewheeling detectives of the period. More revealing was the Pinkerton intent to prepare a case against Burns should the opportunity arise to prosecute it.

The first crisis came in 1917 when the New York State Comptroller's Office decided to hold a hearing on "the revocation of the private detective license of the William J. Burns International Detective Agency, Inc." Formally, the Allied Printing Trades Council was the petitioner, aggrieved over spying on its members. Not far behind the scenes were New York City's district attorney and the Pinkertons. The Brief for the Petitioner aimed at the agency made no bones about its real target, "the most potent force in this Agency, and in the case against it, namely the personality of Burns himself."[46] The agency, of course, was inseparable from its founder, although the conduct under examination was organizational. "If there is operated in this country another Agency that combines equal arrogance, cynical contempt for rights and a willingness in achieving any result for money, with disregard of methods, we have not heard of it. . . . The Burns Agency (which means Burns) is and has been all of these things. . . . There seems to be no result obtainable by foul means or crime that they have not already obtained." [47]

The Burns Agency was accused of six episodes of misconduct: the wiretapping and break-in at the Seymour Law offices in connection with J. P. Morgan's interest in munitions shipments prior to US entry into WW I; new evidence of jury tampering in the Oregon land fraud case uncovered by Attorney General Wickersham; an alleged attempt to discredit a witness, one Dr. Carmen, by getting him to perform an illegal abortion; robbing the mails; working indirectly for the Germans through their Hamburg Line to obtain information on shipments to allies early in WW I; and unethical, if not illegal, conduct in the famous Leo Frank case.

Leo Frank was a twenty-nine-year-old college graduate in engineering who managed the National Pencil Factory in Atlanta, Georgia, where he had moved from New York to take the job. He was married and active in the city's Jewish community. On April 26, 1913, Mary Phagan, a fourteen-year-old girl who worked in the factory, came to collect her paycheck from Frank. She was not seen again until Newt Lee, the African American night watchman, found Mary's bloody remains in the factory basement. Atlanta police initially suspected Lee, although another African American employee, janitor Jim Conley, was also at the scene. Leo Frank was the last person to see Mary alive, and police began to focus attention on him. The investigation was haphazard: evidence was misplaced, witnesses were ignored, and potential leads went unexplored. Frank was an outsider in the South and a Jew. Gossip began to paint him as a seducer of factory girls and a pervert. Concerned for his client's protection, Frank's lawyer hired the Atlanta Pinkerton office to investigate the crime, especially the more likely suspects whom police had already eliminated.

The Leo Frank case became a national sensation. Newspapers covered the salacious details, the anti-Semitism aroused, the vituperative debate over Frank's guilt or innocence, and allegations of justice miscarried. The *Atlanta Constitution*, the state's major newspaper, started a fundraising drive to bring William J. Burns into the vexed investigation. In Europe at the time, Burns welcomed the offer but assigned a man from the Atlanta office. In a long, emotionally charged trial, Leo Frank was judged guilty of murder in August, 1913, and sentenced to hang. Appeals charging a prejudiced trial atmosphere were filed, going all the way to the US Supreme Court without success. Following the final appeal, acting on his conscience, Georgia Governor Stanton commuted the sentence to life in prison in June 1915. One month later, a group of prominent citizens calling themselves "Knights of Mary Phagan," including a county judge and a sheriff, stormed the jail, seized Leo Frank, and lynched him, taking care to document the action on film.[48]

Burns entered the case in March 1914 with a barrage of publicity claiming a police frame-up, a jury swayed by investigative incompetence, and a show trial engineered by ambitious politicians. The *Atlanta Constitution* on May 1, 1914, headlined, "A Horrible Mistake, Says Burns." Burns believed that by assisting the police, the Pinkerton operative actually helped convict his own client. Burns claimed he could produce evidence that would require a new trial. He soon became convinced that the killer was Jim Conley, the janitor observed near the crime scene in bloody clothes who, another factory girl claimed, had confided his guilt to her. Burns employed an African American operative named Owens, who interrogated Conley's wife (or girlfriend) and on Burns's orders took her to Tennessee, where he could quiz her without local interference. Later, Owens said that Burns had told him in writing what the woman should say in her testimony and then chastised him for not destroying the instruction letters. A Burns Agency representative also was accused with offering a bribe for access to defense evidence in the case.[49]

Burns's transgressions in the Frank case were unethical bordering on illegal, although the same might be said of the Pinkerton's role and the official investigation itself. But Burns was guilty of a greater offense in his very public insults of Georgia police, courts, and public officials. The local press vilified him. His state detective license was revoked and the Atlanta office closed. In Marietta, Georgia, he was surrounded by a hostile crowd, struck in the face by a protestor, and forced to flee—for his life, he said, with characteristic drama. In fact, he hid out in a nearby hotel until the crowd was talked into letting him depart on a promise not to return.[50] There is no doubt that Burns injected himself into the Frank case for the publicity it promised, particularly if he were lucky enough to solve a murder that many believed to be unsolved. Others, too, agreed that Conley was the real killer. Burns displayed real courage mixed with grandiosity by taking a stand in support of Leo Frank. It added to his fame. And it added to the growing list of his detractors.

In 1921, after four years of deliberation, the petition to revoke Burns's license in New York was dropped. Unlike Bergoff, Burns had friends, too, and the charges against him were not really up to the (ambivalent) standards of professional misconduct at the time. Indeed, among Burns's powerful friends was Harry Daugherty, whom President Warren Harding had appointed as attorney general in 1920. Daugherty chose Burns to head the Bureau of Investigation (later the Federal Bureau of Investigation), part of the Department of Justice, created in 1908 as a small, progressive branch of law enforcement immune from congressional politics. As "top cop," Burns served in the position for three years, garnering a questionable record. He continued to manage the Burns Agency, with the help of sons Robert A. and W. Sherman, and began farming out government business to the family business. Who better to do the job? During his bureau directorship, the department's staff was reduced from twelve hundred to six hundred, while his agency prospered on government contracts.

But Burns was flirting with higher levels of corruption. Daugherty instructed Burns to initiate a criminal investigation of Montana congressman Thomas Walsh, who had raised questions about oil leases granted by Daugherty's friend and fellow cabinet member Albert Fall. The bureau's probe was transparent retaliation intended to silence Walsh's investigation of corruption, as newspaper reporters soon discovered. Burns dispatched operatives from his private agency to discourage press coverage of the oil leases, producing a scandal of its own and eventually his forced resignation from the bureau. (J. Edgar Hoover succeeded him.)

Teapot Dome, the name of one oil field in the transaction, became synonymous with scandal at the highest government levels. Harry Sinclair, the oil executive whose company received leases, was exposed as party (with Edward Doheny) to a $100,000 bribe that Secretary Fall received for granting the leases. Both Fall and Sinclair were indicted for defrauding the government. Back in the private sector, Burns and son Sherman accepted a job from Sinclair to conduct surveillance of the jury in his trial with the intention of preparing damaging reports about jurors that would compromise them and result in a mistrial. The tampering was revealed by the Burns agent who prepared the false reports but subsequently became a government informant. Fall was fined heavily and went to prison for a year; Sinclair was fined and given a six-month sentence for jury tampering.[51]

The Burns family was treated more delicately, with son Sherman fined $1,000 and William J., whose role was judged indirect, given a sentence of fifteen days in jail. The Supreme Court later reversed the conviction of the elder Burns, but not before condemning the industry's practice. "All know that the men who accept such employment commonly lack fine scruples, often will fully misrepresent innocent conduct and manufacture charges." Characteristically, Burns responded, "Being cognizant of the fact that my government had been doing jury shadowing for years, I certainly thought I had the right to do the same thing."[52] Prophetically, his final controversial act of jury tampering recapitulated his first, the Oregon land fraud case that famously launched his career. But this time he was finished.

### The Industry Transformed

Far from finished, however, were Raymond J. Burns and the William J. Burns International Detective Agency, over which Raymond, the eldest son, now presided. But they represented something new, an industry in transition from the days of unregulated and often unsavory methods to a chastened and self-interested professionalism. A contemporary portrait explains that Raymond Burns

> is a splendid example of the modern investigator. His hip pockets do not sag with the weight of heavy revolvers; neither does he wear thick-soled shoes or the slouch hat. . . . He has the appearance of the successful business or professional man. One might judge him to be a lawyer and be correct in the surmise, for the study of law was considered essential to his qualifications as an investigator. Ninety per cent of the persons who come into contact with the 'brains of the Burns system' probably would say offhand: "Here we have a college professor."[53]

The fall of Burns senior, the retirement of GT-99, and the successful reformist career of Heber Blankenhorn were all markers of a changing American society. The New Deal wrote a social contract aimed at saving capital and insuring labor. The path from 1920s excess to 1930s depression led to an accommodation of industry and labor as well as conciliation within each: corporate liberalism reconciled to collective bargaining and organized labor purged of radicalism. The private detective industry reflected and helped fashion this transition. "By the 1940s, private detective policing had been abandoned by the major corporations in favor of more rationalized and legitimated controls based on compromise, mutual accommodation, and cooperation of labor organizations."[54]

Key to the transformation of detective agencies was a changing structure of opportunities. The former staple of industrial espionage was diminishing, if not all together gone. Crime and its suppression declined sharply when organizing and representing labor were removed from the catalog of crime. Modern police forces included detective divisions with no need for outside investigators. But the transformation did not result in unemployment for private detectives. New opportunities arose and certain older ones assumed new dimensions. The most important of these was protective services, an old practice transformed by its great expansion and modernization. Both the Pinkerton and Burns agencies became nearly synonymous with guards, patrols, watchmen, payroll protection, store and hotel detectives, security personnel for exhibitions, fairs, races, athletic events—all instrumented with alarms, cameras, armored cars, weapons, badges, and uniforms.

Many traditional Pinkerton activities were gone by 1940. Most labor work was against agency policy. Crime detection was being done by others. Small scale detection was available for accounting firms and insurance companies. The Jewelers Security Alliance still retained Pinkerton's. Most activity, however, had shifted to guarding property. Significantly, in 1964 the agency got the largest private security contract in history, guarding of the New York world's fair. Pinkerton's had gone from being thief-takers to being caretakers. Soon, even the designation 'detective agency' would fall from the letterhead.[55]

And there was still investigative work in the domestic economy. The matrimonial field was healthy, not only in the pursuit of grounds for divorce (infidelity in many states) but also for the investigation of suspicious suitors. Insurance companies employed in-house and private detectives to investigate claims involving potential fraud in fires (arson), accidents, and suspicious deaths. Lawyers hired similar investigative work in all manner of litigation. Industrial espionage became less common and shifted its aims to protecting (or stealing) trade secrets and monitoring employee conduct. The list goes on: missing persons, background checks, and simple inquiries beyond the client's abilities. One important consequence of this shift in the nature of private detective employment has been the entry of larger numbers of women investigators, many in domestic inquiries but increasingly in all areas, including management and ownership.[56]

In 1927, while working as credit managers for the Roos Brothers Department Store of San Francisco, Ed Krout and Sam Schneider came up with a new idea: a white-collar detective agency serving business, law firms, and insurance companies. "At the time, there were no professional investigation agencies as we know them today. So-called 'detectives' were tough guys who packed guns and hung around the free lunch counter of the local saloon. They would collect a debt if persuasion were needed. Nearly everyone drove a black Ford."[57] The city directory listed Krout and Schneider as operating the Location Bureau and the General Practice Detective Bureau. Business started slowly when moonlighting cost them their day jobs and the Depression set in. Eventually, insurance companies began using their services to investigate claims. They worked for two companies that constructed the Golden Gate and San Francisco Bay Bridges from 1933 to 1937. Workmen's compensation claims were their specialty, involving the use of cameras to unobtrusively evaluate disability claims. By 1960 the agency had ten branch offices in the major West Coast cities.

Modern detective agencies are organized in trade associations that lobby at the state and federal level on legislation affecting their industry. Eddy McClain began his career with Krout and Schneider as an insurance investigator earning $1.50 per hour and over the next forty-five years rose to chairman of the board. Reflecting the nature of the modern detective agency, McClain's work increasingly centered on the political and regulatory environment of private investigators.

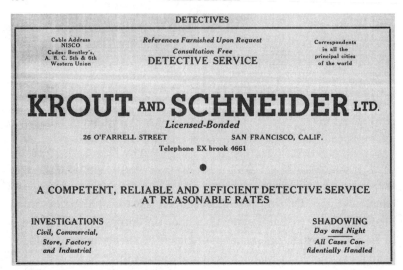

Figure 6.4. An advertisement for one of the new "white-collar" agencies, appearing in the San Francisco City Directory, 1936.

He became active in the California Association of Licensed Investigators (CALI) and, later, in the National Council of Investigative and Security Specialists (NCISS). [58] As trade associations they advocated for legislation to protect, and to prevent limitations on, their ability to investigate the private lives of individuals. Detectives understandably want as much access as possible to data about the people and organizations they have been hired to investigate. But such access is likely to infringe on rights of privacy, resulting not only in unwanted intrusion but also positive harm, as evidenced in cases where, for example, stalkers have obtained celebrity addresses from driver's license records or erroneous credit ratings have destroyed families financially. The debate over rights of privacy vs. the public's right to know is vexed and changing, especially in light of new, more invasive technology. Private detectives are firmly behind greater access, at least for themselves and their clients, and so for less privacy. Civil libertarians struggle to defend privacy. Compromise is elusive for all concerned.

From the early days, detective agencies formed alliances to oppose state licensing laws and, later, federal legislation such as the Wagner Act. In 1910, private detectives gained admittance to the formidable International Association of Chiefs of Police, an affiliation that delivered useful knowledge of tradecraft but little effective representation.

As licensing laws gained popularity, the agencies recognized a need for their own trade association. In Chicago, in 1921, the International Secret Service Association was organized at a meeting of what were described only as "representatives of several large detective agencies in the United States and Canada." Apropos of a developing sense of professionalism, the new association intended to "conduct a drive against questionable detective agencies."[59] The organization lobbied for legislation that would require licenses restricted to honest and law-abiding agencies, at the same time keeping bonding at a reasonable cost and imposing those requirements only on agencies, not individual operatives. With few exceptions, state laws suited these preferences.

On the whole, professionalization led to a more transparent, law-abiding, even more ethical private detective industry. Licensing and regulation regarding civil liberties and privacy are an essential part of this development. Equally important is the evolution of the industry itself. At least in the period of transition, the industry became less repressive, more democratic, more diverse—altogether more civilized. The California Association of Private Investigators (CAPI, later superseded by CALI) was organized in 1947 to represent a new breed of detectives in a new political environment. Mildred Lanore Gilmore, a practicing attorney and experienced private detective, addressed the organization's 1948 convention on the subject of ethics in a changing occupation. "There was a time, and it's been since I entered the business, when the average private detective could barely read or write. That's all changed. Today the average investigator is a college man.... It's time we adopted a code of ethics and enforced the code for the good of the profession." More of the business, she explained, involved guards, protection of property, and prevention of theft, services that also generated lower fees. But the modern agent is smarter and more ethical. In the new environment, "Women make more competent operators than men on most types of cases. They're more conscientious and they look less like operators."[60] One wonders which proposal struck her audience as the more radical, competent women detectives or professional ethics.

Gilmore represented an evolved and arguably more public breed of private detective. As the industry became more civil, its habits of intrigue and menace receded. Respectability, white-collar status, and business acumen became the normative standard, if not always the fact. Yet ironically the pervasive and flourishing public image of the (always male) private eye continued to portray him as a hard-boiled loner, a righter of wrongs, the nemesis of evildoers, a worker, not a genius or Boy Scout. This disparity of image and fact was nothing new, although both image and fact had evolved substantially along separate if intersecting paths. Their symbiotic relationship arose from the mutual pursuit of commercial ends—detective agency business and detective story business, twin born and jointly evolved.

# 7

# THE STORIED DETECTIVE

## Origins of the Detective Story

Edgar Allan Poe invented the detective story in three tales written in the early 1840s, set in Paris and published in the popular press ("The Murders in the Rue Morgue," *Graham's Magazine*, 1841; "The Mystery of Marie Rogêt," *Ladies' Companion*, 1842; "The Purloined Letter," *The Gift for 1845*, 1844). Poe's central characters, C. Auguste Dupin and his nameless roommate and narrator, are the prototypes for Sherlock Holmes and Dr. Watson and many other detective duos to follow. Poe's fictional detective was based on the very real French criminal turned policeman Eugène Vidocq, who went on to establish the first detective agency. "He had read Vidocq, and it is right to say that if the *Mémoires* had never been published Poe would not have created his amateur detective, but one should immediately add that Poe owed to Vidocq only the inspiration that set light to his imagination."[1]

Paris in the mid-nineteenth century was also a prototype, one of urban disorder fed by rapid population growth, immigration, inequality, poverty, and crime. Poe was not alone in finding his inspiration in the streets, salons, and sewers of Paris. Victor Hugo and Honoré de Balzac took the city as their tableau. Poe's contemporary Eugène Sue published *The Mysteries of Paris* in serial form from 1842 to 1843. Sue's plots involve Rodolphe, a fallen aristocrat (like Dupin) who puts his brilliant mind and superior physical strength in the service of the Parisian underclass. Vidocq's influence is powerful; Rodolphe moves easily through the underworld exhibiting an understanding of prostitute and slasher alike. Yet he is also an early Sherlock, outside the mundane urban world and able to redress its evils. Sue introduced a new genre to great commercial response, helping to establish the serial publication format and spawning city-mystery imitators in London and New York. "The first genre to achieve massive success and to dominate cheap fiction was the 'mysteries of the city.' These novels unveiled the city's mysteries by telling tales of criminal underworlds, urban squalor, and elite luxury and decadence."[2]

Poe worked in the nascent American publishing industry in the 1830s and was keenly aware of the need to appeal to popular tastes in commercial literature. He labored as an editor for several struggling literary magazines, wrote poetry, and thought about starting a journal of his own. By the 1840s, he had become a well-known author yet, despite prodigious effort, was never able to earn a living by writing alone. For his classic poem "The Raven," first published New York's *Evening Mirror* in 1845, he was paid a mere nine dollars. His detective stories were yet another effort at commercial success resulting, ironically, in enormous literary achievement but very little income. The Dupin stories conjured Sue's mysteries of the city, with Paris as the quintessential locus of urban crime, chaos, and the struggle for social order—an order achievable through the detective's faculty for deductive scientific analysis. Ratiocination was the unique ability the detective brought to the city's mysteries; observation and logic that together produced solutions, restored coherence, and satisfied the reader's distress over disorder.

Poe's engagement with reality ran deeper than character, plot, and scene in the stories. He believed that events of the world were to be understood by taking a wide view, by attending to the extensive surface of things rather than the intensive depth. Timothy Whalen argues that Poe's epistemology grew out of his critique of a trend toward the commodification of knowledge (and authors) already apparent in antebellum American publishing. The detective story was more than an appealing vehicle for entertainment; it was a way of penetrating the confusion of the modern world. The detective story provided a means to demonstrate his thesis about mass culture.[3]

In "The Mystery of Marie Rogêt," Poe took events of the actual unsolved murder of Mary Rogers in New York in 1841 and transposed them to the fictional world of Paris, where Dupin then set about solving the case—or at least indicating how it could be solved using his methods rather than those of the police. Dupin explains that with the Parisian police, "there is no method in their proceedings, beyond the method of the moment. . . . Vidocq, for example, was a good guesser and a persevering man. But, without educated thought, he erred continually by the very intensity of his investigations. He impaired his vision by holding the object too close [and] necessarily lost sight of the matter as a whole. There is such a thing as being too profound."[4] As the story moves forward, Dupin reviews the evidence as reported in the Parisian (i.e., New York) press. All of the people and places in the New York case have fictional counterparts. Marie Rogêt vanished one day when she failed to show up for a date with her aunt. As an attractive young woman with a suitor as well as a mysterious sailor boyfriend, it was assumed that her disappearance had something to do with her love life. When her body was found floating in a river several days later, suspicion shifted to criminal gangs seen hanging out along the riverside. Dupin finds factual and logical fault with the police investigation, which seized too readily on crime-scene details rather than surveying events in broader perspective, including Marie's previous history, her sailor friend, and his movements following the disappearance.

Poe uses the story to propose a solution to the mystery and, in so doing, offers a critique of the New York police investigation, from the lips of Dupin, of course, and more broadly of conventional ways of knowing. "Marie Rogêt" is more than a mystery story. It is a demonstration of how to obtain more accurate knowledge. Regrettably, it was an incomplete demonstration, as Poe's solution was never tested and the Mary Rogers case never solved. Perhaps the police did not read detective stories, or maybe Poe's epistemology was over their heads. Or, if they knew of his speculation, they may have thought he was out of his depth. Practical consequences notwithstanding, the detective story had its origins in the interplay of real events and imaginative constructions of those events. For Poe it was fiction in the form of scientific method and cultural critique.

Poe was not alone in drawing inspiration from real detectives. Émile Gaboriau, in his 1866 French detective novel, followed Poe by modeling his protagonist, Monsieur Lecoq, after Vidocq. Wilkie Collins's English novel *The Moonstone* (1868), "a founding fable of detective fiction, adopted many characteristics of the real investigation at Road [Hill House]," an English country house where the brutal murder of a child was investigated by the fabled Jack Whicher of Scotland Yard.[5] Charles Dickens's great chronicles of London's underworld drew on actual crimes and on policemen such as Charles Field, one

Figure 7.1. An illustration from a publication of "The Mystery of Marie Rogêt" showing the discovery of the young woman's body. Poe's story is a slightly fictionalized account of a real murder case. (Poe Museum of Richmond, Virginia)

of the first inspectors of the Metropolitan Police. "Dickens had been progressively feeling his way toward detective-story elements from his early Newgate [prison] novel days. . . . It is generally accepted that Inspector Bucket [in *Bleak House*] was drawn from the mannerisms and appearance of Inspector Charles Field of the Detective Department, or 'Inspector Wield' as Dickens dubbed him [elsewhere, in a magazine article]."[6]

Arthur Conan Doyle learned the genre from Poe and Gaboriau. He followed Dickens's practice of selecting a real model from his own experience when it came to developing his protagonist. Sherlock Holmes was endowed with the deductive skills of Dr. Joseph Bell, Doyle's mentor in medical school at the University of Edinburgh. In his autobiography, Doyle recalls,

> I felt now that I was capable of something fresher and crisper and more work-man like. Gaboriau had rather attracted me by a neat dovetailing of his plots, and Poe's masterful detective, M. Dupin, had from boyhood been one of my heroes. But could I bring an addition of my own? I thought of my old teacher Joe Bell, of his eagle face, of his curious ways, and his eerie trick of spotting details. If he were a detective he would surely reduce this fascinating but unorganized business to something nearer an exact science.[7]

The award for the first detective novel has been sharply contested and, recently, in flux. Wilkie Collins's *The Moonstone* (1868) held the title for a time, although Émile Gaboriau's *L'Affaire Lerouge* (1866) had the edge in the all-European field. Both claims seem to have been retired as a result of research by Paul Collins, who has traced the provenance of *The Notting Hill Mystery* to Charles Warren Adams (writing as Charles Felix), who published an eight-part serial version starting in November 1862 and the book-length edition in 1865.[8] Credit for the first American detective novel belongs to Anna Katherine Green, who published *The Leavenworth Case* in 1878.

The question of who was the first detective novelist is a problem for literary historians. The broader sociological problem concerns the cultural and organizational processes that produced the genre and directed its evolution. More significant, perhaps, than who was first, or first in England, France, or the United States, is the impressive near simultaneity of this eruption of mystery and detective yarns in the form of stories, serials, novels, and memoirs. The analytical question is not so much which author drew on which inspiration when, as it is what social forces explain the relatively sudden appearance of a new cultural figure—the detective, whose striking character would evolve over time but whose identity at any one time became widely and readily known.

Before there were detective stories, there were the memoirs of practicing detectives from which the stories in part derived. From the

beginning with Vidocq, real detectives wrote memoirs as literary endeavors, as business promotions, and for their own enjoyment. Allan
Pinkerton inaugurated the genre in the United States with *The Expressman and the Detectives* (1874), the first of a score of titles bearing
his name (though the only one he wrote himself before turning publicity work over to a team of ghostwriters). The writing of *Expressman*
is pretty awful, but it reveals some flashes of Pinkerton's character:
his reluctance to travel in the South owing to his "anti-slavery principles" and his self-description as "a man somewhat after the John
Brown stamp." Very different social sentiments infused *The Molly
Maguires and the Detectives*, which demonized the Irish miners in the
interests of a "sales pitch for Pinkerton's strikebreaking talents,"[9] but
it was nevertheless a commercial success. Arthur Conan Doyle turned
the tables on Pinkerton, taking the Molly Maguires and the figure of
Pinkerton's detective hero McKenna (real life James McParland) as
equally barbarous villains in *The Valley of Fear* (1888). Although Allan
Pinkerton, Doyle's fellow Scot and one-time friend, had died in 1884,
before the novel's publication, son Robert A. Pinkerton registered the
agency's regrets that the Sherlockian version had strayed so far from
reality.[10]

Detective reminiscences proliferated, attempting to capitalize on
the new market for mystery stories. Memoirs provided raw material
for the story writers to build on. George S. McWatters rivals Pinkerton for authorship of the first American detective memoir, although
portions of *Knots Untied*, published in 1872, deal with the experiences
of others and may exceed even Pinkerton's penchant for fiction. The
genre blossomed at the turn of the century with Thomas Furlong and
Charles Siringo.[11] Many more would follow. "The figure of the detective emerges in American popular fiction as a common and recurring
character in the 1870s and 1880s. . . . These early detectives were often
based on and influenced by the semi-fictional narratives of actual
detectives which were published at the same time, among them the
memoirs of George McWatters and Allan Pinkerton."[12]

The relationship of the memoir and the detective story was recip-
rocal and evolving. Poe drew on the memoir as a source of authentic-
ity, and memoirs were fictionalized in efforts to appeal to the reader.
But the connection ran deeper. "Pinkerton's books, like his detective
business, were corporate and cooperative enterprises . . . an attempt
to bolster the agency's prestige and assure Pinkerton's place as spokes-

man . . . to salvage the detective profession from the exaggerated glamor put on detectives by pulp writers. . . . *He was writing in response to detective literature*, hoping to correct some of the misconceptions fostered by the literary products."[13] The same is true of Burns and the many memoirists to follow. They borrowed conventions of the detective story while at the same time writing against it, insisting that real detectives were inaccurately portrayed in popular fiction as too romantic and neglectful of the occupation's professionalism, and that the fiction writers were given to stereotypes and simplifications. Yet, in making their case they adopted their own brand of fiction.

My argument here and throughout this study is that both cultural production and detective work developed as commercial enterprises in one unique American economy; that each enterprise evolved multiple forms, interacting with one another, and all of those converged in the legendary private eye. I do not intend to say that two parallel enterprises combined into one myth or that the analysis is divided in two parts, industrial fact and literary fiction. On the contrary, this is a study of American society and culture that reveals how the detective business arose, fashioning its own fictions, in tandem with a culture industry that was constrained by commercial fact, each a piece of the larger political economy and both subject to an essential interplay. The private detective was imagined in business enterprise as much as commercially conditioned in cultural production. Key is their symbiotic relationship.

### Detective Story Business

The most widely recognized image of the private detective was created and propagated by the publishing industry. In Britain and the United States, publishing as a commercial enterprise aimed at a broad popular audience began in the 1820s and 1830s. Sutherland's study of Victorian novelists and publishers demonstrates the obstacles confronting the publication of inexpensive fiction for the general public. [14] The major publishing houses were convinced that the only way to profit in the fiction market was to produce large, three-volume books (in printed form) that came to be the standard for British novelists such as Dickens, Thackeray, the Brontë sisters, Trollope, and Eliot. Authors were effectively required to produce these tomes by their publishers, who insisted, despite growing evidence to the contrary, that they were the only financially viable format. A rare few like Dickens or Eliot attained huge popularity and some autonomy from publishers' constraints, but the industry as a whole struggled to reach a mass public. By the mid-1830s a breakthrough came with a series of innovations: publication of big novels in parts, circulating libraries, and magazine serialization. Dickens led the movement with the successful serialization of "The Pickwick Papers" in a monthly magazine.

The publishing industry in the United States began its explosive growth in the 1830s with the foundation of the great publishing houses, the profusion of newspapers and magazines, and the emergence of the story paper and the dime novel.[15] This was Poe's era, a period he lamented for the mass production and commodification of literature, just as it was the period that witnessed the eventual great success of his work.[16] Growth of the publishing industry depended on a number of factors. Population expanded rapidly during the nineteenth century: from five million in 1800 to thirteen million in 1830, doubling by 1850 to twenty-three million and tripling to seventy-six million in 1900. The literacy rate for whites was surprisingly high (and possibly over-estimated) and rose from 60 percent in 1800 to 80 percent in 1870 (the first US Census record) and 90 percent in 1900. Literacy was paced by a growing urban middle class society, although the working classes were also readers of the penny press. Public libraries were created and expanded from 2,500 facilities holding twelve million volumes in 1876 to 5,000 libraries with forty million books in 1900.[17] "One of the most remarkable aspects of national life after the Civil War was the tremendous growth of reading, which of course accounted for the rapid expansion of publishing—not only of books, but of magazines and newspapers as well."[18]

Twin forces of technology and commerce drove the publishing industry to new heights in the latter half of the nineteenth century. In printing, manual typesetting was superseded by the linotype machine in the 1880s when it was adopted by the *New York Tribune*. The rotary press, at midcentury, and the offset press in 1870 modernized printing. Paper manufactured from wood pulp, rather than rags, began in the 1840s following independent inventions in Europe and North America. Together these advances significantly reduced costs and increased the efficiency of publishing for an expanding audience. Technology was facilitated by regulatory changes, notably in postal rate reductions in 1863 and 1879 that created different classes of mail and lower rates for newspapers and magazines. Postal-rate incentives facilitated "the real paperback revolution,"[19] with the newspaper weeklies (synonymous at the time with magazines) being the principal vehicle for mass consumption of fiction. The "weeklies" published major novels in serial form at low cost, which expanded the reading public and drove down the price of books. News agents were a key link between publishers and consumers. National distributors like the American News Company contracted with publishing houses and sold directly to news dealers at favorable bulk prices and with generous remaindering policies. An expanding US Post Office provided the vital link in the distribution chain serving subscribers.

Copyright law played an important part. The first US copyright law protected only American authors' works. As a result, international authors were freely pirated and published in cheap editions, the "story papers," or weeklies. The works of British writers, which did not require translation, were particularly vulnerable. American publishers profited from these "free" manuscripts of famous best-selling authors. Yet their reprinting not only denied royalties to the original authors and publishers but also suppressed the market and potential earnings of American authors. Poe complained bitterly of the arrangement, of how it deprived the nation of its own literary wealth, damaged particularly authors who were not independently wealthy, and caused a "fatal resentment" in the heart of literature.[20] Ironically, copyright law finally changed in 1891 when American publishers began to be undercut by even cheaper editions.

John Tebbel's history of American publishing calls the period from 1845 to 1857 "the greatest boom the book business had ever witnessed. Cheap books appeared in profusion from many publishers, some in cloth, others softbound, most selling for less than a dollar. Simultaneous publishing of titles in cloth and paper was common. Piracy did not disappear, but the publishers now drew heavily on American authors; perhaps 70 percent of the output in this period was by native writers, who proliferated in the new atmosphere."[21]

Although the industry suffered a setback in the financial panic of 1857, it was this period that witnessed two great publishing events: the introduction of the original dime novel and the founding of Street and Smith, destined to become the nation's largest publishing firm. Beginning as small-time publishers and bookbinders in Buffalo, Erastus and Irwin Beadle produced a "Dime Songbook" (followed by a dime cookbook, a dime joke book, etc.), leading to a huge success with their first dime novel, *Malaeska: The Indian Wife of the White Hunter*, by Mrs. Ann S. Stephens. In 1859, Francis Scott Street and Francis Shubael Smith were young staff writers for the *New York Dispatch*, a second-rate weekly, when the paper's publisher agreed to turn the company over to the aspiring publishers for a share of any profits.[22]

Street and Smith, with a circulation of 30,000, faced strong competition from the upscale magazines like *Harper's Weekly* (120,000) and Frank Leslie's *Illustrated Weekly* (140,000). But the partners had ambition, energy, and complementary skills—Street the businessman and Smith the writer and editor. Together they introduced a series of publishing innovations. After changing the paper's name to the *New York Weekly*, they advertised, including in the pages of their rivals; developed the cliffhanger in serialized stories; offered free copies of the first segment of a serial; paid well for the best authors; and contracted for exclusive rights to their authors' works. Sometimes they pirated British material, but they also developed an instinct for popular tastes. "They knew what the masses wanted to read. They wanted to read of girls pursued (but never quite caught) by villains, of poor boys who managed to overcome all obstacles to achieve wealth. . . . [Poe's stories in *Graham's*] touched off the imagination of many writers for the various weeklies, and Francis Smith, with his genius for anticipating trends, knew immediately that detective fiction was something on which his readers would feed avidly. He gave it to them."[23] By 1869, the *New York Weekly*, with Buffalo Bill gracing the front page, dominated the competition with a circulation of 300,000, and Street and Smith had a growing list of magazine and dime novel publications.

The detective of American popular culture was fashioned in the "pulps," in the popular press of story weeklies, magazines, and dime novels published on low-grade paper. There were, of course, earlier sources of detective fiction in novels and in the respectable London magazines and the mainstream US weeklies that published the early stories of Poe and Green. But it was in the cheap popular magazines that the detective story developed and achieved its most familiar form, beginning with adventure stories featuring a detective hero who appealed to working-class, adolescent, and leisure readers.

"The Old Sleuth," begun in 1872, was the first successful and continuously running detective series in the era of weeklies. The series launched with the person of Old Sleuth, a private and elusive master

Figure 7.2. "The Old Sleuth," a series created by Harlan Page Halsey, appeared in *Fireside Companion* magazine in 1872 and later in its own publication, the *Old Sleuth Library*, both published by George Munro and Sons. The series then moved to Arthur Westbrook's *Old Sleuth Weekly*, where it ran for more than two hundred issues, from 1908 to 1921. Pictured is an issue from 1910.

detective with extraordinary powers of strength, intelligence, and disguise. Over time, plot and character evolved, turning to the adventures of the master's pupils, young men and boys similarly endowed with superpowers—and even a few young women able to disguise themselves as men.[24] Street and Smith hired Old Sleuth creator Harlan Page Halsey to write for *New York Weekly*. Because domestic copyright law protected the Old Sleuth brand of its original publishers, Halsey wrote under pen names and created other characters from the same mold. Unknowing readers reported that these stories were much better written than "Old Sleuth."[25] Street and Smith found their own superhero in Nick Carter, a youngster of prodigious talents trained by his own shadowy father.

> He began, of course, by being the best marksman in the world. He could, and often did, defeat as many as twenty or thirty ruffians single-handed. Nick Carter could imitate the appearance and the speech of a western farmer, a Chicago businessman, a French government official, a Russian spy, a Japanese nobleman or a cowboy. Reading lips in three different languages was just one of his minor parlor tricks. In addition to this, Nick was a good boy. He neither drank, smoked, swore nor lied."[26]

Debuting in 1886, Nick Carter became the most successful character in the genre, appearing in magazine stories, dime novels, and, later, radio shows that ran until the 1940s. Although the pulps featured tales of adventure, romance, and westerns, the detective story dominated in popularity with dozens of magazines with titles incorporating such descriptors as "True," "Real," "Dime," and "Front-Page."

For decades, the pulp fiction industry thrived owing to an eager reading public, cheap editions, and a distribution network of mail, news agents, and newsstands. The demand for stories was so great that commercial publishers began employing teams of writers to feed the plethora of weekly magazines and dime novels. A dozen people wrote Nick Carter stories alone. "The trend was toward industrial production based on division of labor and corporate trademarks, the pseudonyms of the market."[27] The incongruous "literary factory" was invented to insure a steady flow of stories on demand for the voracious pulps. The editor of *Publishers Weekly* for August 1892 offered a vivid account of one factory and its workers:

This literary factory was hidden away in one of the by-streets of New York. . . . It employs over thirty people, mostly girls and women. For the most part these girls are intelligent. It is their duty to read all the daily and weekly periodicals in the land. . . . Any unusual story of city life—mostly the misdoings of city people—is marked by these girls and turned over to one of three managers. These managers, who are men, select the best of these marked articles, and turn over such as are available to one of a corps of five women who digest the happening given to them and transform it to a skeleton or outline for a story.

The chief manager would then send the story "shell" to any one of "a hundred or more writers" with a letter asking the writer to turn the germ into a story of so many parts and so many pages to be delivered by a specified date for a set fee.[28]

The creative side of the business was made up of a few prominent authors whose actual names or pen names appeared with their published stories. Named authors usually had a following. Then came hundreds of anonymous producers and ghostwriters who worked outside the factories. Pulp editors welcomed submissions conforming to certain well-understood themes and parameters. Hundreds of freelancers responded to publisher requests for ideas, outlines, or complete stories produced at piece rates ranging from one to four cents per word. "The vast majority receive a cent a word for their yarns: from thirty to fifty dollars for a short story; one to two hundred and fifty for novelettes. A bargain is usually struck between the editor and the unknown writer for complete novels adaptable to serial use: anywhere from two to five hundred dollars."[29] Known writers commanded the higher rates, but they were few and their output could not sustain the demand. Lower paid "hacks" wrote under a franchise name, which readers nevertheless believed to be a favorite author. Occupational lore in the pulpwood industry talks of the million-words-a-year writer who (if he or she actually existed) earned a healthy annual income of ten thousand dollars. That was unlikely; at one cent per word it assumes an average 2,739 words per day and continuous employment. Named authors enjoyed higher rates; four cents per word was exceptional.

In addition to the pivotal role of publishers, the business was shaped by a market composed of consumers and producers, readers and writers. Who read detective stories? The question preoccupied publishers, yielding to unexpected answers. Consumers formed several cate-

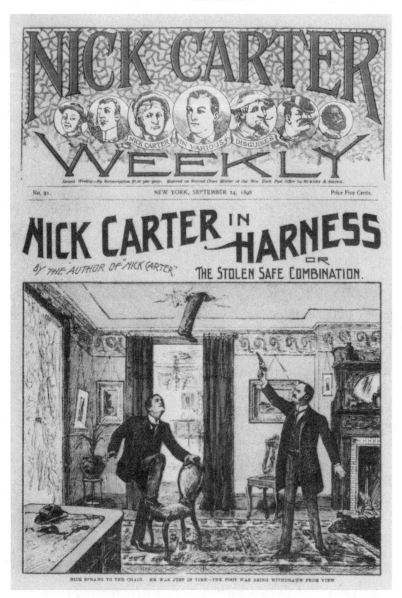

Figure 7.3. A representative issue of Street and Smith's Nick Carter Weekly (September 24, 1898). Master detective Nick Carter appeared over decades in pulp magazines and on radio in the 1940s.

gories, the most numerous of which were working-class men. In the nineteenth century, "the evidence suggests that the bulk of the dime novel audience were young workers, often of Irish or German ethnicity, in the cities and mill towns of the North and West; and that dime novels and story papers made up most of their reading matter. . . . Nor were dime novels limited to working class readers; they were read by clerks, shopkeepers, local professionals, small farmers and their families."[30] Erin Smith's innovative "reconstruction" of the pulp reader analyzes advertisements appearing in *Black Mask* during the 1930s and 1940s. The ads mainly promoted correspondence schools, work clothes, and "he-man accessories" for the working man and "promised job training and bodybuilding to reconstitute the fading culture of autonomous, manly artisans. . . . *Black Mask* ads and fiction were presented as almost seamlessly connected."[31]

Although adolescents constituted an important segment of the audience, retailers reported that office boys were often followed to the newsstands by their employers, bankers and lawyers.[32] A survey by the University of Chicago library school in 1930 demonstrated that over half the population of pulp readers had only a grade-school education; another 30 percent had finished high school.[33] These readership estimates encounter a sampling problem in that detective stories also appeared in "slick," as opposed to pulp, publications. The venerable *Saturday Evening Post* published crime and mystery stories, including articles by William J. Burns (or his surrogates).[34] *McClure's Magazine* featured "the adventures of the two greatest detectives in the world: Burns, the foremost living detective in America, and Gilbert K. Chesterton's 'Father Brown,' the most brilliant conception of the unraveler of criminal mystery in fiction since Sherlock Holmes."[35] The detective story had an appreciable middle-class following.

A profile of detective story writers suggests they were working men and women who earned modest amounts from writing and usually supported themselves with a day job. They produced a commodity at piece rates for a publisher who retained ownership of the product — both the story and the pen name under which it appeared. A minority of several hundred or so made a living exclusively from writing. A very few authors became famous and moved up to quality publishers, where they earned more and received royalties. Dashiell Hammett went to Knopf in 1929 with his first novel and soon earned handsomely. But the great bulk of work that defined the modern detective story was produced by work-a-day writers: "the dime novel . . . was a commercial product of a burgeoning industry employing relatively educated professionals—writers who also worked as journalists, teachers, or clerks."[36] In 1942, *Writer's Digest* published the results of a survey done by the Pulp Writers' Section of the Authors' League of America. Six hundred responding writers reported that a "good average" word rate was three-quarters of a cent; a few top writers received two-and-a-half cents per word, down from the good average of four cents per word in the 1929 peak year. The average annual income was eighteen hundred dollars. Nationwide, about 450 were full-time writers. A much larger number of part-timers were employed in various professions. Seventy-five percent held college degrees. Gender was not reported, although men certainly predominated judging from the most common educational backgrounds—law and engineering.[37]

What sort of product did the pulp industry produce? In his insightful study of the dime novel and working-class culture in the nineteenth century, Michael Denning notes that "there are two bodies of narratives in this field of fiction, the popular, commercial, sensational stories that captured the reading public, and genteel, moralistic narratives that attempt to use the dime novel format with varying degrees of success to recapture and reorganize working class culture."[38] The pulps featured both Old Sleuth and Horatio Alger's tales of youngsters whose virtues are rewarded with success. Master detective Nick Carter combines these traits, a good boy who doesn't't smoke or swear but turns into preternatural action figure when justice requires. The genre imagined a detective hero who possessed both swashbuckling physical skills and high moral standards.

Such was the product that publishers believed the mass public demanded, the commodity they solicited from their producers. Writers would receive requests "for *fresh, bold, daring* stories [but] if they submitted anything 'off trail,' outside the ordinary, they were usually reprimanded to read recent issues of the magazine to get a better idea of what the editor was looking for."[39] *Writer's Digest*, the trade journal that informed authors about trends in the industry, reported in 1930 that "*Ace-High Magazine* is broadening its policy to include a slight amount of woman interest. While physical masculine action, viewpoint and appeal must be paramount, if a woman is necessary to the plot and does not overshadow the other elements, she is permissible. But she must always be a secondary character and kept in the background." Publishers advised authors to "study our needs before submitting."[40] Editors knew what they wanted and conveyed such expectations to authors. One writer lamented, "The resultant story, while it has my name on it, is really the work of the editor who ordered it. . . . He has simply used my knack of writing to get the story *he* wants, in the way *he* wants it, for what he considers *his* public."[41]

### Rise of the Hard-Boileds

The modern portrait of the private detective derives primarily from the "hard-boiled" school that made its appearance in the 1920s, achieved legendary cultural status in the next two decades, and lives on in the collective imagination. The tough-guy detective developed with the times: World War I, Prohibition and the underworld it generated, urban-industrial society, corporate trusts, labor union struggles, federal policing, and, notably, the dramatic growth of real detective agencies staffed by business entrepreneurs and more than a few real tough guys.

Julian Symons's history of the detective story describes the 1920s as the first Golden Age for detective fiction, a period in which the classical cerebral sleuth yielded pride of place to the hard-boiled private eye, from Sherlock Holmes to Sam Spade.[42] The eccentric genius held sway in S. S. Van Dine's Philo Vance, Rex Stout's Nero Wolfe, Ellery Queen, and more in the British canon. But the popular success of the pulps advanced something new, the everyman's detective from the city streets in place of the upper-class dilettante in a New York townhouse. The hard-boiled detective had shed the prissy morals of Nick Carter—he smoked, drank, and shot people. The shift should not be overstated, though. The clever, clue-following, puzzle-solving detective persisted in vividly drawn characters like Earl Derr Biggers's Charlie Chan (based on a real Honolulu police detective), who was allowably eccentric by dint of being Chinese.

Credit for the first hard-boiled detective story should be shared between Carroll John Daly and Dashiell Hammett, who were verging on a new kind of character in the pages of *The Black Mask* in 1923. Daly's popular protagonist Race Williams had no manners and no doubt about who he was:

Under the laws I'm labeled on the books and licensed as a private
detective. Not that I'm proud of the license but I need it, and I've
had considerable trouble hanging onto it. My position is not exactly
a healthy one. The police don't like me. The crooks don't like me.
I'm just a halfway house between the law and crime; sort of working
both ends against the middle. Right and wrong are not written on
the statutes for me, nor do I find my code of morals in the essays
of long-winded professors. My ethics are my own. I'm not saying
they're good and I'm not admitting they're bad, and what's more
I'm not interested in the opinions of others on that subject. . . . Race
Williams—Private Investigator—tells the whole story.[43]

*The Black Mask,* birthplace of the hard-boiled detective story and
the most famous of the mystery pulps, was launched in 1920—oddly
enough, by the publishers of a slick magazine, *The Smart Set.* Editors
H. L. Mencken and George Jean Nathan were struggling to keep the
firm financially healthy and saw the Street and Smith pulp *Detective
Story* as a successful model to imitate. Within the year, Mencken and
Nathan sold the magazine at a profit, but the new editors struggled to
find a winning style in a field of 178 existing mystery-detective-crime
magazines.[44] Under the successive editorships of George W. Sutton
and Philip C. Cody, the magazine discovered its profile in the work of
a group of young authors experimenting with hard-edged characters
like Race Williams and the Continental Op, whose exploits appeared
in multiple issues. Another early favorite was Erle Stanley Gardner, a
practicing lawyer who turned from writing westerns to the engagingly
original Ed Jenkins, Phantom Crook series. The *"Black Mask* Boys"
included a dozen authors whose work appeared regularly under the
direction of four editors, all of whom had a keen sense of the market.
*The Black Mask* and its stable of authors enjoyed great commercial
success—and in some instances critical appreciation.

The decade-long editorship of Joseph T. ("Cap") Shaw is best
known for building on its predecessors, perfecting the hard-boiled
genre, and achieving magazine celebrity. Although he hoped to be a
writer and knew nothing about *The Black Mask* when hired in 1926,
Shaw proved an extraordinary editor with an unfailing eye for talent
and a sensibility that commanded the respect of his authors. In the
first issue under his direction, Shaw set down the predicate for the
hard-boiled detective. His editorial entitled "The Aim of *Black Mask*"

Figure 7.4. The *Black Mask* issue for January 1929, with stories by Dashiell Hammett and Erle Stanley Gardner.

(the article had been dropped) announced the magazine's plans "to establish itself as the only magazine of its kind. . . . Detective fiction, as we view it, has only commenced to develop [and] must be real in motive, character and action . . . plausible . . . clear and understandable. . . . Word has gone out to writers of our requirements of plausibility, of truthfulness in details, of realism."[45] Other pulps insisted their authors obey a morals code: law and order always prevail, gangsters have no redeeming qualities, male heroes are courageous and women chaste. When *Black Mask* serialized Hammett's novel *The Glass Key* about city machine politics, Shaw was criticized for glorifying corrupt politicians. He replied forcefully in *Writer's Digest*, arguing that the novel performed a public service: "Not until the public realizes that modern crime, modern gangs, cannot exist without the collusion of corrupt and equally criminal police and public officials, will it be possible to cure what is undoubtedly one of the most serious illnesses, to put it mildly, that our body politic has ever suffered from."[46] Shaw, and Hammett, whose work he was defending, brought a new brand of realism to the detective story, which acquired its edge from indulging the seamy side of contemporary society.

By featuring Daly and Hammett, Shaw sent a message to the pool of aspiring writers about what *Black Mask* considered the commercial ideal in detective stories. In letters of acceptance and rejection, he stressed "character" in addition to action and realism. Writers strived to satisfy these requisites, although they were necessarily general and elusive. Gardner, who later created the Perry Mason franchise and became the richest of all the crime writers, wrote to Shaw in 1926 about the new editor's interests. Shaw had seen several of Gardner's stories in draft and confided to another editor that although he thought them fluent, "he allows himself to drift a bit. . . . Mr. Gardner would increase his effectiveness if he opened all his stories in action."[47] Gardner learned of Shaw's impression, thanked him for the advice, and expressed interest in the magazine's direction:

> I know that you're taking hold with a vision of increased magazine sales and I want to cooperate with you. Anything that gives me a slant on your tastes and ideas is a value because we are both working to the same end and for the same purpose. I'd like to be in Black Mask every month and if you'll take the trouble to tell me just what you like in what I send in and just what you don't like I think I can

cooperate with you pretty closely. Remember that what I'm trying to do is write stories that'll sell magazines—hold the readers you have and help you reach for more.[48]

In a preface to these lines, Gardner declared "I am a fiction factory." Both author and editor saw their ambitions satisfied.

J. A. Sutherland's study of Victorian novelists and publishers cites a very similar exchange between a young Thomas Hardy and his formidable editor, Alexander Macmillan. Macmillan complimented the aspiring writer on his "description of country life among working men" but also warned of certain "fatal drawbacks," particularly his characters, which were "wholly dark" and therefore untrue. Anxious to publish a novel with Macmillan, Hardy replied, "Would you mind suggesting the sort of story you think I could do best, or any literary work I should do well to go on upon."[49] Gardner's exchange with Shaw demonstrates the same alacrity of an ambitious author, one who would later become famous for his creative originality, to shape his work to the demands of genre and market. The Victorian publishers Sutherland describes promoted the big novel in three-volume bulk and sprawling plot, written and priced for the upper middle classes. Jane Austin, the Brontës, Dickens, and Trollope wrote about the manners and fortunes of their own social class, including their relationship to lower orders. They might be compassionate but not too dark. The pulp publishers channeled their authors in an entirely different direction. Dark was good, provided it conveyed a sense of realism. Males of the working and middle classes were the target audience, although occasional professional readers and women were welcome.

Hammett, whose talents were already widely recognized when Shaw took over, was looking beyond the pulps to the literary world of Knopf and the *Saturday Review of Literature*. He needed to be convinced that Shaw was up to something new and worthwhile. Shaw persuaded him that *Black Mask* was both, and working together the two men became fast friends. Part of the reason Hammett decided to return to *Black Mask* was an advantageous publishing deal. Shaw offered to publish Hammett's forthcoming first novel (on labor conflict in "Poisonville") as a three-part serial before its appearance as Knopf's *Red Harvest* in 1929. Hammett's great novels all appeared originally in this form, the first of which was dedicated to Shaw. But unlike Shaw, Gardner, and most of the *Black Mask* gang, Hammett

Figure 7.5. A 1936 dinner in Los Angeles for *Black Mask* authors, who signed the frame of the image: Standing are R. J. Moffat (a guest), Raymond Chandler, Herbert Stinson, Dwight Babcock, Eric Taylor, and Dashiell Hammett; seated are Arthur Barnes, John K. Butler, W. T. Ballard, Horace McCoy, and Norman Davis. (UCLA Special Collections)

was no slave to the market. He began writing in order to earn a living, but he was also a social critic, artistic independent, political radical, and a bit of a rogue. When one of his stories was rejected in 1924, he thanked the editors for "jolting [me] into wakefulness." He had succumbed to commercialism. "This sleuth of mine has degenerated into a meal ticket. . . . I've fallen into the habit of bringing him around whenever the landlord, or the butcher, or the grocer shows signs of nervousness."[50]

Hammett was special in many respects. He was original (as was Daly) in his effort to transform the detective story. Hammett drew on his own Pinkerton experience for an authentic sense of character, scene, and dialogue. The verisimilitude of *Red Harvest* and *The Maltese Falcon* demonstrate the extent to which experienced events infused the stories: the corporate agency, political corruption, industrial violence, and everyday routine were brought from the authors' experience into the detective story. And Hammett was good, so good that he enjoyed early success and growing critical acclaim. He wrote for a living in a collective endeavor and commercial milieu but knew when to rescue his sleuth from literary corruption.

In one respect *Black Mask* remained traditional. Detective heroes were exclusively men. At the beginning of his editorship, Shaw flirted with the idea of reaching the female reader. In a letter to Gardner, he shared, "A thought that especially appeals to me—as it would provide something we lack—is a touch of feminine interest that would not let down our he-man readers and would at the same time bring in a swarm of new ones of both genders."[51] Gardner replied helpfully, suggesting Nell Martin: "That girl can create a female detective that'll hit dead center with Black Mask readers and if you put it to her right she'd do it at a reasonable word rate."[52] Martin was a successful writer of lighter fare for magazines, novels, and film. She also happened to be Dashiell Hammett's lover when they were living in New York. Hammett dedicated *The Glass Key* to her. The historic opportunity was lost, however, when Shaw explained that he had been misunderstood, that he was suggesting that Gardner write feminine characters into his own stories and that "this magazine is by no manner going to be feminine."[53] Nevertheless, over the years women authors joined the ranks of *Black Mask* and pulp crime contributors. Among the better known were Georgiana Ann Randolph Craig (pen name Craig Rice), Dorothy Dunn, and Kathleen Moore Knight.[54]

Shaw put together a school of writers known as the "Black Mask Boys," who together developed the hard-boiled detective genre as a commercial enterprise. It was a fortuitous conjunction of magazine vehicle, editor, and a team of writers drawn to the distinctive style and appearance of the new publication. Hammett produced a series of stories, including the first appearance of the Continental Op.[55] Hammett and Daly attracted submissions from other aspiring writers. The young writers brought experience from other professions and from World War I military service. Gardner was a lawyer writing stories at night. Despite a classical education, Raymond Chandler was working unhappily as a bookkeeper and oil company executive when he was fired for drunkenness. In doldrums, he came across a copy of *Black Mask* that revived his long-cherished ambition to be a writer. His first submission, "Blackmailers Don't Shoot," amazed Shaw for its encapsulation of the magazine's persona. [56]

*Black Mask* was a collective endeavor. All of the editors cultivated and worked closely with a relatively stable group of authors who, in turn, enjoyed the camaraderie as well as the work. Daly and, especially, Hammett led the way, but their inspiration was shared and elaborated by a developing school of popular culture creators. Authors read one another and shared ideas. The cover art, much of it by Fred Craft and J. W. Schlaikjer, lent the magazine an unmistakable noir allure. The figure of the private detective, shaped by a network of people working together, became increasingly recognizable, understood, and savored. The private detective was imagined, of course, but that is the point. In characteristically lapidary prose, Raymond Chandler described it best:

> Down these mean streets a man must go who is not himself mean, who is neither tarnished nor afraid. The detective in this kind of story must be such a man. He is a hero. . . . He must be, to use a rather weathered phrase, a man of honor—by instinct, by inevitability, without thought of it, and certainly without saying it. . . . He is a relatively poor man, or he would not be a detective at all. He is a common man or he could not go among common people. He has a sense of character, or he would not know his job.[57]

### Detectives in Radio and Film

The print version of the detective story migrated readily to other branches of the culture industry, but not without transformation in form and substance. Radio was the first step, an obvious move taken initially by Street and Smith in 1930 as circulation of the industry-leading *Detective Story* magazine began to decline along with the pulp market generally. The publishers hired writers to develop *Detective Story Hour*, a program featuring stories taken from the magazine and introduced to the radio audience in the mysteriously ominous voice of the Shadow. The narrator intoned, "Who knows what evil lurks in the hearts of men? The Shadow knows!"—trademark lines familiar to legions of fans. The resonant radio voice belonging to actor Frank Readick, who was succeeded briefly by Orson Welles, became more memorable than the stories it introduced. Indeed, the Shadow was so popular on radio that *The Shadow Magazine* appeared in 1931 to complete the circuit. A comic book version followed for the youngsters. With a growing audience, the Shadow was reincarnated as a fully formed character on radio, first as a mysterious figure with an Asian "power to cloud men's minds" and so make himself invisible, and later in the guise of wealthy urban socialite Lamont Cranston—the predecessor of Batman.[58]

Print and broadcasting industries overlapped in ownership and content. As the audience changed and radio listening became a national habit, the detective story also changed. The Shadow's voice introduced audio effects as prominent features in 1940s radio drama. *The Whistler*," a spinoff mystery show, was prefaced by the sound of footsteps, a person whistling, and the nameless character who confides, "I know many things, for I walk by night. I know many strange tales hidden in the hearts of men and women." Radio sound effects accented the spoken words. Intrigue generated in a short space of time moved the broadcast through thirty- or sixty-minute segments interspersed with advertising. The effect was an evocative scene rather than a literary cadence. In the 1940s, Nick Carter and Sam Spade were brought to radio, but as amiable wise-cracking guys with female associates rather than "he-men" of the hard-boiled genre.

Sponsors had to be indulged. Daytime radio dramas, with a largely female audience, were often sponsored by makers of soap and detergent, giving rise to the term *soap operas*. Afternoon shows for adolescents advertised breakfast cereal, and the evening offered an adult fare of music, variety, and comedy brought to you by automobiles, appliances, and cigarettes. Sponsors now played the role of shaping theme and content that market-conscious publishers once had. And as networks of local stations developed, another filter was added to the process of screening and shaping content. Unlike the variety of print selections offered for the reader's choice, radio produced a single program schedule for the entire country (though sometimes with separate East and West Coast network programming). The result was greater homogeneity of language and taste. Political censorship was not unknown. When Hammett went to jail for five months for refusing to reveal to a federal judge the names of fellow members of the Civil Rights Congress, NBC canceled the Sam Spade radio series.[59]

The detective story in film was equally transformed, albeit in ways unique to the medium. Fundamentally, film is a more powerful medium with the potential to reach and affect a wider audience than the individual radio program, pulp, or novel. "When sound came to domi-

nate Hollywood around 1930, detective films flourished, but they employed thematic norms quite different from the 'hard-boiled' fiction
popular at the time, even when they used that fiction as their source.
Most 1930s detective movies tended to leaven the gruesome aspects
of their mystery with light comedy, and many appeared in series for-
mats that focused largely upon the charm of the detective."[60] The story
changed in 1941 when John Houston directed a third attempt to bring
*The Maltese Falcon* to the screen. The first two versions, in the light-
comedy, charming-detective style, flopped. "Houston's film is altogether different in tone and points to a major trend for detective films
to follow. Except for dark and cynical wisecracks, there is little comedy and hardly any seduction."[61] Although there were antecedents in
European film and radio drama, Houston's *Maltese Falcon* established
film noir as a distinctive and influential style. It also established the
movie detective in the person of a jaundiced Humphrey Bogart as Sam
Spade and many cinematic detectives to come. After 1941, it was hard
to imagine Sam Spade as anyone other than Bogart.

Yet even Houston was constrained in what could be put on the
screen by the film studios and the self-censoring Production Code
Administration of the Motion Pictures Producers and Distributors
of America. The code's chief enforcer, Joseph Breen, wrote to Jack
Warner, head of Warner Brothers Pictures, who produced *The Maltese Falcon*, explaining, "We have read the final script and regret to
advise that while the basic story is acceptable, a picture based upon
this script could not be approved . . . because of several important ob-
jectionable details." Among those details the letter cited were Spade's
line "damn her"; unnecessary drinking; "the characterization of
[Peter Lorre's character] Cairo as a pansy, as indicated by the lavender
perfume [and] high-pitched voice"; a line suggesting a previous sexual
affair between Spade and Brigid O'Shaughnessy; and "Spade's speech
about the District Attorneys [which] should be rewritten to get away
from characterizing most District Attorneys as men who will do anything to further their careers. This is important."[62] The influential film
noir style pervaded movies of the 1940s and 1950s with particular rele-
vance for the detective story. James M. Cain's novels *Double Indemnity*
and *The Postman Always Rings Twice* became noir classics. Raymond
Chandler's Phillip Marlowe and Ross McDonald's Lew Archer went
from hard-boiled protagonists in print to noir movie private eyes.

Nowhere is the film detective story more fully exemplified than in Roman Polanski's 1974 classic, *Chinatown*. The American Film Institute ranks *Chinatown* twenty-first among the one hundred best American movies and *The Maltese Falcon* thirty-first—both detective stories. Polanski's remarkable achievement captures the essence of noir filmmaking in a story that reimagines the Chandler detective novel as a vehicle for telling the historical tale of how the development of Los Angeles was made possible by seizing a distant water supply. Recall the true story (see chapter 5) of the Los Angeles Aqueduct that tapped Eastern Sierra water sources for export to the city despite the mobilized resistance of rural communities. Protesting rural towns and farms petitioned officials for redress and, when all else failed, bombed the aqueduct and occupied the flood gates, dumping the expropriated water supply. The incidents of 1924 led the Los Angeles Department of Water and Power to hire the Pyles National Detective Agency for an undercover operation to identify the rebels and stop the resistance movement. The detectives failed to make a difference; the rebels were already well known and local officials refused to prosecute them. The resistance movement continued, eventually developing into a long legal struggle.[63]

*Chinatown*, based directly on these events, rewrote history as a detective story. Robert Towne, author of the original screenplay, moved the conflict from the Eastern Sierra to Los Angeles and moved its timing from the 1920s to 1937, the look of which could still be found and photographed in 1974. The water and development story was replotted as a murder mystery arising from the death of the city's water agency head, an honest man who refused to build a storage dam on geologically unstable ground. The Pyles National Detective Agency is replaced with the independent detective firm of Jake Gittes (played by Jack Nicholson), a replica of Chandler's Marlowe, whose "métier," he explains, is marital infidelity. The murder mystery is further embedded in a tale of incest perpetrated by the powerful tycoon behind the water grab (played by John Houston, to add more irony), itself symbolizing the political incest behind the corrupt business of water and real estate development. Gittes's heroic effort to save the incest victim and expose the city's incestuous corruption both fail in film noir fashion, ending in futility. Hugely popular and enduring, *China-town* revivified the hard-boiled detective—the Chandlerian working man engaged in a seamy business, cynical about the human condition and faced with a recognition of the futility of fighting the rich and powerful who are capable of overriding the public interest.[64] Like the metaphorical Chinatown, the ways of power are inscrutable. The modern detective story began to engage social criticism.

## Reprise

Social and literary theorists debate the meaning of the detective story; whether it is an expression of social control or an exposé of inequity, whether it bolsters or challenges the prevailing social order. Earnest Mandel, the luminary Marxist economic theorist and mystery story aficionado, holds to the first, domination theory. The crime story began as homage to the noble social bandit, the Robin Hood of feudal times, but evolved with the rise of capitalism and the criminalization of attacks on property. Eugène Sue's protagonist, the forerunner of the master detective, was a transitional figure, advocating for the poor but, as Mandel's criticism of Sue argues, defending bourgeois society in the end. The "rising place of crime stories in popular literature corresponds to an objective need for the bourgeois class to reconcile . . . the inevitability of crime, with the defense of and apology for the existing social order."[65] In less rhetorical terms, the detective story intends to reassure readers that some societal aberration has been discovered and put right, order restored.[66]

The Cuban government inadvertently devised a test of Mandel's theory. "In 1972, the Ministry of the Interior had announced a competition to develop the [crime] genre in Cuba: 'The works that are presented will be on police themes and will have a didactic character, serving at the same time as a stimulus to prevention and vigilance over all activities that are antisocial.' The heroes were to be champions of the people, so upright that they even refrained from swearing." The contest attracted no entries. Cuban authors wanted to write about repression, corruption, and poverty, not produce propaganda. The more successful ones were able to undermine the official scheme by publishing abroad, where their critical successes made news and filtered back home to liberalize literary sanctions.[67] The proposition that books on police themes would prevent antisocial activities was never confirmed in Cuba and fares poorly elsewhere.

The social control theory fails the reality test. From Hammett to *Chinatown*, modern detective stories regularly challenge social institutions and practices, exposing without rectifying, settling nothing and leaving the reader uncomfortably enlightened. More to the point, the detective story genre typically struggles with opposing tendencies to challenge injustice and to commend law enforcement. Mandel's kind of story would not sell very well, at least to a modern audience that has seen the world and the genre change. Michael Denning's study of the dime novel and working-class culture gets it right: "The commercially produced dime novels were a product of a nascent culture industry, not the creation of workers. Whom do they speak for? Whom do they represent? The dime novels were, I suggest, neither the vehicle of workers' self-expression nor the propaganda tools of capitalists; they were a stage on which contradictory stories were produced, with new characters in old costumes, morals that were undermined by the tale, and words that could be spoken in different accents."[68] Although Denning is careful not to extend his analysis of the dime novel to include the pulps, his framework based on oppositional cultures applies as well to the later period and, most important, captures the workings of the culture industry. The evidence shows that publishers labored in a competitive business to create salable magazines and books with little thought of their social meaning, apart from their alignment with readers' preferences and pocketbooks. Reader tastes were probably influenced by the needs of social control (law, policing, morality), as well as the satisfactions of recusancy and the standards of entertainment. The industry sought to appeal to consumers by capturing some admixture of sentiments in engaging and accessible ways.

The detective story is explained best by the activities of people working together, in the work of those who produce it and the patronage of those who consume it under evolving historical conditions. The figure of the private detective is a product of the culture industry, a commodity fashioned in a changing marketplace. The story began nearly two hundred years ago with the 1828 memoirs of Vidocq. Over time and across borders, it developed in the hands of some lauded authors and a great many working writers and editors. The memoir begins a sequence of representational vehicles, from short stories, novels, and pulp magazines to radio and film. Through it all, the detective story is a commercial enterprise laboring to keep pace with the market, to innovate in product design and content. The memoir, from Vidocq to Pinkerton, was advertising for profit, embellished accounts that obscured skullduggery in a fiction about why the detective provided a necessary service.

Poe and the story writers sought a mass audience with tales of intrigue that penetrated and resolved social disorder. Dime novels combined a cheap paper format with innovations in distribution and yarns that mixed morality plays with working-class sentiments. The story paper cum pulp magazine invented fiction factories, piece-work writers, franchised characters, and editors who schooled writers on what readers wanted. Editors learned by trial and error to cultivate talent. Talented writers like Hammett and Chandler tailored their work to the genre just as their originality transformed the detective for a more sophisticated middle-class public. The signal and enduring accomplishment of the hard-boiled school was to join the detectives' disreputable practices with moral ends, dirty work with just results. Howard S. Becker explains, "The stories were looking for a kind of hero who would embody the doer of dirty work in the private eye character and, when they finally hit on the optimal combination of willingness to do that dirty work and the moral sensibility to recognize it for what it was (as in Spade and Marlowe and all the variations on them) the genre solidified around it and persists to this day more or less in that form."[69]

As the pulps began to fade, publishers like Street and Smith moved their product to radio, where new effects in sound and drama changed the story again. A single broadcast audience called for a less hardboiled or more intriguing mystery figure. Film produced another transformation with the power to assimilate and recreate. The private detective is still an outsider, able to penetrate if not correct society's evils. Sam Spade personifies the noir city; *Chinatown* is the fated history of Los Angeles. The modern detective is both a jaundiced loner and a social critic, "a kind of poor man's sociologist," as Ross McDonald once observed.[70]

# 8

# MAKING A LEGEND

Every Sunday for nearly forty years, Don Herron has met on a San Francisco street corner with enthusiasts for the now-famous Dashiell Hammett Tour. For several hours Herron guides the devotees through the places Hammett inhabited and wrote about, regaling them with stories of John's Grill, where Sam Spade ate pork chops in *The Maltese Falcon*; the corner above the Stockton Street tunnel, where Brigid O'Shaughnessy shot Miles Archer; the Flood Building on Market Street that housed the Continental Detective Agency and the Old Man, the Continental Op's boss.[1] A nostalgia trip to be sure, but also an experience bringing together Hammett admirers, detective fiction buffs, local historians, urban sociologists, international connoisseurs, visiting detectives and diverse tourists—a group of people acting together on the basis of their common understanding of what they are there to see and do.

The Dashiell Hammett tour and myriad events like it are occasions of collective action made possible by the subculture that surrounds them and by the legend that gives them meaning. The private eye inhabits a global subculture sustained by an extensive network of actors with interests that derive from the detective's origins in society and story. From a changing society comes private policing by agencies given to publicity, trade associations, journals, lobbying, correspondence schools, and memoirs of alleged exploits. From evolving stories come genre, publishers and pulps, radio and film detectives, literary societies and product promotions. All of these are chronicled in magazines about detectives and mystery fiction, specialized bookstores, and even PI museums. The private detective suffuses popular culture.

ON APPROXIMATELY THIS SPOT

MILES ARCHER,

PARTNER OF SAM SPADE,

WAS DONE IN BY

BRIGID O'SHAUGHNESSY.

Figure 8.1. San Francisco street marker commemorating the city's most famous detective story and Dashiell Hammett's legendary private eye.

Paramount, of course, is memoir-inspired adult fiction followed by mystery fiction aimed at adolescents, a winning genre of its own that exudes moral lessons. Generations of American youngsters were raised on adventures of the Hardy Boys and Nancy Drew. Edward Stratemeyer created the Hardy Boys in 1926 and sold the franchise to Grosset and Dunlap publishers, who employed first one or two and later a dozen authors to draft short books from Stratemeyer's outlines, all under the name of Franklin W. Dixon. The first three titles appearing in 1927 scored such a solid commercial hit that the same team created the Nancy Drew series in 1930, stories centered on boys and girls solving mysteries with the occasional help of their parents. Both series ran to over one hundred titles, selling millions of copies in twenty-five languages.

In the same period, the detective appeared on radio. Real detectives moved to the airways with Boston's James Wood Jr., who wrote for *Startling Detective Adventures* magazine and adapted the stories for radio plays.[2] Strategically located in Los Angeles, the resourceful Nick Harris published *In the Shadows*, a collection of true detective stories, and then adapted the adventures for a regular series of fifteen-minute programs on KFI radio.[3] Far greater commercial success and cultural diffusion attended fictional magazine characters who moved from pulps to radio and film in the 1930s. Publishers Street and Smith produced the radio program *The Detective Story Hour*, which introduced *The Shadow*. Nick Carter and Sam Spade were adapted for radio and film in the 1940s. Charlie Chan went from six Earl Derr Biggers novels beginning in 1925 to radio, comic books and thirty films.[4]

Newspaper and magazine comics aimed at children also attracted ascending age groups. Dick Tracy, created by Chester Gould in 1931, is aptly described as "an American cultural phenomenon," a private detective who fought crime and aided police with uncanny skill and gadgets like the two-way wrist radio that has recently become a reality. From comics to pocket books and film, Dick Tracy was responsible for "a proliferation of moral storytelling".[5] The detective hero invaded the world of children's fantasy in the service of breakfast cereal promotions. "There was Quaker Puffed Rice's Dick Tracy Secret Service Patrol that gave youngsters the chance to 'be a master detective like Dick Tracy.' For a dime and four box tops, kids got a Dick Tracy Secret Code Book, the Patrol Pledge, a Badge, [and] the Secret Detecto-Kit."[6] Post Cereal Company ran a rival promotion for membership in Post's Junior Detective Corps, which included a manual and lots of neat stuff, all for only two box tops of Post Toasties. The Junior Detective pledged "to keep myself strong and healthy by eating the food my mother and father want me to eat, because I know detectives must have strong bodies and sound minds".[7] Rare were the children of mid-century America who did not absorb an understanding of private detectives and their service to society.

Adult detective enthusiasts share an equally rich cultural world. Literary societies bring together studious aficionados of the genre. Best known are the Baker Street Irregulars, their name taken from a phrase Arthur Conan Doyle coined to describe a group of street urchins led by one Wiggins who sometimes assisted Sherlock Holmes. The society was formed in 1934 in New York, enlisting editors, writers, and readers with a scholarly interest in the Holmes canon. A designated Wiggins presides over meetings. Members present research papers exploring the fine-grained details, lacunae, and mysteries within the Holmes mysteries at annual society dinners. Not to be denied its cultural patrimony, the Sherlock Holmes Society of London was organized in 1951, reviving an earlier initiative. The Society gathers Sherlock enthusiasts for dinners, discussions, films, and London

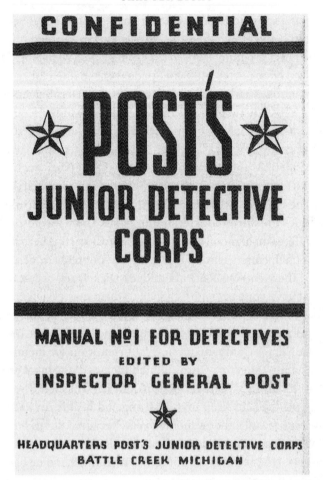

Figure 8.2. Front cover of Post Cereal's *Junior Detective Corps Manual* providing children with the corps pledge, instructions on detecting and finding clues, corps' secret writing code, signs, and password, a whistle, and the examination form required (with four more box tops) for advancement to Detective Sergeant.

walking tours. More recently, the Vidocq Society was established by a trio of forensic scientists in Philadelphia with the aim of examining actual cold cases of deaths and disappearances. Vidocq Society Member (VSM) deliberations take place over monthly luncheons at the historic Union League of Philadelphia.

There is *PI Magazine* for professional investigators who want to keep up with developments in the field, including legislative changes in privacy laws, and *Mystery Scene* magazine for news from the world of fiction writing (successor to the more scholarly *Armchair Detective*). In San Diego, California, Ben Harroll runs the PI Museum on Wheels and Café Noir dedicated to preserving the history and artifacts of the profession. Austin, Texas, has the more eclectic Spy and Private Eye Museum. Recently, the Museum of London put on an attendance record–breaking exhibition, *Sherlock Holmes: The Man Who Never Lived and Will Never Die*. The professional detective's trade is taught in various schools and correspondence courses, successors to the Nick Harris Professional Detective School. In sum, the private eye is a living and evolving cultural phenomenon—a legend.

Legends are collections of stories handed down over time and transformed by diversely motivated storytellers of succeeding generations. They tell of important past events, yet do so in purposeful ways that embellish, commend, condemn, and otherwise color their subject. They are understood as caricatures, perhaps as tall tales, but also as metaphorical truths. The legend is a historically evolved story, both widely embraced and critically interrogated; the product of many authors with diverse interests, cultural fact and controversy. Legends invite inquiry, reinterpretation, and redeployment in changing conditions. They leave room for the participant. That is what makes them engaging, and is the source of their appeal whether as education or entertainment, discussion or argument.

Case comparisons illustrate these general features of the legend as well the uniqueness of the legendary detective. Consider the classic legend of Robin Hood. The story begins in the veiled history of thirteenth-century England. British historian R. C. Holt found reliable if fragmentary evidence of the forest outlaw's existence and of the story's gradual reinterpretation over the centuries. Initially, Robin's tale thrived as a form of entertainment rather than social protest in households and taverns and among traveling minstrels, who spread the story, adding new meanings in the retelling. For a long time Robin Hood was chronicled as an outlaw and the nemesis of feudal lords. Five hundred years passed before he was credited with robbing the rich and giving to the poor, an improvement added by early book and folio publishers looking for a mass market.

> Composition and repetition were intermingled. . . . These robust simple stories constitute singularly delicate and complex evidence: about Robin, what he was thought to have been and about the social

context in which the telling of his deeds was born and nurtured . . . a story is not fixed in time and place. It provides a continually shifting point of focus. As circumstances that sustain it change—the audience, the means of communication, the social assumptions and conventions, the intellectual milieu—so the story changes. . . . *Legend is fact of a very peculiar kind* . . . . The fancy present in all legends falsifies. . . . In bridging the gap between the real and ideal world . . . it achieve[s] an enduring confidence trick. Playwrights may surrender to it. Sociologists may compound it. We all can enjoy it. But it is also useful to uncover it and understand what made it possible.[8]

Similar figures color American history and populate our imagination. The cowboy rivals the detective in cultural prominence and can be traced through myriad circumstances that explain his origins and interpretation. The cowboy grew from a narrow empirical foundation to a vast legend because it provided a convenient narrative of conquest and expansion in the American West.[9] Eric Hobsbawm argues that many countries had a history of cattle and sheep herders (*vaqueros*, gauchos, drovers), "but none of them has generated a myth with serious international popularity, let alone one that can compare, even faintly, with the fortunes of the North American cowboy."[10] In those countries frontiersmen were not associated with settlement of new lands, and their ranks sometimes included rebels and barbarians, less opportune subjects for legend making. Real cowboys in the United States were few in number, confined to a brief period in the late nineteenth century before cattle drives were superseded by expanding railroads and meatpacking plants. Yet the cowboy came to represent freedom and settlement of the West, a feat better credited to the U.S. Army and government-subsidized railroads. The idealized cowboy appealed to journalists and showmen, who began to sell eastern audiences a picaresque story of Indian wars, buffalo hunts, defense of white women, and defeat of rustlers by gunslinging lawmen.

Buffalo Bill cover stories became a popular feature of Street and Smith's *New York Weekly*. Louis Warren's study, *William F. Cody and the Wild West Show*, traces the western legend from its origins on the Kansas plains after the Civil War to international popularity in the early twentieth century. "The Wild West show made cowboys into symbols of whiteness only through a balancing act, combating their [Mexican] border image on the one hand and portraying them as

aggressively physical and autonomous on the other."[11] Like the popularized private detective, the cowboy embodied ambiguity, a well-
founded skepticism about whether he was western hero or eastern
entertainment. Warren interprets the very recognition of this duality
as part of the legend's appeal. Consumers enjoyed the play of fact-or-
fiction in portraits of western figures. But age has not been kind to
the cowboy. Despite a century-long run, the cowboy along with the
fabled West eventually lost their resonance. The western novel and
cowboy legend have faded, corrupted in commercial advertising and
ideological politics, overshadowed by the more palpable detective.
Hobsbawm says Sam Spade killed the cowboy. In any case, the private
eye has proven more durable, superseding the cowboy in popular culture, morphing into new places and purposes, not least because detectives have served the purposes of profitable industrial and cultural
enterprises.

The "Okie" is another legendary phenomenon. James Gregory's
compelling study of the 1930s Dustbowl migration concludes, "The
Okie is an invention, a work of collective imagination . . . assembled
from many sources."[12] The many sources that Gregory traces to the
Okie image include the Dust Bowl migration of poor and dispossessed
southwesterners, their conflictual encounter with the California migrant labor market, political scapegoating during the Depression that
blamed them for the state's economic troubles, the rustic portraits
in Steinbeck's fiction, social ridicule, and ostracism. But out of self-
preservation, the Okies' story was fashioned in their own tenacious
pursuit of a decent living and community regard. In fundamentalist
churches, country music, and dance hall socials, they created a subculture that spoke solidarity; a positive identity concocted of western
symbolism, Okie toughness, and Americanism.

Comparative cases help explain how legends develop in similar
and contrasting ways. Holt demonstrates the conditions that "made
possible" the Robin Hood story, how legend provides a record of
changing historical memory. Both Hobsbawm and Warren describe
the cowboy's story as less a product of conditions on the range than
an invention of Wild West shows. Gregory gives a fuller explanation
of the Okie legend and of the subculture in which its meaning was
fashioned. All these legends begin with the concrete historical cir-
cumstance of a particular social group, occupation, or population.
Their experience is chronicled in colorful ways that suit the interests

of storytellers. As historical conditions change, so do the stories and their purposes. A decisive moment in the development of legends comes with the printed word; an entrepreneurial initiative that reproduces oral tradition for mass audiences in forms ranging from medieval folios to modern pulps. Some legends flourish, finding renewed celebrity, while others fade as their social supports collapse. Legends thrive on the strength of their protagonists and the variety of interests they serve.

The legendary private detective reflects this portrait and adds something to the general explanation. Unlike the comparative cases, the private detective's legend was reproduced by major industries in the fields of business and culture. Their legends are more central to modern society but equally imbued with the "fancy that falsifies" of Robin Hood. Like the Okie or the cowboy or Robin Hood, the private detective is a historical agent, a job and social role, as well as a literary invention and cultural commodity—a real actor reinterpreted in congeries of stories. But the detective legend is maintained by two vigorous industries providing it with a durability lacking in the cowboy, who had no industrial base, or the Okie, supported only by a local subculture. The legendary detective is a multipurpose invention, a synthesis of images produced in commercial activity and maintained in cultural memory. The legend encompasses kindred figures from criminal associate to master sleuth, superhero to working man or woman, hard-boiled private eye to social critic—Robin Hood–like in character changes over time.

The detective agency industry and the culture industry are symbiotic enterprises; businesses that grew from a common root and continued to interact as they developed along distinct pathways. From the beginning, the detective story exploits the mysteries of the city that engaged the original private eyes. Real detectives and agencies produced memoirs and magazine articles written in response to (other) fiction, claiming the real occupational world of the private investigator was nothing like its depiction in mystery stories. Indeed, real detectives presented themselves as professionals and business people, not "gumshoes" or hard-edged ops. Yet ops wrote fiction, too, in their memoirs, their client solicitations, and even their investigative reports. Moreover, fiction writers take plots from real events: Hammett wrote about labor conflicts, municipal corruption, and shipping thefts; Doyle about violence in the coalfields; Poe about murder in

Figure 8.3. Allan Pinkerton's memorial in Chicago's Graceland Cemetery marking the resting place of "the Founder in America of a noble profession."

New York. The two industries operate in a larger context influenced by society and economy and by one another, aware of their counterpart and ready, at once, to borrow from the other's repertoire or assert its own distinctive character. Both businesses operate in a commercial world, fashioning products and services for the marketplace.

What is symbiotic in the development of these enterprises? What is it about the detective business that is explained by the story business, and vice versa? In the first instance, the detective business provides the empirical bases of stories. Vidocq supplied Poe and others with the setting, protagonist, and problematic. Hammett introduced a realism that Shaw nurtured in the hard-boiled genre. The story business, in turn, provided a model for a long line of memoirists, from Pinkerton and Siringo to Burns and GT-99. Fiction contributed to the language of agencies and operatives offering the crime-story model to self-aggrandizing memoirs. From a broader comparative perspective, the enterprises operated differently in different societies, illustrating how social conditions affected their interaction. Relatively early, France and Britain developed municipal police forces, rather than private eyes, and police inspectors became the protagonists of Dickens and Wilkie Collins (and even Sherlock's plodding colleagues). The absence of national police and slow development of municipal detectives led to the predominant American private detective agencies and spawned their fictional counterparts Nick Carter and Sam Spade. Intra-nationally, as society changed, so did legend; as collective bargaining was established and industrial work of the great American agencies declined, the hard-boiled private eye morphed into a more amiable presence in radio and film.

The beauty of legend is that it simultaneously collects our stories and invites their examination. Legends are not fact but ways we think about fact—invitations to appreciate, argue, demur, and reinterpret. The deconstruction of legends offers a useful strategy for explaining cultural change and collective action—and that by contrast to facile refutations of myth. On closer examination, legends synthesize a wealth of evidence about the social world, much of it in disparate and conflicting ensembles. Legends illustrate how social complexity and contingency come together, how contested narratives coexist.

And finally, legend preserves its constituents, history's agents. The private detective figure is an amalgam that embodies the criminal associate, labor spy, strikebreaker, leg breaker, jury tamperer, frame-up artist, braggart, entrepreneur, advocate, and reformer. It is a universally compelling legend that effortlessly unites a storied past. But it is also a collection of stories not to be submerged in collective portraits, a cast of memorable events and characters: Allan Pinkerton, the British Chartist and American abolitionist; William J. Burns, progressive, intriguer, and defender of Leo Frank; James Wood Sr., investigator of child slavery; Cora Stayer, founder of an agency for ladies in need of advice; Heber Blankenhorn, public servant, investigator, and reformer; Pinkerton women who defended fellow workers at the World's Fair; Mildred Gilmore, who urged ethics on the profession; Dashiell Hammett, a writer who served in the army and in jail for defending civil rights; and the ebullient Nick Harris, journalist, detective, pitchman, and counselor, who bid the public "let's talk it over." They all pursued respectability; some of them deserved it.

# NOTES

## Introduction

1 Huberman 1937, p. 6.
2 Hammett 1929, p. 117.
3 Crowley 2008.
4 "$125,000 in Gold Coin Stolen on S.F. Liner," *San Francisco Examiner*, November 23, 1921, pp. 1, 2; Layman 2005, pp. 47–50.
5 Hammett et al. 2000, p. 264.
6 Chandler 1934, p. 14.
7 Lukas 1997, p. 14.
8 Hughes 1962, pp. 6–7.
9 Hobsbawm and Ranger 1983, p. 1.
10 Morton 2004.
11 Adorno 2001.
12 Eagleton 1983, p. 216.
13 Hobsbawm 2013, p. 285.

## Chapter One

1 Morton 2004, p. 19.
2 Chevalier 1973.
3 Cobb 1970, p. 18; Shpayer-Makov 2011.
4 Vidocq 1828.
5 Chevalier 1973, p. 7.
6 Thompson 1966, pp. 662–63.
7 Miller 1973.
8 Oughton 1961, p. 36.
9 White 2011.
10 Contract between the Illinois Central R.R. Co. and Pinkerton & Co., February 1, 1855, Pinkerton Archives.
11 *Chicago Democrat*, March 5, 1861, quoted in Morn 1982, p. 41.

12   Gutman 1966, p. 40.

13   White 2011.

14   Gutman 1966, pp. 295–96.

15   Kenny 1995, p. 31.

16   Green 2006.

17   Siringo 1914, pp. 3–5.

18   Boyer 1978, p. 125.

19   Lukas 1997, p. 77.

20   Crapsay 1871, p. 190.

21   Krause 1992.

22   Hogg 1944.

23   Pinkerton 1884, p. xix.

24   Pinkerton Papers, microfilm reel 1.

25   Hogg 1944.

26   Dowell 1969.

27   Crapsay 1871, p. 197.

28   Beet 1906, p. 439.

29   Hunter 1922, pp. 283ff.

30   Train 1922.

31   Pinkerton 1884, p. 16.

32   Furlong 1912, p. 5.

33   Burns 1913, p. 319.

34   McWatters 1872, pp. 643ff.

35   Siringo 1914, p. 107.

36   Jeffreys-Jones 1972, p. 240.

37   Weiss 1986, p. 87.

38   Jeffreys-Jones 1972, pp. 245–47.

39   Burns 1913, p. 11.

**Chapter Two**

1   Siringo 1912.

2   ibid., pp. 16–21.

3   ibid., p. 325.

4   Siringo 1914, p. 93.

5   Morn 1982, pp. 162–63.

6   Lukas 1997, p. 593.

7   Siringo 1912, p. 518.

8   Lukas1997, p. 176.

9   Ibid.; Kenny 1998.

10   Kenny 1995.

11   Lukas 1997, p. 188.

12   ibid., pp. 194–95.

13   Hunt 1990; Caesar 1968.

14   Hunt 1990, pp. 3–5.

15  Bean 1952; Fradkin 2005.

16  Hichborn 1915.

17  Hichborn papers, investigative report, July 21 and 22, 1909, box 23, folders 1031and 2116.

18  "How Burns' Men Get Evidence for Him," *San Francisco Chronicle*, April 27, 1907, p. 1.

19  Hichborn papers, investigative report, October 13, 1907, box 23, folder 2116.

20  "Detectives in Calhoun Trial," *San Francisco Chronicle*, March 17, 1909, p. 18.

21  Hunt 1990, pp. 47–48.

22  Gatlin 1911.

23  Bean 1952, p. 309.

24  Steffens 1907, p. 625.

25  Hunt 1990, p. 53.

26  La Follette Civil Liberties Committee, hearings, pt. 15B, pp. 6,075, 6,091.

27  La Follette Civil Liberties Committee, hearings, pt. 65, supplementary exhibits, pp. 23,724–40.

28  Holter 1985, p. 246.

29  La Follette Civil Liberties Committee, report 6, "Strikebreaking," p. 65.

30  ibid., pp. 76–84.

31  La Follette Civil Liberties Committee, hearings, pt. 15B, p. 6,079.

32  Morn 1982, 54.

33  "Hired a Woman Detective," *New York Times*, February 27, 1890, p. 1.

34  "Women Detectives Capture Two Men," *New York Times*, November 14, 1926, p. 24.

35  "Hired Spy of 'Merchant Princes' Expelled by Girl Clerks," *The Day Book* (Chicago), June 27, 1913, p. 1.

36  La Follette Civil Liberties Committee, report 46, pt. 3, p. 49.

37  Reda 2005.

38  La Follette Civil Liberties Committee, April 1936, p. 338.

39  Whatley 1993.

40  Correspondence, Railway Audit and Inspection Company to Fulton Bag Company and Cotton Mill, January 8, 1920, Fulton Bag and Cotton Mills Collection, box 1, folder 24.

41  Siringo 1914, pp. 2–3.

42  Lucas 1949.

43  P.I. Museum collection, San Diego, CA.

44  Detective License Department Minute Books, p. 219.

45  For example, Mosley 1990.

## Chapter Three

1  Warren 1917.

2  Ibid., emphasis in original.

3  Ibid., pp. 19–21.

4  Ibid., p. 34.

5    Ibid., following p. 42.

6    Ibid., pp. 69–73.

7    Murray 1955.

8    Interchurch World Movement 1920.

9    Interchurch World Movement 1921, pp. 57–61.

10   US Commission on Industrial Relations, records, 1915, microfilm reel 4.

11   Howard 1924. The original Cabot Report has disappeared, although at one time the La Follette committee had a copy, which it summarized. Later, Sidney Howard wrote a short, popularized version.

12   Detective License Department Minute Books.

13   US Census of Business 1939, vol. 3, table 1A; and US Census of Business 1948, vol. 6, table 1G.

14   La Follette Civil Liberties Committee, hearings, pt. 15A, pp. 5,264–67.

15   Ibid., pt. 8, p. 2,800.

16   Ibid., pt. 15A, pp. 5,326 passim.

17   Ibid., pp. 5,761, 5,199.

18   These documents, later bound, are available via ProQuest.

19   Auerbach 1966.

20   La Follette Civil Liberties Committee, report 46, pt. 3, "Industrial Espionage," p. 30.

21   Ibid., hearings, pt. 2, 663.

22   Ibid., pt. 8, p. 3,066.

23   Ibid., p. 3,067.

24   Ibid., pt. 15B, "Corporations Auxiliary Co., Pinkerton's National Detective Agency, Inc.," p. 6,151.

25   Ibid., pt. 65, pp. 23,697–98.

26   Ibid., pt. 15A, p. 5,723.

27   Ibid., report 398, pt. 4, pp. 1,330–84; Starr 1996, pp. 180–88.

28   Train 1922, p. 91.

29   Friedman 1907, p. vii; Lukas 1997.

30   Friedman 1907.

31   Ibid., pp. 190–93.

32   Pinkerton's National Detective Agency records, microfilm reel 18.

33   "Union Places Its Own Spies," *Milwaukee Journal*, April 16, 1936, p. 2.

34   F. W. Stockman, correspondence to C. E. White, April 21, 1921, Fulton Bag and Cotton Mills Collection.

35   White 2011, pp.453–54.

36   Reda 2005.

37   Wood Detective Agency papers, box 7.

38   Nick Harris Detectives advertisement, *Los Angeles Times*, December 3, 1911.

39   "Café Operator Sues Detective Agency for Loss," *Los Angeles Times*, July 28, 1934, p. A3.

40   Detective License Department Minute Books, April 22, 1927.

41   "Woman Puzzles Police Surgeon," *Los Angeles Times*, December 23, 1910, p. 1.

42   "Divorce Gained By Jocelyn Lee," *Los Angeles Times*, April 4, 1931, p. A2.

43  Kim Cooper, "Red Light Raid," *On Bunker Hill.* http://www.onbunkerhill.org /redlightraid.

44  "Let's Talk It Over" (advertisement), *Los Angeles Times*, March 23, 1924.

45  "Blue Beard Case Will Be Discussed" (notice), *Los Angeles Times*, January 25, 1936, p. A2

46  "Detective Is Sold (In Which Nick Solves Deep Motor Mystery)," *Los Angeles Times*, September 26, 1926, p. G8.

47  "Men So Prominent You Cannot Doubt Them" (advertisement), *Los Angeles Times*, April 30, 1924, p. 5.

48  "Nick Harris Police Whistle Save Actress" *Los Angeles Times*, April 30, 1924, p. 10.

49  Harris 1923.

## Chapter Four

1  Yellow Aster Mine records.

2  Ibid., report, September 30, 1903.

3  Ibid., report, October 1, 1903.

4  *Randsburg Miner*, January 16, 1904.

5  Panama Pacific Exposition records.

6  Interchurch World Movement 1920.

7  La Follette Civil Liberties Committee, hearings, pt. 15A, p. 5,248.

8  Friedman 1907, p. 14.

9  Ibid., p. 17.

10  GT-99 1937, p. 48.

11  Interchurch World Movement 1921, p. 49.

12  La Follette Civil Liberties Committee, hearings, pt. 15A, pp. 5,580–82.

13  Ibid., p. 5,367.

14  Spielman 1996, pp. 76, 80.

15  GT-99 1937, p. 11.

16  Ibid., pp. 28–29.

17  Ibid., p. 53.

18  La Follette Civil Liberties Committee, hearings, pt. 15A, p. 5,380.

19  Ibid., pp. 5,243–44.

20  Wager 1918.

21  Hammett 2001 [1923], p. 905.

22  Ibid., pp. 905–11.

23  Burns Agency report, February 25, 1914.

24  Ibid., February 28 and March 3, 1914.

25  Walton 1992.

26  La Follette Civil Liberties Committee, hearings, pt. 15A, p. 5,640.

27  Ibid., p. 5,641.

28  Ibid.

29  Panama Pacific Exposition records.

30  Ibid., carton 61, folders 2–6.

31  Ibid., report, April 12, 1915.

32   Ibid.

33   Ibid., March 22 and March 24, 1915, box 28, folders 10–15.

34   GT-99 1937, p. 53.

35   La Follette Civil Liberties Committee, hearings, pt. 15A, p. 5,366.

36   Ibid., pp. 5440–41.

37   Siringo 1912, 1914.

38   Spielman 1996, p. 125.

39   Howard 1924, p. 80.

40   Oscar Elsas, president of Fulton Bag and Cotton Mills, letter to Railway Audit and
     Inspection Company, May 15, 1914, Fulton Bag and Cotton Mills Collection.

41   Adams 1966; Blum 2008.

42   Hunt 1990.

43   Burns 1913, p. 65.

44   Ibid., pp. 10–11.

45   William J. Burns, correspondence to Hiram Johnson, February 11, 1913 (letter),
     March 24, 1913 (telegram).

46   Friedman 1907, p. 17.

47   McLellan 1930, p. 31.

48   Davis 1987.

49   GT-99 1937, p. 289.

## Chapter Five

1    Frost 1968; Gentry 1967.

2    Kennedy 1980, chap. 1.

3    Levi 1983, p. 27.

4    *San Francisco Examiner*, July 23, 1916.

5    *San Francisco Chronicle*, June 13, 1916.

6    Gentry 1967, 28–29.

7    Frost 1968, 22–23.

8    Ibid., 34–36.

9    *San Francisco Examiner*, July 27, 1916.

10   Frost 1968; Gentry 1967; Mooney-Billings Report 1931; Densmore Report 1919.

11   Gentry 1967, p. 441ff; Hopkins 1932.

12   Dowell 1939.

13   Spence 1996, p. 94.

14   Ibid., p. 100.

15   Ibid.

16   Murray 1955.

17   Adams 1966.

18   Frost 1968, p. 266.

19   Quoted in Frost 1968, p. 267.

20   Watson 2005; Donner 1990, p. 31.

21   Friedman 1907; Lukas 1997.

22   Mooney Billings Report.

23  La Follette Civil Liberties Committee, report no. 6.

24  The Modesto Frame-Up.

25  *Los Angeles Times*, December 3, 1911.

26  La Follette Civil Liberties Committee, report no. 6, pt. 1, p. 8.

27  Ibid., p.23.

28  Ibid., preliminary report, p. 11.

29  Ibid., pt. 15A, pp. 5240–5241.

30  Velke 1997.

31  La Follette Civil Liberties Committee, preliminary report, p. 10.

32  Levinson 1935; Norwood 2002.

33  Levinson 1935, p. 219.

34  Trimble 2007.

35  John Craig, "The Violent Art of Strike-breaking," *Newspaper name*, article date, page.

36  Levinson 1935, p. 219.

37  La Follette Civil Liberties Committee, report no. 6, pt. I, p. 84.

38  Levinson 1935.

39  Quoted in Levinson 1935, p. 169.

40  Levinson 1935, p. 220.

41  La Follette Civil Liberties Committee, report no. 6, pt. I, p. 74.

42  Final Report and Testimony, US Commission on Industrial Relations, pp. 5,011–17; 4,994–99.

43  Detective License Department Minute Books, September 3, 1926.

44  *Los Angeles Times*, February 9, 1929.

45  La Follette Civil Liberties Committee, report no. 6, pt. III, p. 95.

46  Ibid., pp. 191–221.

47  Final Report and Testimony, US Commission on Industrial Relations, p. 5,013.

48  *New York Times*, April 22, 1916, p. 8.

49  Ibid., January 27, 1917, p. 1.

50  Ibid., January 14, 1916, p. 24.

51  Ibid., April 22, 1916.

52  Burns, correspondence to Anderson Electric Corporation, June 6, 1917. Pinkerton's National Detective Agency records, microfilm reel 19.

53  Warren 1917.

54  La Follette Civil Liberties Committee, report no. 6, pt. I, p. 112.

55  Final Report and Testimony, US Commission on Industrial Relations, p. 4,966.

56  Hughes 1962.

## Chapter Six

1  Blankenhorn 1919.

2  Gall 1983.

3  Interchurch World Movement 1920, p. 98.

4  Ibid., p. 249.

5  Ibid., pp. 231–32.

6   Ibid., pp. 245–51.

7   La Follette Committee, appendix revised with index, pp. 337–44.

8   Ibid., p. 339.

9   Howard 1924.

10  US Commission on Industrial Relations, Final Report and Testimony, 1916, vol. 1, p. 57.

11  Adams 1966, p. 226.

12  Ibid.

13  US Commission on Industrial Relations, records, 1912–1915, microfilm reel 4.

14  Huberman 1937, pp. 165–69.

15  Blankenhorn Letter in Gall 1982, p. 248.

16  Ibid., p. 249.

17  Ibid., p. 249.

18  Ibid., p. 250.

19  Ibid., p. 248.

20  Gall 1983, p. 524.

21  Auerbach 1966, pp. 49–50.

22  Ibid., chap. 9.

23  Auerbach 1966, p. 203.

24  Quoted in Gall 1982, p. 253.

25  La Follette Civil Liberties Committee, hearings, pt. 15A, p. 5,500.

26  Ibid., p. 5,501.

27  Ibid., pp. 5,513–14.

28  Ibid., pt. 8, p. 3,145.

29  Ibid., p. 3,146.

30  Ibid., pt. 15A, p. 5,737.

31  Ibid., pt. 15B, p. 6,295.

32  Platforms of the People 1924.

33  Holter 1985, p. 251.

34  La Follette Civil Liberties Committee, hearings, pt. 6, p. 103.

35  Ibid., p.132.

36  "Bill Too Drastic for Detectives," *San Francisco Chronicle*, March 15, 1913, p. 3.

37  "The Public Service," *Los Angeles Times*, March 10, 1915, p. B12.

38  "'Spotter' Measure Passes in the Assembly," *San Francisco Chronicle*, March 10, 1915, p. 9.

39  La Follette Civil Liberties Committee, hearings, pt. 6, p. 134.

40  "Bergoff License Revoked by State," *New York Times*, October 11, 1935, p. 10.

41  La Follette Civil Liberties Committee, hearings, pt. 65, p. 23,772.

42  Wood Detective Agency papers, "Agency History."

43  GT-99 1937, p. 289.

44  Frost 1968, p. 28.

45  Pinkerton's National Detective Agency, "Investigation of Improper Activities," microfilm.

46  Ibid., "Brief for the Petitioner" to State Comptroller's Office, microfilm.

47  Ibid.

48   Dinnerstein 1966.

49   Pinkerton's National Detective Agency, "Brief," microfilm.

50   "Burns Takes a Hand in Frank's Behalf," *New York Times*, May 2, 1914, p. 1.

51   McCartney 2008.

52   "Sinclair to Serve Six Months More for Shadowing Jury," *New York Times*, June 4, 1929, p. 1.

53   "R. J. Burns Looks More Like Business Man Than Hunter of Criminals," *San Francisco Chronicle*, October 13, 1921, p. 9.

54   Weiss 2007/08, p. 3.

55   Morn 1982, p. 192.

56   *PI Magazine*, various issues.

57   Krout and Schneider website; San Francisco City Directory, 1936.

58   Hailey 2002.

59   "Detective Agencies Get Together," *New York Times*, March 17, 1921, p. 14.

60   "'Private Eyes' Adopt Code of Ethics," *San Francisco Chronicle*, June 27, 1948, p. 9.

## Chapter Seven

1    Symons 1972, p. 34.

2    Denning 1998, p. 85.

3    Whalen 1999.

4    Poe 1981, p. 67.

5    Summerscale 2008, p. 267.

6    Flanders 2011, p. 177–78.

7    Klinger 2005, p. xxiv.

8    Collins 2011.

9    Kenny 1997, p. 31.

10   Morn 1982.

11   Furlong 1912; Siringo 1912.

12   Denning 1987, p. 139.

13   Morn 1982, p. 80, emphasis added.

14   Sutherland 1972.

15   Tebbel 1987.

16   Whalen 1999.

17   Tebbel 1987, p. 81.

18   Ibid.

19   Ibid., pp. 68–69.

20   Whalen 1999, pp. 36–37.

21   Tebbel 1987, p. 71.

22   Denning 1987, pp. 10–12.

23   Reynolds, 1955, pp. 22, 55.

24   Roberts et al. 1990.

25   Reynolds 1955, p 40.

26   Ibid., p. 65.

27   Denning 1987, p. 23.

28  "Fiction Factories," *Publishers Weekly*, August 13, 1892, p. 231.

29  Hersey 1937, p. 33.

30  Denning 1987, p. 45.

31  Smith 2000, p. 72.

32  Locke 2004.

33  Smith 2000, p. 23.

34  Burns 1925.

35  "The McClure Writers," *McClure's Magazine*, May 1912, p. 56.

36  Denning 1987, p. 45.

37  Locke 2004, p. 114.

38  Denning 1987, pp. 60–61.

39  Locke 2004, p. 65, emphasis in original.

40  Ibid., p. 29.

41  Locke 2004, p. 78, emphasis in original.

42  Symmons 1972.

43  Daly 1927, p. 1.

44  Nolan 1985, p. 267.

45  Ibid., p. 25.

46  Reprinted in Locke 2004, p. 31.

47  Erle Stanley Gardner, correspondence to Joseph T. Shaw, August 23, 1926, Ransom Collection.

48  Ibid.

49  Sutherland 1976, pp. 214–15.

50  E. R. Hagemann Collection, Hammett, August 1924, box 32, folder 4.

51  Shaw, correspondence to Gardner, May 31, 1926.

52  Gardner, correspondence to Shaw, October 27, 1927.

53  Shaw, correspondence to Gardner, May 1, 1934.

54  Pronzini 1998, pp. 17–19; Walton and Jones 1999.

55  Nolan 1983.

56  Nolan 1985.

57  Chandler 1934, p. 18.

58  Gibson 1979; Goulart 1972.

59  Nolan 1983, p. 222.

60  Luhr 1995, p. 7.

61  Ibid.

62  Layman 2005, pp. 291–92.

63  Walton 1992.

64  Eaton 1997.

65  Mandel 1984, p. 8.

66  Haycraft 1941.

67  Anderson 2013, p. 67.

68  Denning 1998, p. 81.

69  Howard S. Becker, correspondance to the author.

70  *The Wycherly Woman* (Knopf, 1961).

**Chapter Eight**

1   Herron 2009.
2   Wood Detective Agency papers.
3   Harris 1923; "Slave Girl Story," *Los Angeles Times*, February 2, 1936, p. C8.
4   Huang 2010.
5   Roberts 1993.
6   Ibid., 271–72.
7   Wood Detective Agency papers, Post's Junior Detective Corps.
8   Holt 1982, pp. 16, 189–90, emphasis added.
9   Warren 2005.
10  Hobsbawm 2013, p. 276.
11  Warren 2005, p. 234.
12  Gregory 1989, p. 247.

# BIBLIOGRAPHY

## Books and Articles

Adams, Graham, Jr. 1966. *Age of Industrial Violence, 1910–1915*. New York: Columbia University Press.

Adorno, Theodor. 2001. *The Culture Industry: Selected Essays on Mass Culture*. London: Routledge.

Anderson, John Lee. 2013. "Private Eyes: A Crime Novelist Navigates Cuba's Shifting Reality." *New Yorker*, October 21, 60–71.

Auerbach, Jerold S. 1966. *Labor and Liberty: The La Follette Committee and the New Deal*. Indianapolis, IN: Bobbs-Merrill.

Bean, Walton. 1952. *Boss Ruef's San Francisco: The Story of the Union Labor Party, Big Business, and the Graft Prosecution*. Berkeley: University of California Press.

Beet, Thomas. 1906. "Methods of American Private Detective Agencies." *Appleton's Magazine*, 8 (July–December): 439–45.

Blankenhorn, Heber. 1919. *Adventures in Propaganda, Letters from an Intelligence Officer in France*. Boston: Houghton.

Blum, Howard. 2008. *American Lightening: Terror, Mystery, the Birth of Hollywood, and the Crime of the Century*. New York: Crown.

Boyer, Paul. 1978. *Urban Masses and Moral Order in America, 1820–1920*. Cambridge, MA: Harvard University Press.

Burns, William J. (1913) 2010. *The Masked War*. New York: Doran. Reprint, Whitefish, MT: Kessinger.

———. 1925a. "Hotel and Bank Crooks." *Saturday Evening Post* 197, no. 49 (June 6): 46–52.

———. 1925b. "The Trail of the Bank Swindler." *Saturday Evening Post* 197, no. 50 (June 13): 43–126.

Caesar, Gene. 1968. *Incredible Detective: The Biography of William J. Burns*. Englewood Cliffs, NJ: Prentice-Hall.

Chandler, Raymond. 1934. *The Simple Art of Murder*. New York: Vintage.

Chevalier, Louis. 1973. *Laboring Classes and Dangerous Classes in Paris during the First Half of the Nineteenth Century*. Princeton, NJ: Princeton University Press.

Cobb, Richard. 1983. *The Police and the People: French Popular Protest, 1789–1820*. Oxford: Oxford University Press.

Collins, Paul. 2011. "The Case of the First Mystery Novelist." *New York Times Sunday Book Review*, January 7.

Craige, John H. 1910. "The Professional Strike-Breaker." *Collier's Weekly*, December 3, 20–25.

Crapsay, Edward. 1871. "The Nether Side of New York." *Galaxy* 11, no. 2 (February):188–97.

Crowley, Jack. 2008. "*Red Harvest* and Dashiell Hammett's Butte." *Montana Professor* 18, no. 2 (Spring): http://mtprof.msun.edu/Spr2008/crowl.html.

Daly, Carroll John. 1927. *The Snarl of the Beast*. New York: Harper Collins.

Davis, Natalie Zemon. 1987. *Fiction in the Archives: Pardon Tales and Their Tellers in Sixteenth-Century France*. Stanford, CA: Stanford University Press.

Denning, Michael. 1998. *Mechanic Accents: Dime Novels and Working-Class Culture in America*. Rev. ed. London: Verso.

Dinnerstein, Leonard. 1966. *The Leo Frank Case*. New York: Columbia University Press.

Donner, Frank. 1990. *Protectors of Privilege: Red Squads and Police Repression in Urban America*. Berkeley: University of California Press.

Dowell, Eldridge F. 1969. *A History of Criminal Syndicalism Legislation in the United States*. New York: Da Capo.

Eagleton, Terry. 1983. *Literary Theory: An Introduction*. Minneapolis: University of Minnesota Press.

Eaton, Michael. 1997. *Chinatown*. London: British Film Institute.

Flanders, Judith. 2011. *The Invention of Murder: How the Victorians Revelled in Death and Detection and Created Modern Crime*. London: Harper Press.

Fradkin, Philip L. 2005. *The Great Earthquake and Firestorm of 1906: How San Francisco Nearly Destroyed Itself*. Berkeley: University of California Press.

Friedman, Morris. 1907. *The Pinkerton Labor Spy*. New York: Wilshire.

Frost, Richard H. 1968. *The Mooney Case*. Stanford, CA: Stanford University Press.

Furlong, Thomas. 1912. *Fifty Years a Detective*. St. Louis, MO: C. E. Barnett.

Gall, Gilbert J. 1982. "Heber Blankenhorn, the La Follette Committee, and the Irony of Industrial Repression." *Labor History* 23, no. 2 (Spring): 246–53.

———. 1983. "Heber Blankenhorn: The Publicist as Reformer." *Historian* 45, no. 4 (August): 513–28.

Gatlin, Dana. 1911. "How Abe Ruef Confessed," *McClure's*, February.

Gentry, Curt. 1967. *Frame-Up: The Incredible Case of Tom Mooney and Warren Billings*. New York: Norton.

Gibson, Walter B., and Anthony Tollin. 1979. *The Shadow Scrapbook*. New York: Harcourt Brace Jovanovich.

Goulart, Ron. 1972. *Cheap Thrills: An Informal History of the Pulp Magazine*. New York: Arlington House.

Green, James. 2006. *Death in Haymarket: A Story of Chicago, the First Labor Movement, and the Bombing That Divided America.* New York: Anchor.

Gregory, James N. 1989. *American Exodus: The Dust Bowl Migration and Okie Culture in California.* New York: Oxford University Press.

GT-99. 1937. *Twenty Years a Labor Spy.* Indianapolis, IN: Bobbs-Merrill.

Gutman, Herbert G. 1966. *Work, Culture, and Society in Industrializing America: Essays in American Working-Class History.* New York: Vintage.

Hailey, Kitty. 2002. "Profile: Eddy McClain Statesman of the Investigative Profession," *PI Magazine*, July/August, 10–13.

Hammett, Dashiell. (1923) 2001. "From the Memoirs of a Private Detective," *Smart Set* 70 (March): 87–90. Reprinted in *Hammett: Crime Stories and Other Writings*, edited by Steven Marcus, 905–9. New York: American Library.

———. 1929. *Red Harvest.* New York: Knopf.

———. (1930) 2001. "Suggestions to Detective Story Writers." In *Hammett: Crime Stories and Other Writings,* edited by Stephen Marcus, 910–14. New York: American Library. Compiled from Crime Wave, New York Evening Post.

———. 1931. *The Glass Key.* New York: Knopf.

———, Kirby McCauley, Martin Harry Greenberg, and Edward Gorman. 2000. *Nightmare Town: Stories.* New York: Vintage.

Harris, Nick. 1923. *In the Shadows: Thirty Detective Stories Showing Why "Crime Doesn't Pay"; A Series of Famous Cases.* Los Angeles: Times-Mirror.

Haycraft, Howard. 1941. *Murder for Pleasure: The Life and Times of the Detective Story.* New York: Appleton-Century.

Herron, Don. 2009. *The Dashiell Hammett Tour.* San Francisco: Vince Emery Productions.

Hersey, Harold Brainerd. 1937. *Pulpwood Editor: The Fabulous World of the Thriller Magazines Revealed by a Veteran Editor and Publisher.* New York: Stokes.

Hichborn, Franklin. 1915. *The System: As Uncovered by the San Francisco-Graft Prosecution.* San Francisco, CA: Barry.

Hobsbawm, E. J. 2013. "The American Cowboy: An International Myth?" In *Fractured Times: Culture and Society in the Twentieth Century.* London: Little, Brown.

Hobsbawm, Eric, and Terence Ranger. 1983. *The Invention of Tradition.* New York: Cambridge University Press.

Hogg, J. Bernard. 1944. "Public Reaction to Pinkertonism and the Labor Question." *Pennsylvania History* 11 (July): 171–99.

Holter, Daryl. 1985. "Labor Spies and Union-Busting in Wisconsin, 1890–1940." *Wisconsin Magazine of History* 68, no. 4 (Summer): 243–65.

Hopkins, Ernest Jerome. 1932. *What Happened in the Mooney Case.* New York: Brewer, Warren & Putnam.

Howard, Sidney (with the assistance of Robert Dunn). 1924. *The Labor Spy.* New York: Republic.

Huang, Yunte. 2010. *Charlie Chan: The Untold Story of the Honorable Detective and His Rendezvous with American History.* New York: Norton.

Huberman, Leo.1937. *The Labor Spy Racket*. New York: Modern Age.

Hughes, Everett. 1962. "Good People and Dirty Work." *Social Problems* 10, no. 1: 3–11.

Hunt, William R. 1990. *Front-Page Detective: William J. Burns and the Detective Profession, 1880–1930*. Bowling Green, OH: Bowling Green State University Press.

Hunter, Robert. 1922. Violence and the Labor Movement. New York: Macmillan.

Jeffreys-Jones, R. 1972. "Profit over Class: A Study in American Industrial Espionage," *Journal of American Studies* 6, no. 3 (December): 233–48.

Kennedy, David M. 2004. *Over Here: The First World War and American Society*. Oxford: Oxford University Press.

Kenny, Kevin. 1995. "The Molly Maguires in Popular Culture." *Journal of American Ethnic History* 14, no 4 (Summer): 27–46.

———. 1998. *Making Sense of the Molly Maguires*. New York: Oxford University Press.

Klinger, Leslie S. 2005. *The New Annotated Sherlock Holmes*. New York: Norton.

Krause, Paul. 1992. *The Battle for Homestead, 1880–1892: Politics, Culture, and Steel*. Pittsburg, PA: Pittsburg University Press.

Layman, Richard. 2005. *Discovering "The Maltese Falcon" and Sam Spade*. San Francisco, CA: Vince Emery Productions.

Levi, Steven C. 1983. *Committee of Vigilance: The San Francisco Chamber of Commerce Law and Order Committee, 1916–1919*. Jefferson, NC: McFarland.

Levinson, Edward. 1935. *I Break Strikes: The Technique of Pearl L. Bergoff*. New York: Robert M. McBride.

Locke, John. 2004. *Pulp Fictioneers: Adventures in the Storytelling Business*. Silver Springs, MD: Adventure House.

Lucas, Robert. 1949. "The Crime Files of Sheridan Bruseaux." *Ebony* 4, no. 5 (March): 60.

Luhr, William, ed. 1995. *The Maltese Falcon*. Directed by John Huston. New Brunswick, NJ: Rutgers University Press.

Lukas, J. Anthony. 1997. *Big Trouble*. New York: Simon and Schuster.

Mandel, Ernest. 1984. *Delightful Murder: A Social History of the Crime Story*. Minneapolis: University of Minnesota Press.

McCartney, Laton. 2008. *The Teapot Dome Scandal*. New York. Random House.

McLellan, Howard. 1930. "The Shadow Business," *North American Review* 230, no. 1 (July): 29–35.

McWatters, George S. 1872. *Knots Untied; or, Ways and By-Ways in the Hidden Life of American Detectives*. Hartford, CT: Burr and Hyde.

Miller, Wilbur R. 1973. *Cops and Bobbies: Police Authority in New York and London, 1830–1870*. Columbus: Ohio University Press.

Moffett, Cleveland. 1898. *True Detective Stories from the Pinkerton Archives*. New York: Dillingham.

Morn, Frank. 1982. *The Eye That Never Sleeps: A History of the Pinkerton National Detective Agency*. Bloomington: Indiana University Press.

Morton, James. 2004. *The First Detective: The Life and Revolutionary Times of Vidocq, Criminal Spy and Private Eye*. London: Edbury / Random House.

Mosley, Walter. 1990. *Devil in a Blue Dress*. New York: Simon and Schuster.

Murray, Robert K. 1955. *Red Scare: A Study of National Hysteria, 1919–1920*. New York: McGraw-Hill.

Nolan, William F. 1983. *Hammett: A Life at the Edge*. New York: Congdon and Weed.

———. 1985. *The Black Mask Boys: Masters of the Hard-Boiled School of Detective Fiction*. New York: William Morrow.

Norwood, Stephen H. 2002. *Strikebreaking and Intimidation: Mercenaries and Masculinity in Twentieth-Century America*. Chapel Hill: University of North Carolina Press.

Oughton, Frederick. 1961. *Ten Guineas a Day: A Portrait of the Private Detective*. London: John Long.

Panama-Pacific International Exposition. 1915. Illustrated Souvenir Book. San Francisco, CA: Robert A. Reid.

Park, Robert E. 1936. "Human Ecology." *American Journal of Sociology* 42, no. 1 (July): 1–15.

Pinkerton, Allan. 1875. *The Expressman and the Detectives*. Chicago: Keen, Cook.

———. (1877) 1973. *The Molly Maguires and the Detectives*. New York: Carlton. Reprint, New York, Dover.

———. (1878) 1969. Strikers, Communists, Tramps, and Detectives. New York: Carleton. Reprint, Arno / *New York Times*.

———. (1884) 1975. *Thirty Years a Detective*. New York: Carleton. Reprint, Montclair, NJ: Patterson, Smith.

"Platforms of the People." 1924. *Outlook Magazine*, April 9, 594–95.

Poe, Edgar Allan. 1981. *The Complete Tales of Mystery and Imagination*. London: Octopus.

Pronzini, Bill. 1998. "Women in the Pulps." In *Deadly Women: The Woman Mystery Reader's Indispensable Companion,* edited by Jan Grape, Darryl Dean James, and Ellen Nehr, 17–19. New York: Carroll & Graf.

Reda, Paul. 2005. "Cora Stayer." paulreda.com/corastrayer/.

Reynolds, Quentin. 1955. *The Fiction Factory*. New York: Street and Smith.

Roberts, Garyn G., Ray B. Browne, and Gary Hoppenstand, eds. 1990. *Old Sleuth's Freaky Female Detectives: From the Dime Novels*. Bowling Green, OH: Bowling Green State University Popular Press.

———. 1993. *Dick Tracy and American History: Morality and Mythology in Text and Context*. Jefferson, NC: McFarland.

Shpayer-Makov, Haia. 2011. *The Ascent of the Detective: Police Sleuths in Victorian and Edwardian England*. London: Oxford University Press.

Siringo, Charles A. (1912) 1988. *"A Cowboy Detective:" A True Story of Twenty-two Years with a World-Famous Detective Agency*. Chicago, IL: Conkey. Reprint, Lincoln: University of Nebraska Press.

———. (1914) 1975. *Two Evil Isms: Pinkertonism and Anarchism*. Facsimile Reproduction, Austin, TX: Steck-Vaughn.

Smith, Erin. 2000. *Hard-Boiled: Working-Class Readers and Pulp Magazines.* Philadelphia, PA: Temple University Press.

Spence, Richard. 1996. "K. A. Jahnke and the German Sabotage Campaign in the United States and Mexico, 1914–1918." *Historian* 59, no. 1 (Fall): 89–112.

Spielman, Jean E. 1923. *The Stool-Pigeon and the Open Shop Movement.* Minneapolis, MN: American Publishing.

Starr, Kevin. 1996. *Endangered Dreams: The Great Depression in California.* New York: Oxford University Press.

Steffens, Lincoln. 1907. "William J. Burns, Intriguer." *American Magazine* 65, no. 1 (November): 614–25.

Summerscale, Kate. 2008. *The Suspicions of Mr. Whicher: A Shocking Murder and the Undoing of a Great Victorian Detective.* London: Bloomsbury.

Symons, Julian. 1972. *Bloody Murder: From the Detective Story to the Crime Novel.* London: Penguin.

Tebbel, John. 1987. *Between Two Covers: The Rise and Transformation of American Book Publishing.* New York: Oxford University Press.

Thompson, E. P. 1966. *The Making of the English Working Class.* NY: Vintage.

Train, Arthur. 1922. *Courts and Criminals.* NY: Charles Scribner's Sons.

Trimble, Paul. 2007. "Richard Cornelius, Division 205 and the Great URR Strike of 1907." *Bay Area Electric Railroad Association Journal* 2 (Spring): 21–41.

United States Census of Business. 1939. Washington, DC: U.S. Government Printing Office.

Velke, John A. 1997. *Baldwin-Felts Detectives, Inc.* Richmond, VA.

Vidocq, François-Eugène. 1828. *Memoirs of Vidocq.* London: Hunt and Clark.

Wager, Leroy H. 1918. *Confessions of a Spotter.* St Louis, MO: Wilson.

Walton, John. 1992. *Western Times and Water Wars: State, Culture, and Rebellion in California.* Berkeley: University of California Press.

Warren, Leslie. 1917. *Industrial Society and the Human Element.* Boston: Sherman Service.

Warren, Louis. 2005. *Buffalo Bill's America: William F. Cody and the Wild West Show.* New York: Vintage.

Watson, Bruce. 2005. *Bread and Roses: Migrants and the Struggle for the American Dream.* New York: Penguin.

Whalen, Timothy. 1999. *Edgar Allan Poe and the Masses: The Political Economy of Literature in Antebellum America.* Princeton, NJ: Princeton University Press.

Whatley, Warren C. 1993. "African-American Strikebreaking from the Civil War to the New Deal," *Social Science History* 17 no. 4 (Winter): 526–58.

White, Richard. 2011. *Railroaded: The Transcontinentals and the Making of Modern America.* New York: Norton.

Weiss, Robert P. 1986. "Private Detective Agencies and Labour Discipline in the United States, 1855–1946," *Historical Journal* 29, no. 1: 87–107.

———. 2007–8. "From Cowboy Detectives to Soldiers of Fortune: Private Security Contracting and Its Contradictions on the New Frontiers of Capitalist Expansion." *Social Justice* 34, nos. 3–4: 1–19.

## Archival Documents

Detective License Department Minute Books. 1915ff. California State Board of
Prison Directors. California State Archives, Sacramento.

E. R. Hagemann Collection. UCLA Library Special Collections, University of
California, Los Angeles.

Fulton Bag and Cotton Mills Collection. Georgia Historical Society. georgiahis
tory.com.

Hichborn, Franklin. Papers. UCLA Library Special Collections, University of
California, Los Angeles.

Johnson, Hiram. Papers. Bancroft Library, University of California, Berkeley.

Labor Archives and Research Center. San Francisco State University.

Pinkerton's National Detective Agency. Records. Part A, Administrative File,
1857–1999, University Microfilm, reels 19–21. Library of Congress.

Pinkerton, Allan. Papers. Newberry Library, Chicago.

Panama Pacific Exposition. Records. Bancroft Library, University of California,
Berkeley.

Ransom Collection. Harry Ransom Center. University of Texas at Austin.

Yellow Aster Mine. Records. California State Library, Sacramento.

Wood Detective Agency. Papers. Harvard Law School Library Historical and
Special Collections.


## Reports

Densmore, John. 1919. *Connection of Certain Department of Labor Employees with
the Case of Thomas J. Mooney* [Densmore Report]. US House of Representatives Document 66-157, parts 1 and 2.

Interchurch World Movement Commission of Inquiry. 1920. *Report on the Steel
Strike of 1919*. New York: Harcourt, Brace and Howe.

———. 1921. *Public Opinion and the Steel Strike: Supplementary Reports of the
Investigation*. New York: Harcourt, Brace and Howe.

Joint Marine Modesto Defense Committee. [1936]. *The Modesto Frame-Up*.
San Francisco, CA: Joint Marine Modesto Defense Committee. Labor Ar-
chives and Research Center, J. Paul Leonard Library, San Francisco State
University.

[La Follette Civil Liberties Committee] Violations of Free Speech and Rights
of Labor Subcommittee. 1937–1940. Hearings and Reports to the Committee on Education and Labor. Washington, DC: US Government Printing
Office.

US Commission on Industrial Relations. 1912–1915. Unpublished Records of the
Division of Research and Investigation: Reports, Staff Studies, and Background Research Materials. Microfilm. University Publications.

———. 1916. *Final Report and Testimony*.US Senate Document 64-415 (microfilm).

Wickersham Commission. (1931) 1968. *Mooney-Billings Report.* Submitted to the National Commission on Law Observance and Enforcement. June. Montclair, NJ: Patterson Smith.

William Burns Detective Agency. 1914. *Asiatic Exclusion* [Burns Report]. Report to Mark Sullivan, February–March. Records of the US Commission on Industrial Relations, reel 11.

# INDEX

Wadell-Mahon Detective Agency, 48, 113
Wagner, Robert F., 135
Wagnet Act, 135–38, 150
Walsh, Frank, 133
Walsh, Thomas, 146
W. A. Mundell International Detective Agency, 60
Warne, Kate, 48–49
Warner, Jack, 178
Warner Brothers Pictures, 2, 178
Warren, Louis, 188–89
Washington Detective Bureau, 118
Weinberg, Israel, 104
Weiss, Robert, 28–29
Wells, Orson, 176
Western Federation of Miners (WFM), 34, 38
Whalen, Timothy, 154
Wheatland Riot, 65, 118
*Whistler, The,* 177
White, Stanford, 117

Wicher, Jack, 155
Wickersham, George, 41, 144
William J. Burns International Detective Agency, 2, 20, 50, 60; finances of, 63–64; founding of, 45, 59; investigations, 88–89, 94–97, 113, 121–23
Williams, Race, 169–70
Wilson, W. B., 131
Wilson, Woodrow, 99, 131, 133
Witzke, Lothar, 107
Wohlforth, Robert, 138
Wolfe, Nero, 169
Wood, James, Jr., 142, 184
Wood, James R., Sr., 20, 45, 70–71, 142, 192
Wood, Leonard, 100
Wood, William, 111
*Writer's Digest,* 168

Yellow Aster Mine, 77–81